Photo: Gillianne Tedder

Alistair Mant was born and raised in Sydney. He attended Sydney Grammar School and the University of Sydney, where he shone in Arts and failed abysmally in Law. His educational breakthrough occurred on the Snowy Mountains Scheme, where he started work at the age of nineteen as a 'fitter's assistant'. This was his first and most important exposure to big, complicated and important systems. He worked also as an account executive in advertising before the IBM Corporation transferred him to Europe. Subsequently, he carried out research at the Tavistock Institute of Human Relations and was elected Dean of Faculty at the South Bank University, also in London.

Intelligent Leadership follows the critical acclaim of *Leaders We Deserve*, *The Rise and Fall of the British Manager* and *The Experienced Manager*, for which he was awarded the British Institute of Management's Bowie Medal.

Alistair divides most of his time between Australia and Europe, helping public and private organisations to develop strategies which are people-friendly and therefore likely to work in practice. His wife is a developmental psychologist and his daughters are, respectively, a musician/musicologist and a theatre director.

D1333920

For my father
Gilbert Mant 1902–1997

INTELLIGENT LEADERSHIP

ALISTAIR MANT

ALLEN & UNWIN

First published in 1997 by
Allen & Unwin
9 Atchison Street
St Leonards NSW 1590
Australia
Phone: (61 2) 8425 0100
Fax: (61 2) 9906 2218
E-mail: frontdesk@allen-unwin.com.au
Web: http://www.allen-unwin.com.au

National Library of Australia
Cataloguing-in-Publication entry:

Mant, Alistair.
    Intelligent leadership.

    ISBN 1 86448 167 6

    1. Leadership. 2. Organizational change. I. Title.

658.4

Set in 11/14 pt Casablanca by DOCUPRO, Sydney
Printed by Griffin Press, South Australia

10 9 8 7 6 5 4

Contents

Preface

This book is primarily about intelligence—not the sort of 'intelligence' measured by IQ tests or formal examinations, but the kind of practical intelligence which creates opportunities and steers around potential cockups and blunders. The presumption of the book is that all of us are grateful for leadership which is possessed of useful intelligence. Leaders have to do many things but if they are stupid, we are sunk.

It is hard to see how to write about practical cleverness without discussing its obverse—operational stupidity. The problem with this is that most of us are very sensitive about the subject of stupidity, I think because most of us have been made to feel *personally* stupid at some time in our lives by parents, siblings, teachers, officials and bosses. This is the moment to assert that I am not trying to be clever or superior about this—I have to deal with the subject. But the focus is always on *systemic* stupidity—the way that otherwise smart people can be rendered *apparently* stupid by dysfunctional or amoral *systems*. Of course, those responsible for such systems are not, collectively, exactly brilliant.

Every single human being possesses some kind of cleverness or other but we delude ourselves if we assume that we are all equal in this respect. Leaders of great enterprises, and that goes for countries like Australia too, need to be highly intelligent. The book assumes that we all need to be clearer about what *kinds* of intelligences (plural) they need.

The year of publication, 1997, happens to include two highly significant fiftieth anniversaries for me and for the book's contents. The first of these is the fiftieth birthday of the Snowy Mountains Scheme, where I worked for a while in a very lowly manual role in 1958–59. This book is not an autobiography but I can say that my involvement in that great national enterprise set me firmly on the path to understanding the special demands of leadership in Australia. I live overseas these days and this is the first book I have written initially for an Australian audience. My other writings have migrated to Australia from Europe; this book is designed as an Australian export, after suitable improvements have been made by those who love and/or hate what it has to say. Sir William Hudson, the first Commissioner of the Snowy Scheme is my first example of intelligent leadership.

The other fiftieth birthday is that of the Tavistock Institute in London, where I worked for some years, in a slightly less lowly role, in the 1970s. The Tavistock was the outgrowth of the extraordinary ingenuity stimulated by the Second World War. Great emergencies sometimes unleash great creativity. 'Socio-technical systems' theory— one of the 'Tavi's' main exports—represented a revolutionary way of connecting technical and operational systems with *human nature*. The problems the Institute addressed are perennial—each new generation of leaders has to learn how to make organisations purposeful and congenial for *people*.

Accordingly, there are numerous references in these pages to the great names at the Tavistock, some of them now dead of course— Wilfred Bion (on the psychodynamics of groups), Ken Rice, Harold Bridger and Eric Miller (on experiential leadership learning), Elliott Jaques (on stratified systems theory and the time-span of discretion) and perhaps most significant of all, Eric Trist and Fred Emery (on socio-technical systems theory). The glory days of the Tavistock as an organisation are long past but we forget the lessons at our peril. (Fred Emery died in April 1997 but his wife Merrelyn, from a Canberra base, continues to address the big questions concerning representative, participative democracy.)

The two fiftieth birthdays symbolise for me firstly the peculiar genius of Australia and secondly those unchanging realities about the human condition which every generation has to learn. Put the two together and you have a powerful engine for change. I firmly believe that this country has unique assets which equip it for world leadership in some arenas. The coming of the millennium, and the Olympics, and the remaking of the Constitution all symbolise the opportunities to be seized. But we could miss the chance if we fail to mobilise all the latent intelligence and the leadership potential. This is a good time for the 'clever country' to re-examine the *kind* of cleverness it needs.

Bryce Courtenay tells the apocryphal story of a conversation between President Clinton and that great Australophile Edward de Bono. The President asks: 'What would be the elements of an ideal country in the twenty-first century?' De Bono is supposed to have replied: 'Well—it would have to have a population of less than twenty-five million people, it would have to use the English language, it would have to be located on the Pacific rim, it would have to possess a well-entrenched democracy, and it would have a strong tertiary education system. Oh—by the way—it exists already—it's called Australia!'

Alistair Mant
April 1997

Acknowledgments

There are far too many people to thank by name for my recent re-education in Australian political and managerial life. They know who they are. Let me single out my two daughters, Eleanor and Isabel, each of whom has travelled around Australia with me recently and whose half-Australian insights, shaped by their mother's keen eye, have been extraordinarily helpful to me. I want to mention also my publisher Joshua Dowse, a publisher who understands writers. I recommend this. I am also grateful for the extended hospitality of my friend Angela Nordlinger, in whose home I have met an amazing array of creative eccentrics, some of them installed in the book.

Charles Handy, the doyen of the management writers, advised on the text and made one crucially important structural suggestion for which I am very grateful. My old friend Alan Walker has done a superb job of indexing very complex material.

Finally, and most important, I am indebted to the outstanding Australian entrepreneurs who have lent their personal and professional stories to this little enterprise. They are, as they say, part of the solution rather than part of the problem.

Introduction

I want to be the leader!
I want to be the leader!
Can I be the leader?
Can I? I can?
Promise? Promise?
Yippee! I'm the leader!
I'm the leader!
OK, what shall we do?

Roger McGough, b. 1937

There goes the mob! . . . I am their leader—I must follow them!

French revolutionary leader (in cafe), circa 1848

As the millennium approaches, there is evidently some kind of problem about 'leadership'. The evidence suggests that confidence in political leaders is diminishing, to the point where the democratic process itself is threatened. If very substantial numbers of people (as in the United States) don't bother to vote at elections, something must be seriously wrong. It is not just politics. Confidence in the morals and capability of business leadership has also diminished. The 'Tomorrow's Company' movement is dedicated to the idea that if the free-enterprise limited liability public corporation doesn't reform

1

itself, it will surrender all legitimacy. It doesn't stop there. Confidence in public administrators, trade unions, senior military officers, church leaders, teachers and even parents has been shaken by the manifest failure of all kinds of institutions to cope intelligently with change.

This book begins from the assumption that there is a good deal of stupidity about. You can make an argument that most of the problems confronting society are ethical problems. I don't want to deny the importance of the moral dimension, merely to stress the intelligence angle and to say something helpful *about* intelligence—what it really is and how it can be tweaked to good effect. The great psychoanalyst Wilfred Bion argued that arrogance and stupidity were pretty much the same thing, because the one invariably causes the other. I think he was right. Just now there are many excellent books coming out on the subject of business ethics and morals. I don't want to add to the pile and, anyway, I think we are more likely to make progress if we focus on practical operating intelligence. In other words, the main reason why leaders fail is that those who do are often *not up to the job*—they lack the intellectual firepower (a concept explained fully later on) needed to cope with the complexity. They may have parallel failings, but this is the real killer when blunders and cockups occur.

This doesn't mean that I will neglect the ethical dimension. It crops up repeatedly in these pages because it would be stupid to ignore the issue. How you approach this depends, I think, on your belief system. Believers, in the religious sense, look on human intelligence as a *function* of the moral universe. The higher-order system is God and He determines the nature of intelligence. Skeptics, on the other hand, argue that our ethical beliefs are a function of our intelligence, which is all we have to call on in coping with a naughty world. We invent gods to help allay our fears about the imponderable. I am not taking sides. I hope that *anybody* who cares about quality and standards and human compassion and enduring success will find it helpful to focus on the intellectual aspect of leadership, whatever their starting point. The *real* enemies are those who don't care—those whose survival needs cut them off from thoughtfulness. They don't read books anyway.

Margaret Thatcher's great project for Britain, presented as a *moral* crusade against 'socialism', was to make it more like the United States, a country she uncritically admires. Unfortunately, she succeeded in replicating the *worst* of the United States, the bits that threaten its long-term prosperity—the brutal, tooth-and-claw, materialistic fractiousness, rather than the wonderful folksy generosity and community spirit. An Australian writer, Robert Hughes, has described this aspect of American culture much more succinctly than any of the locals (in *The Culture of Complaint*). He paints a picture of a permanently infantilised population, wanting gratification now but unwilling to pay the long-term costs; always needing someone to blame for life's reverses. This is the well-known 'dumbing' of America—the widespread loss of capacity to see the connection between the immediate and the longer term. If all politics is driven by competing interest groups squabbling in a marketplace, what is the place for long-term vision or for intelligent leadership?

In both the United States and the United Kingdom there has been a huge widening of the gulf between the richest and the poorest in society. A new book, Robert Frank's *The Winner-take-all Society*, suggests that the top few per cent of the American wealthy are now sucking out nearly *half* of the disposable wealth each year. This is not only morally dubious, it is also *inefficient* because it makes society very expensive to manage. The United States, for the first time, now has more of its citizens in jail or on remand than in college. This is very expensive. The same drift to splitting rich and poor is apparent in Australia but, as yet, things have not gone so far. On 6 November 1996, the *Australian Financial Review* revealed that the chief executives of Australia's top fifty companies had, in the space of a decade, increased their average salary from thirty-six times the average salary of employees in their own firms to forty-nine times the average. That was before taking account of fancy new stock options, partly paid shares and other perks. The top fifty CEOs' A$35 000 per *week* now equals the *annual* average Australian wage. Even within big firms, the winners are increasingly taking out a disproportionate share of the spoils. At the bottom end of those firms, the staff are likely to exist precariously on short-term, part-time contracts, or casual work.

In the old days, the CEO's rewards were often fixed by the chairman—frequently the ex-CEO and quite interested in protecting his own reputation vis-à-vis the interloper. Nowadays, a 'remuneration committee' comprising other *inner circle* top dogs and 'remuneration consultants' (also in the loop) ratchets up the figures, to mutual advantage. In Britain and Australia, prime ministers wring their hands and publicly disapprove of 'fat cats', especially in recently privatised public utilities. In Japan, the average employee vs CEO multiplier tends to be much smaller; in the United States, it can run into the hundreds, except in certain principled organisations (like the office design firm Herman Miller, where the CEO's salary is *pegged* to twenty times average earnings in the firm). With luck and good management, Australia may preserve its traditional values of egalitarianism, fairness and sympathy for the underdog. All this is a question of leadership (and, of course, intelligence). Australia doesn't *have* to copy the United States and the United Kingdom, even though there are worrying signs that some political leaders can't think what else to do.

POWER, AUTHORITY AND MODES OF THOUGHT AND OPERATION

In 1977 I published a book called *The Rise and Fall of the British Manager*. This was an attempt to say something helpful to the English, in whose midst I had been living for ten years or so. By that time, I had discovered that the Scots, the Irish, the Welsh and the citizens of the north of England were the salt of the earth. These were the people who provided the *best* of the original Australian immigrant population stock. But the people who called all the shots in Britain— the financiers and captains of industry—clustered around London and, surrounded by flatterers and chatterers, were in my judgement mostly bad news. They were charming and witty and altogether seductive. Most of them were crooks, but in a very gentlemanly way. They had a mindset so distinctive that I had to coin a term to describe it. The word was 'binary'. Their kith and kin provided Australia with the *worst* of its bad habits. The so-called 'bottom of the harbour' financial scams of the 1980s always remind me of the 'South Sea Bubble' and other spectacular English ripoffs. Nick Leeson, of Barings Bank infamy, is just a modern Francis Drake.

One beauty of the word 'binary' was that it could be expressed graphically, thus: ∞. It described a relationship characterised and dominated by interpersonal influence. Binary meant: if I win, you lose; or if we scratch each other's backs, we can screw the rest—as in on–off binary notation. Its fundamental assumption is of Darwinian *survival*. Its most obvious manifestation was the 19th century capitalists' abuse of power, an abuse that bedded-in the fear and resentment that was to characterise British industrial relations there-after. The Scots always understood the principle of *industrial democracy*—creating a three-cornered constitutional framework (you versus me but within the constitution) to give the workers some say, usually via representation, in the policy formulation process. This diminishes the sense of a feudal 'master vs servant' relationship. The Scots are engineers at heart, and value the *real* 'masters'—the work outputs and the constitutional framework. The English genius is for money and power, and true democracy always threatens vested interests.

The other form of binary relationship was characterised by *seduction* rather than the naked abuse of power. In fact the main subject of *The Rise and Fall of the British Manager* was the emergence of the highly seductive 'management' movement—an English invention which did much harm in Britain and seeped out damagingly to all the other English-speaking economies, including the United States and Australia. The main role of 'management' was to separate re-spectable *owners* from the dreadful depredations visited on 19th century *workers*. The Germans, without a management movement, or management 'profession', or management education industry, or even a *word* in the language for 'management', prospered by focusing on the *outputs* the customers needed and the *rights* the workers merited.

After World War II, Mercedes-Benz built their reputation for safety and integrity by crash-testing hundreds and hundreds of cars, when all the British and American manufacturers cared about was styling and salesmanship. Of course, both engineering and salesman-ship are important; the trick is to get the balance right. The English got to be brilliant at salesmanship—the ultimate binary skill—but they needed to, as the engineering got progressively worse. Increas-ingly, the boards of British companies were dominated by the money men; on German boards, the engineers still held the balance of power. From the middle of the 19th century, the Germans also began to embrace the principles of industrial democracy—an idea they mainly picked up from Scots writers and businessmen. Luckily for us Anglo-Saxons, the virus of 'management' is now seeping into German language and culture. In time, it may sap their vitality.

The opposite mindset to the binary I dubbed 'ternary', borrowing this use of the term from the anthropologist Gregory Bateson. He used it to describe certain kinds of three-cornered relationships,

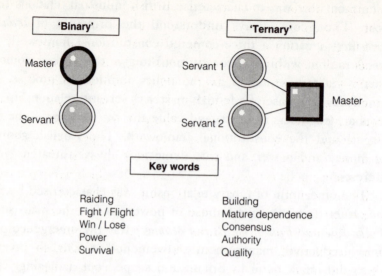

Figure 1   Modes of operation

In the binary mode of thought somebody always comes out on top. In the ternary mode the product or purpose or ideal comes out on top. The central binary question is: 'Will I win?' The central ternary question is more *intelligent*: 'What's it *for*?'

where absolute power is softened or governed by the *authority* of particular roles like non-commissioned officer or nanny. The idea of the ternary relationship was that it was governed by the *purpose* or *object* of the relationship or by its constitutional representation, rather than by interpersonal power. This too could be expressed graphically, thus: 8□. Mercedes was a ternary organisation because all its human relationships were governed by the ambition to make perfect motor vehicles. Its main bankers were on the board and committed to very long-term investment in the future. The British motor industry (which effectively no longer exists, now that BMW has acquired Rover, the last British-owned volume manufacturer) was binary because its relationships were dominated by greed, ambition and flashiness. The short-term imperatives of the stock market drove the enterprise. The honest engineers were there of course (many of them Scots), but were underrecognised, underpaid and undersupported by long-term development resources.

The simplest way to illustrate the binary/ternary distinction is to refer back to the democratic process. If you vote according to what you take to be your own or your family's best interests, you are voting binary—if you gain, somebody else is bound to lose. If you vote according to what you take to be best for your *country*, even if you expect to disadvantage yourself in the short term, then you are voting ternary—the relationship of everybody to the higher-order ideal takes precedence over the win/lose relationships between people or sectional interests. By the way, the ternary route is more *intelligent*; it demands more *thought*. It requires the citizen to connect personal desire with the duties of citizenship. Not voting at all is binary by definition.

Doctors and health service managers found the binary/ternary idea particularly helpful because it explained why they kept having the same kinds of repetitive arguments without ever making any progress or arriving at an agreed conclusion. Doctors see themselves as ternary (dedicated to a precious 'third corner'—the sanctity of human life) and managers as binary (dedicated only to bean-counting). The managers, on the other hand, are often outwitted by senior consultants, who have cunning and highly political (binary) ways of securing their own clinical interests. The unfortunate manager, who knows that funds are not unlimited, usually aims merely to optimise health expenditure for maximum equity. That is his or her 'third corner'. So long as both sides believe themselves to be absolutely in the right, there can be no progress.

Paul Keating's 1996 election slogan, *'You don't have to like him but you've got to respect him!'*, played on the binary/ternary tension. Liking is interpersonal, hence binary. If they are pretty sure their candidate is unlikeable and disliked, the spin doctors' trick is to shift the ground to the 'third corner' by focusing on *task* and *destination*. Respect is gained through effort and dedication to a purpose. If the public believe that the purpose is to better the nation, then they may respect a leader who is perceived as 'tough but fair' in pursuit of the purpose. I did my best to persuade my Conservative friends in the United Kingdom that they could usefully adapt the Keating slogan for John Major: 'You can't respect him but you can't help liking him!' This idea has not gone down well.

Perhaps the most important aspect of the ternary idea was that it focused attention away from the *behavioural* angle of leadership and put the weight on the *purpose* of organisations. Once you accept the idea that managerial *authority* (as opposed to naked power) flows from the third corner, then you have to ask: *what does this organisation exist*

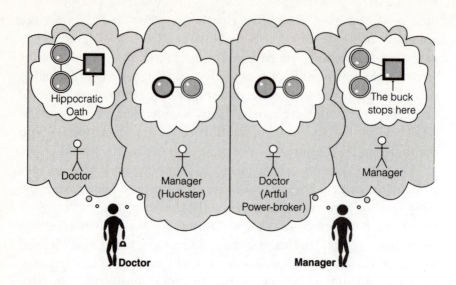

Figure 2   This illustrates the potential usefulness of the binary/ternary idea in practice. When doctors and health service managers habitually disagree, each side is always 'in the right'. The diagram shows how this arises with each side thinking of the other in binary mode. So long as this binary state persists there can be no intelligent progress—all arguments are *low grade* arguments that go nowhere fast. Once both sides see and appreciate the meaning of the diagram they may be able, and prepared, to ascend to the ternary position in order to have a *high grade* argument—that is, a *realistic* one. Thus a diagram on the binary/ternary idea can have the effect of helping to convert binary behaviour into ternary intelligence.

to do? If the purpose of the organisation is essentially frivolous (as in most parts of the perfumery business) or pernicious (as in tobacco), then a ternary focus is likely to be embarrassing. In such organisations, 'leadership' is bound to be defined in terms of (binary) persuasiveness. If, on the other hand, the output or purpose of the organisation is manifestly *useful*, as in most parts of public service, then the personal aspect of leadership doesn't have to be persuasive because the overall purpose is *good* (or persuasive) *enough*. It isn't quite so simple, however. Some organisations supply outputs that are intrinsically valuable (life insurance, for example) but the *way* in which the product is distributed turns out sometimes to be reprehensible. The simple matrix in Figure 3 sets out the possible combinations.

The Rise and Fall of the British Manager was a surprise success in

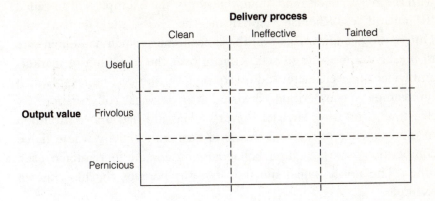

Figure 3 **Possible output value/delivery process combinations**

Real (inner) motivation flows from commitment or attachment to a
valuable *purpose*. The *authority* of the ternary leader flows from the
purpose. If the purpose is frivolous or pernicious, it follows that the
leadership is likely to revert to binary. Even if the purpose is
intrinsically good, the delivery process may still be naughty. Life
insurance, for example, is fundamentally useful but the *practices* of
some life companies and sales representatives are tainted. You can
locate any organisation's purpose and mode somewhere on the grid.

Britain, considering its subject matter. Possibly, many of its readers
were Scots or other such honest folk, or women, whose orientation
tends to be ternary, for reasons explained in Chapter 11. The
binary/ternary idea evolved as a simple but powerful way of describing
some of the issues mentioned above. It is not a 'theory', nor is it
essentially new—merely a reframing of ideas which have been with
us since Plato, and before. You could say that binary relationships
channel *power*, and ternary relationships create and depend upon
authority. The authority derives from the common 'third corner'. The
full flowering of the idea came with the publication of a subsequent
book, *Leaders We Deserve*.

This book first came out in 1983. By then, I had enjoyed many
discussions and arguments about the meaning of the binary/ternary
split. It had become clear that it was a pretty good way of thinking
and talking about *leadership*. By the early 1980s an increasing number
of political and industrial leaders were being exposed as corrupt or
incompetent or, very frequently, both. Business leadership in the
Anglo-Saxon world was beginning to look a little shaky in comparison

with the Asian 'tigers' and, more relevantly, the exemplars of so-called 'Rhineland' or 'Rhenish' capitalism—the Swiss, the Germans, the Dutch, the Scandinavians—all those economies which had taken care to preserve a measure of state control over the operation of markets and which were characterised by strong local sub-economies in which intercompany competition coexisted with regional collaboration. By this time, Professor Michael Porter of Harvard had drawn attention to the existence of regional *clusters* of economic activity where fierce competition *and* farsighted collaboration seemed to reinforce each other. The north Italian tile industry was perhaps the best known example.

In his original presentation of the binary/ternary notion, Bateson wrote:

> There is a very profound contrast between such (symmetrical) competitive systems of behaviour and complementary dominance–submission systems—a highly significant contrast for any discussion of national character. In complementary striving [what I would call *binary*] the stimulus which prompts A to greater efforts is the relative *weakness* in B; if we want to make A subside or submit, we ought to show him that B is stronger than he is. In fact, the complementary character structure may be summarized by the phrase 'bully-coward', implying the combination of these characteristics in the personality. The symmetrical competitive systems [what I would call *ternary*] . . . are an almost precise functional opposite of the complementary. Here the stimulus which evokes greater striving in A is the vision of greater *strength* or greater striving in B.

This was what Michael Porter described in northern Italy—the co-existence of binary competitiveness and ternary collaboration. If your competitor is strong, it makes you strong too—and your region.

Note that Bateson was writing about, amongst other matters, national character. You don't have to spend too long in the 'Rhineland' economies to realise that, although business activity is highly competitive, both within and between nations, these are highly civilised places in which to live and work. In these countries, the bosses are not exactly softies. The point is that, generally speaking, they are invested with *authority* by the existence of proper constitutional working relations. When most people are asked to describe past bosses they recall with respect and gratitude—'good bosses'—they come up with the same two words repeatedly: 'tough' (or firm) but

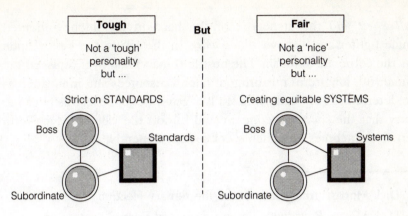

Figure 4   The good boss

> When most people recall past good bosses (or teachers, or parents) it is surprising how often they spontaneously come up with: 'Tough (or firm) but fair'. You don't necessarily have to *like* a boss who is intelligent enough to insist on high standards and to create fair systems, at least at the time. But, afterwards, you are likely to remember that (ternary) boss with gratitude and affection and to think of him or her as a 'leader'.

'fair'. This has very little to do with personality or 'leadership style' and everything to do with concern for *standards* and respect for *fairness*. As Figure 4 shows, these are ternary elements. If the boss is consistent in these matters, sooner or later he or she will come to be regarded as an admirable *person* and as a 'leader'.

By contrast with the Rhineland economies, the United States, particularly in the Reagan/Bush period, went Darwinian, on the very dubious assumption that markets, left to themselves and utilising supposedly perfect knowledge, will operate in the short term with the same kind of 'efficiency' as evolutionary processes which generally take millions of years to wreak their effects. Natural selection was tough on more species than we know about. The difficulty is to know, in the short term, if you (or your species, or your corporation, or your model of economics) are doomed. As long as it lasted, the full-blown American Darwinian period favoured the binary type of person. The flavour of the month was Gordon Gecko, the anti-hero of the cult film

Wall Street and the archetype of the hard-driving, money-oriented jungle fighter and—above all—a *bully*. In the 1980s, the key weapon was the corporate ambush. The hostile (binary) takeover replaced the thoughtful, long-term nurturing of talent, resources and innovation as the determinant of 'leadership skills'. A number of observers began to worry that the shortsightedness could kill off the valuable, long-term (ternary) outcomes on which *all* of society depends.

Dick Morris, 'triangulation' and the ternary election

Dick Morris, President Clinton's disgraced former electoral strategist, provides a near-perfect example of the relationship between the binary and ternary modes, at both the personal and the institutional level. His 1996 book *Behind the Oval Office* reveals how his relationship with the President veered from mutually seductive backscratching to an impressively detached shared understanding of American history. The personal relationship, in other words, flipflopped between binary and ternary. Because Dick Morris got caught trying to impress a Washington prostitute with his presidential connections, he will probably go down in history merely as a binary fixer. He certainly was a master of binary *fight/flight* psychology, as all good spin doctors are. The complication is an independent variable—he is *also* a highly intelligent man. This means that, when he needed to, he could ascend to the ternary, and take the President with him.

At the start of the campaign Clinton *ought* to have been a lame duck, trailing a string of scandals behind him. Morris addressed the problem by a strategy of what he dubbed 'triangulation'. The Republicans' greatest error, in his view, was the mistaken *binary* belief that in order to beat Clinton they had to destroy him. The Morris stratagem was to flood the media with a continuous drip-drip of TV advertisements during the slack eighteen months before the campaigning got going in earnest. Every single advertisement addressed the 'values agenda'—issues like welfare reform, tuition tax credits, family leave, the environment, tobacco and so on. Clinton's role was to stay aloof from all the attacks on his reliability as a man: the Gennifer Flowers/Paula Jones sex scandals, Whitewater, 'travelgate', the draft, pot-smoking, etc. The President's *aides* discussed these matters with the media—the President himself, never. Morris's mantra was: 'Public values defeat private character attacks'.

The point was that most of Clinton's indiscretions were in the distant past. The trick was to position the President's *current* achievements alongside the already securely established 'values agenda'. According to Morris, 'verbs always beat adjectives'. By the time the Republicans mounted a serious offensive, after the party conventions, the attack was almost entirely adjectival—condemning Clinton and praising Dole. By then the public had absorbed the message that the President had apparently been *doing* something about the issues that most concerned them (according to Morris's polling). Morris understood that at that stage the only effective Republican counter to his strategy would be to steal or appropriate the 'values agenda' so carefully nurtured over the previous year and a half.

General Colin Powell would have been the Republican secret weapon, were he to gain the nomination, because he was already associated in the public mind with *ternary* values. When the news came through that Powell had failed to get the support needed (this was a whole *year* before polling day), Morris announced: 'The election is now over!' Turning to the President, he said: 'Congratulations, you've won!' The twelve people around the table in the White House met this with an astonished silence, then derisive laughter. In his book Morris wrote: 'The President remained silent. He looked up at me over his reading glasses. Then, having silently calculated that I was probably right, he resumed reading his agenda book without saying a word. The outcome of the election, if not our actual margin of victory, was established that day and was never seriously in doubt afterward.'

The Democrats' success in 1996 may be an important harbinger of things to come. Because of Morris's strategy, and the failure of the Republicans to counter it intelligently, the election was won largely on the basis of higher-order *ternary* values—the 'values agenda'. That is how democracy is supposed to work—the people voting for longer term collective advantage rather than for selfish gratification of immediate appetites. In that sense, it was the most ternary election in recent American history. Maybe we shall see the same shift elsewhere; for example in Australia in 1999? The point is not that American politics has suddenly gone all mushy and sentimental— the 1996 battleground was as tough and binary as in any election in history. It was just that the *binary* battle was won by the *intelligent* application of a *ternary* agenda. No person, not even a spin doctor like Dick Morris, is *either* binary *or* ternary. Intelligence dictates which of the two makes more sense, and when.

ABOUT THIS BOOK

In 1993 and 1994 I was spending much more time back in my homeland, working directly with clients or through the major business schools and the Leadership Consortium of blue-chip Australian firms. As a result, I got wind of a number of individuals who were exercising, it seemed to me, a peculiarly Australian, and effective, form of leadership. Any one of them would have been worthy of a full-scale biography. It was an attractive idea to use these stories to illustrate some important general themes about leadership in Australia. The main point about the people described in this book is that they all demonstrate the particular quirky or maverick kind of intelligence that Australia will need to make use of if the country is to prosper in the next century. 'Intelligence' takes many forms; these people help us to appreciate the intelligence of the future, whilst acknowledging the contribution of other kinds of 'brightness' in the past.

The book's essence

I encourage the reader to read the whole book because all the stories and diagrams are woven into the central argument. A rough navigational route map is provided below.

The following seven basic elements represent the main features to be taken in along the way. They are arranged in a causal sequence; that is, each element plays a part in causing the others. Taken together, they add up to the cause of successful leadership. Like the geographical features seen on a journey, the fact that they hardly change doesn't reduce the pleasure of seeing them afresh. This book exists partly to remind us of the basic truths which don't change.

1. *Authority*
Successful leadership depends on the leader acting with authority or authoritatively. This has nothing to do with autocracy or authoritarianism. It just means that the people authorise the leader to get on with it because they trust him or her. We need to understand what causes that kind of trust.

2. *Purpose*
The ternary symbol ⅋□ appears at the top of every page as a reminder that, while leaders need all kinds of skills, their authority derives ultimately from the useful purpose. If the purpose is good enough and

the leader can see how to get to it, he or she doesn't need 'charisma'—that will come in time.

3. *Judgement*

No one can define good judgement, but most of us know it when we see it. It is the *sine qua non* of effective leadership. Essentially, it is the mental ability to grapple at speed with complexity. There are well-proven methods for identifying this capacity and predicting its development in people.

4. *Systems ('frog') thinking*

The evidence suggests that sound judgement is mainly a function of 'systems thinking'—the ability to focus on the particular whilst holding the context in mind. The particular task in hand is *what* to do; the context supplies the *why*. If you understand why, you can exercise judgement and thus provide a lead towards a new, more intelligent direction.

5. *Sanity*

This book devotes a lot of attention to psychological damage because this is the most significant source of interference into otherwise sound judgement. When the complexity gets too much for the leader, that is when any lurking psychopathology is likely to erupt.

6. *Broad-band intelligences*

If we examine the childhoods of the leaders described in this book, we see intelligence developing in a broad way, stimulated by a wide variety of influences and activities. This has implications both for infant education and for broadening the thinking/doing range of adults.

7. *The virtuous circle*

Individual leaders who are clever and sane in the pursuit of valuable goals create circumstances which encourage a critical mass of other people to develop in the same way. In time, this may imbue whole institutions and societies with a sense of purpose. In this setting, new generations of purposeful and resourceful leaders emerge quite naturally.

How to navigate the book

Because leadership and intelligence are such complex and subtle subjects, the road ahead (for the reader) is a winding one. I apologise in advance for any time the reader may spend in the undergrowth, just off the road. Because the 'leadership' route is so interesting, I think the undergrowth is interesting too. But be warned.

The basic structure of the book is as follows.

Part I deals with meaning and interpretation. What do we *mean* by the central concepts of 'intelligence' and 'leadership'? And what is the place of 'systems thinking'? I wouldn't have bothered to write this book if I hadn't felt that we need, urgently, to look at these concepts from a new angle—from a *number* of new angles, as it happens. It is easy to say, as people do, 'He's a *natural* leader!' or 'She's really *bright*!', but what does this mean? One person's 'bright' may be another's airhead. Some people distrust, even *detest*, leaders that others will follow to the ends of the earth. In this part of the book I look at the key issues from a number of different angles because I know from experience that different people *construct* things differently. Accordingly, I employ a number of metaphors—from monkeys, via leprechauns, to rugby scrums.

Part II—the 'engine room' of the book—comprises the stories, along with reflections on related matters. Each story concerns a real, flesh-and-blood 'leader'—most of them Australians. These stories are deliberately longer than the cameos that usually illustrate leadership in books. The reason for this is that leadership must involve a powerful *personal* dimension if it is to make any sense. Leadership as a concept is too woolly unless you can get to grips with the formation of the leader–follower *process* inside and between people. I hope the reader will share with me the excitement of meeting these remarkable people. I am much in their debt. They do *not* represent a comprehensive or exhaustive list of outstanding leaders—they are merely *interesting*. Three are dead (including the monkey), one (I think) is in jail, and the three women show the way forward to the ternary future.

Part III contains a number of 'helpful hints' about how to nurture and sustain the kind of intelligent leadership celebrated in the book. This isn't a how-to-do-it sort of book, but it would be churlish not to share a few tricks of the trade that have worked for me and my colleagues around the world. There is nothing fancy here; just a few practical methods which grow directly out of the concepts outlined in Part I.

That is the basic structure, but the book isn't quite as neat as that. The stories run throughout the book and there are a great many cross-references and anticipations of themes yet to come. This is deliberate. I find much of the management literature pretty unreadable, on the grounds that most of the popular books contain just one big idea padded out to a couple of hundred pages. The exceptions amongst the big names, like Tom Peters and Charles Handy, grapple with complexity and offer pretty good stories. As my central thesis on intelligence concerns *making connections*, the sensible way to write about it is to make multiple connections in the text. The sensible way to read this book is therefore to jump about a bit. When I get letters from readers, I find they often pick up on what seem to me (but not to them) to be minor themes. That is fine by me—the world is a complicated place and not to be understood via simple formulae. Some readers may even prefer to dip into the stories before tackling the logic of intelligent leadership.

PART I

Intelligent leadership: no oxymoron

Much has been written about leadership. I have tried to read most of it, from inspirational stories about generals and admirals to convoluted accounts of psychological experiments. I have come to the conclusion that the subject needs to be examined from a variety of angles. That is the intention of this first part of the book. My hope is that at least some of these perspectives, if not all of them, will make sense to my readers. The *experience* of leadership and followership is powerful and simple—almost primitive. Understanding the meaning of it all and working out what to do about it is not so simple.

It is easy to be distracted by the 'great leaders' of history, most of whom come under immense pressure and some of whom fall from grace spectacularly. A good many of the best known have been tyrants. The point is that intelligent leadership is exercised, day by day, by thousands of humble people in modest roles—using their ingenuity to surmount problems and running calculated risks when it seems right to do so. For them the possession of intelligence and the exercise of leadership are certainly not contradictory.

1

Redefining leadership

The psychologists say, turning logic on its head, that every victim requires a murderer. This is the principle of *reciprocity*. So it is that every follower—and that means all of us some of the time—requires a leader sometimes. When we consider leadership, we are dealing with two quite separate aspects: the *process* that goes on between leader and follower (which is mainly emotional, although there is an intellectual aspect as well); and the *context* of the leadership (this concerns the *destination* towards which the leader points, which is usually rational but may contain highly emotional elements too).

It is surprising how many books and articles on leadership fail to draw this distinction clearly. If we view leadership as a human process, deeply rooted in our instinctual nature, then we can say that leadership exists whenever the human instinct to follow is triggered. Leadership, as a phenomenon, is thus defined by followership. There may, or may not, be a defensible purpose to it. Adolf Hitler was an extraordinarily successful leader because he succeeded in persuading many millions of devout German citizens to turn *away* from their cherished beliefs and values. Together with his stage manager, Dr Goebbels, he was arguably the first political leader fully to understand the black art of combining communications technology with theatre in order to affect mass psychology. The *process* was managed brilliantly. The *destination* was crazy.

Long ago, that great populariser Robert Ardrey, in *The Social Contract*, said something very wise about the human instinct to follow a lead, however primitive:

> A mob transcends its leaders, becomes a single wild happy thing satisfying identity, stimulation, the following response, xenophobia, australopithecine joys of the hunt and the kill, a thing that through delirious social self-approval discards all neocortical inhibition. To describe a mob as sub-human is incorrect; it simply ceases to behave like individuals. To regard it as a storm of disorder is equally incorrect, for a mob is as orderly a human phenomenon as one will ever encounter; let a single voice of rational dissent be raised within it, and observe what happens to the dissenter.

It is a good description of the primitive behaviours sometimes observable in boardrooms and on factory floors. Some people love it. If you think the context, purpose and destination are important too, then you could say that it is the task of leadership to express that rational dissent whenever necessary, at whatever risk.

THE LEADERSHIP PHENOMENON AS PHYSICS OR CHEMISTRY?

The leadership field has always been dogged by trait theory. Most learned studies of 'leaders' adopt this line. This is the *physics* approach to the subject: if you collect together all the right elements—courage, dedication, vision, confidence, energy, perseverance, etc.—it *must* work, just like an experiment in the laboratory. The trouble is that the followership angle makes the process *chemical*—when it works, somehow the *chemistry* works between the followers' needs and the 'leader's' capacity (or need) to channel them. This is very complicated and unpredictable. Some of the most powerful leaders in history have broken all the 'rules', which makes *predicting* leadership success very difficult. By the way, adolescent boys usually fall into the trap of adopting physics assumptions in their approach to girls—in the hope that the dogged application of formulae will get them somewhere. The girls generally know better—the trick is in the mutual *chemistry*;

you can't invent a relationship—you have to discover it! Boys should be taught these things in school.

With honourable exceptions, much of the American literature on leadership is based on physics principles. Even 'contingency theory', which asserted that situations differ and different folks require different strokes, managed to come across as a technical trick—first figure out the contingency and then apply the rules. The most honourable exception of all is the great American political scientist (and biographer of F. D. Roosevelt), James McGregor Burns. In his magisterial *Leadership* (first published in 1978) he drew the distinction between 'transactional leadership', which was all about interpersonal influence and persuasiveness, and 'transformational leadership', which concerned destinations as well. The archetype of the transactional was LBJ, who was described by Godfrey Hodgson (in *In Our Time*) thus:

> . . . a legislator whose vote was needed would find himself literally surrounded by a one-man army of Lyndon Johnson. His birthday would be remembered, his vanity flattered, his shoulder squeezed. He would be reminded, subtly or brutally according to the estimate made of his temperament, of his political problems at home or of his hopes of advancement on Capitol Hill. Every scrap of information would be retrieved, every tactic used, until the wretched man did what was wanted of him; then he would be overwhelmed by signs of the majority leader's gratitude and admiration.

McGregor Burns' transactional/transformational leadership paralleled my own invention of the binary/ternary idea at about the same time. The latter is explained in the Introduction. Its principal advantage is that it can be expressed visually ⅄ vs ⊶; this makes it easier to understand for people whose intelligence leans towards the *spatial*. You can see by looking at it that the left-hand symbol might be two people simply interacting and the right-hand symbol might be the same two interacting (in *role*) in a particular *context* or for a particular *purpose*. McGregor Burns' 'transformational' leadership was likewise focused on the *destination* to which the leader points. His ideas were copied by many imitators, most of whom turned them into slick (binary) consultancy packages.

LEADING FROM BEHIND

The leaders celebrated in this book are all 'natural' leaders in the sense that people are generally prepared to follow them. But none of them has learned the techniques of leadership as such. What distinguishes them is that they *leave things different*—like the dramatic hero in the play—not just the relationships but the whole situation. I will return to the theatrical metaphor later on because it is a good way of explaining the occasional impact of superficially 'uncharismatic' people. However, most of the books on leadership lean uncomfortably towards the 'Johnson treatment' in their assumptions about learning how to lead. President Truman famously said: 'A leader is a man who has the ability to get other people to do what they don't want to do and like it!' That is the essence of leading from the front. My leaders have the capacity to absorb themselves in something so interesting and valuable that other people begin to take notice after a while. This seems to me to be an attractive model of leadership for a culture like Australia which values the unconventional and the underdog. My leaders are not very 'clubbable' in the ordinary sense and none of them was really designed by nature for the executive suite of the big corporation. They are too impatient.

One of the more interesting of the new books about leadership comes from Professor Howard Gardner—*Leading Minds*. He distinguishes between 'direct' and 'indirect' leadership, which allows him to put politicians and scientists together as leaders, on the grounds that both sometimes leave the national or world stage different. Margaret Thatcher is listed as a 'direct' leader because the political process affects people directly and J. Robert Oppenheimer as an 'indirect' leader because it was his scientific works that did the affecting, long after his passing. In my terms, Thatcher was almost the ultimate 'binary' (persuasive/interpersonal) leader and Oppenheimer the classic 'ternary' (attached to task and role). This book (mine) proposes that ternary leadership is more interesting and, in the future, more important. Some of my leaders are 'direct' and some 'indirect', but they are all basically ternary (much more concerned about the important thing to be done than about influencing people), though all of them can turn on the 'Johnson treatment' when they have to.

Margaret Thatcher is an interesting and important case when 'strong' leadership is the subject. She performed a crucially important service for Britain in taking on and defeating the over-mighty trade union bosses. Their role was supposed to be a ternary one (improvement of industrial relations), but most of the big boys played it as a binary exercise in boss-bashing. In Thatcher they encountered a super-binary and came off second-best. That battle was inevitable and it was necessary that she win it.

The point is that this was a major set-piece battle in a long war to rescue the British socio-economic system. Sometimes, the war historians tell us, the best battlefield commanders don't translate well to strategic leadership, where the problems are more complex and the time-spans longer. Many of Thatcher's admirers now wish she had withdrawn from the fray at the top of her form, in the mid- to late-1980s. She would have gone down in history as one of the great prime ministers.

As things turned out, she went on to make the kinds of mistakes that overstretched CEOs are prone to—the application of too-simple formulae to too-complex problems. Perhaps the most damaging of these was the slavish adherence to monetarist economic theory (or dogma). In the end these ideas were quietly dropped by her successors but, by then, the damage had been done in the form of an emasculated manufacturing base and destabilising boom/bust cycles. Margaret Thatcher was a *strong* political leader but, as this is a book about leadership intelligence, we should note that history is likely to judge her as being *wrong* too often on the big questions.

PECKING ORDERS AND 'SIBLING' LEADERSHIP IN ORGANISATIONS

To anticipate the quirky and individualistic leaders in the book, it may help to invoke the metaphor of sibling pecking orders. The reader should be warned that it doesn't help to approach this too literally—we are dealing here not with family life but with the way that psychology affects organisational life. Leading from the front is, metaphorically speaking, the province of the first-born child. Leading from behind is the younger sibling's speciality. The psychologist Alfred Adler described the first-born as characteristically a *'power-hungry conservative'*. The newly first-born baby is 'powerful', even though physically helpless. First-time parents almost always lack confidence and tend to be 'led' from the start by the imperious newcomer. Most often, the key event, a year or so into this tyranny, is the arrival of the younger child. Suddenly the first-born has to yield the mysterious power to the newcomer. Watch a two-year-old watching its newborn sibling—it cannot understand its powerful feelings, which veer between a sort of 'love', simple curiosity and murderousness.

The psychological life's work for the first-born from then on (unless it is old enough by then to understand and manage feelings of rivalry) is to *get the power back*. It is no coincidence that the executive suites of public and private-sector organisations all around the world are peopled by so many first-borns. If you need power, you will work relentlessly to get it. The second- to nth-born child enters a much more complex family situation than the first-born. It is more like an elaborated *authority structure* than a crude power nexus. The younger sibling is generally less conscientious, more self-possessed, more interested in things for their own sake, and much less anxious to please adults. The cry of the younger sibling down the ages is: *'It's not fair!'* This presupposes that families are democracies of a sort. The best ones are.

This is just a metaphor for illustrating the difference between *anointed* leadership and *emergent* leadership. This book is primarily about the second of these because emergent leadership depends on ingenuity, not position. Quite a few scientific revolutionaries like Newton and Einstein were first-borns, but it has been argued that the 'emotional' revolutions that alter our way of perceiving ourselves are different. *All* the famous evolutionists, or those quickly converted to Darwin's view, were, like him, younger brothers. Almost all the eminent scientists who opposed the evolutionary doctrine were first-borns. Frank Sulloway, in *Born to Rebel*, argues that the Copernican and Freudian revolutions, which similarly disturb comforting notions about ourselves, demonstrate the same birth-order effect. He argues that nearly all the true revolutionaries, if they are not younger siblings, turn out to be first-borns brought up to reject their fathers or first-borns whose fathers were themselves revolutionaries.

Sulloway's data and opinions are highly contentious (no doubt especially in the eyes of first-borns) but, as I say, birth order is just an engaging metaphor for examining the relationship of *power* to *ingenuity*. The capacity of managers to hang on to power, however cunningly, is not as important as the capacity to be truly creative—to make exciting things happen. It is crucial therefore for systems—corporations, governments, countries—to allow ingenuity to flourish, even though there are likely to be powerful impediments, some of them unconscious. In a sense, *all* women are younger siblings when they make it into the upper ranks of male-dominated organisational systems. They are latecomers, they tend to be excluded from the locker room ethos and they certainly complain, 'It's not fair!' You could argue that Australia as a whole remains a kind of younger sibling, at least until the Republic arrives.

LEADERSHIP OF THE BIG (WORLD) GAME—THE RUGBY METAPHOR

If the family analogy is not to your taste, consider the rugby field. On the surface, the contest is between two fairly matched teams of fifteen men. Look under the surface and you can see a much more subtle and significant contest between the heavy *forwards* of both sides (whose project is to tighten or close the game up) and the fleetfooted *backs* of both sides (who aim to open things out, have a bit of fun, and entertain the people who really matter). The analogy works pretty well for corporate life. Remember that when the game emerged, on the playing fields of Rugby School, it was important that *all* the boys should be kept occupied, or out of mischief, on winter afternoons. This meant the big, slow, lumbering and possibly dangerous boys as well as those who were naturally graceful athletes.

Thus was the scrum invented. Getting your head down, (male) bonding and shoving steadily forward against the opposition describes late 20th century corporate life pretty well, at least in the eyes of women. Studies of big corporate blunders almost invariably involve all-male 'groupthink'—the process by which individually smart people sometimes lose their wits in gung-ho groups. But all the best 're-engineering' success stories involve creative collaboration *across* organisational boundaries by the mentally fleet-of-foot. That means that the true leaders of the future are likely to collaborate with the most interesting people *outside* their immediate systems in formal and informal strategic alliances. Insiders often doubt the 'loyalty' of such clever or unconventional people. Chapter 10 contains the story of John Latham of IBM whose broad networks *outside* the company might have been used to save the company from its only big blunder in sixty years of operation. But he was usually regarded in the firm as a kind of *spy*, because too few people understood his 'big game' motives. Most observers date the major problems of the IBM Corporation from the early to mid-1980s. Latham knew exactly what was going to happen, and when, *in 1971*!

I appreciate that my use of the rugby metaphor precludes many women and all those who hew to other football codes, and is bound also to irk those whom God meant to be heavyweight *forwards*. Of course, not all forwards are slow, dangerous or lacking in individuality; some of them are amongst my best friends. The scrum simply illustrates mindlessness and head-down doggedness better than any other example I can think of. It also prepares us for the metaphor of the *bicycle* and the *frog*, which is all about how the parts of a system relate to the whole. If you happen (metaphorically speaking) to be stuck in an organisational scrum, you *have* to preserve, somehow, a connection with the big game.

Intelligent leadership, I argue, is not just about who wins the narrow contest, but about the magnificence of the *whole game*. Accordingly, this book is not primarily about how to make old-fashioned corporations more flexible or ingenuity-friendly. There are a number of very good books emerging on the concept of the 'intelligent organisation'—not least Gifford Pinchot's new book, *The End of Bureaucracy and the Rise of the Intelligent Organisation*. My aim is to focus more closely on the makeup of the new kind of leader—the kinds of people who generate shared enthusiasm rather than merely wield influence. The obvious contest is that between corporations, fighting in marketplaces, just as in the rugby example. From a national perspective, the *real* underlying struggle may be between the emergent leadership of gifted juniors right across the corporate world and the established *cadres* of seniors, networked together not just within firms but right across the upper echelons of business, government, the professions and all the other elements of the Establishment.

To give an example from an Australian perspective, I would be much more interested in the international networks established by ingenious and entrepreneurial *scientists* or *engineers* (for example, in the sixty-plus federally-funded Cooperative Research Centres) than in executive 'teamwork' within corporations. Whenever there is a gung-ho team, there is usually a disaffected knot of non-members grumbling about the energetic wrong direction the team is taking. In my experience, *some* of the grumblers are usually right. The best of them may have difficulty in explaining their position, not necessarily because they lack eloquence, but because what they have to say is *complicated*. It is complicated because it refers to an *external* logic. This is the oldest problem for leadership. Winston Churchill was a great leader partly because he habitually surrounded himself with brilliant, cranky, fearless insubordinates. He loved it. Margaret Thatcher, who constantly compared herself with Churchill, could not abide cleverness. If you said something complicated (about a truly complicated subject), you were deemed 'wet'. Before long, you were out of the Cabinet, or whatever. This really was a brain drain.

It follows that this is not likely to be a useful book for anyone who thinks, 'I want to be the leader!—I want to be the leader!' (as McGough's words have it). There certainly was a time when it was possible to maintain ascendancy by mastering the Machiavellian tricks of political power. In the future, the only reliable pathway to influence and satisfaction will be via ingenuity in the pursuit of interesting and valuable ends. The leaders in these pages are all people who have taken this route, sometimes with great difficulty. They are all good role models, in my opinion, for future success. In the Introduction I set out the distinction between 'binary' and 'ternary' leadership. This offers a simple language for thinking about human influence in terms of its two main manifestations—one (the ternary) generally useful and healthy; the other (the binary) often exploitative and divisive.

THE ABB COMPANY—THE NEW CORPORATE MODEL

Much has been written about Asea Brown Boveri, the Swiss/Swedish trams-to-power-stations conglomerate. On the surface, it is simply a big multinational firm. Look more closely, and you see a loose federation of over a thousand smallish units, each of them with the coherence and shapeliness of a quick-moving rugby *back line*. ABB describes itself not as 'multinational' but as *multidomestic*. The aim is not 'globalisation' but *global localisation*. Because ABB doesn't have a superstructure of bureaucracy, it has no big, slow, lumbering *forwards* to dominate the game. Instead, the company is led by the fleetfooted *backs*, out in the field. The dynamic is not 'export-push' from the (scrum) centre but 'import-pull' from the forty-plus countries in which

ABB operates. The optimum size for a manufacturing plant is regarded as no more than about 300 people. As a result, there is no executive undergrowth from which to launch an ambush. The kind of in-fighting found in most big corporations is notably lacking in ABB because there is no place for skulduggery to take root; everything is in the open. If you have a successful career, it will probably be because you are effective, not because you male-bonded with all the other influential top dogs.

Few of the leaders described in these pages are, or were, corporate executives. The importance of the ABB example is that it shows the possibility of fleetfooted creatives surviving in big firms. It would be too easy for the executive reader of this book to write off my individual examples of leadership as harebrained boffins. Hewlett-Packard and Xerox are two other contemporary examples of big corporations that have succeeded in keeping the 'forwards' at bay and opening up space for the 'backs'. Significantly, the late and much lamented founder of H-P, Dave Packard, was exactly the same kind of product/purpose-driven boffin as I describe. The famous 'H-P way' was always designed to open up possibilities, encourage ingenuity and make crude careerism a dangerous activity. It is the ternary principle made flesh because it transcends the people and the products—it is what the company *stands for*. Dave Packard *hated* the bureaucratic careerists and made sure that the clever scientists, on whom the company depended, had a generous stake in all the stock schemes.

The Herman Miller corporation, a Michigan-based office furniture maker/designer, not only limits the bureaucracy, it formally pegs the chief executive's salary to twenty times average earnings in the firm. It may sound generous but it means that the wonderfully witty and approachable Kerm Campbell earns significantly less than most of his peers in other companies. Nobody in Herman Miller, Campbell included, would have it otherwise. The effect of this is to give the whole firm a coherence and *integrity*, and to reinforce a sense of *fairness*. I would guess that all my leaders could flourish in Herman Miller and that is why the company buzzes. But Herman Miller adopted the 'Scanlon Plan' back in the early 1950s. This was the brainchild of Joseph Scanlon of MIT. It was based on the need to ensure that the precious individual *identity* of every single member of staff should be nurtured (against the bureaucracy), that every

employee should *participate* directly in the company's decision processes, that the principle of *equity* should govern all role relationships
(Kerm Campbell's salary being the most obvious example), and that
the identification and nurturing of *competence* should govern all staff
deployment, from top to bottom (that principle determined the company's employment of only the very best design skills).

In reading my selection of intelligent leadership tales, bear in
mind that those I describe would not survive for long in most big
corporations. But bear in mind also that this is not just a matter of
their individual eccentricities, it is also the *fault* of organisations
dominated by generally well-meaning plodders. Inevitably, such
organisations become happy hunting grounds for amoral careerists.
Look at the terrible things that go on in scrums.

THE FABLE OF THE POLYPLOID HORSE

The ABB Company is a good example of a system reclaiming its
natural properties. Before the coming of the big bureaucracies (mainly
in the 19th century) nearly all organisational systems were shapely
and comprehensible. This meant that they had a human scale and
you could stay in touch with the extremities. Before the 19th century,
nearly all economic activity was centred on the *household*. For most
people, an adequate subsistence depended on a complex of various
forms of task work and wage labour. Regular, full-time employment
at a single job was highly unusual. The viability of the household,
which might involve more than one extended family, was the crucial
priority in life and the work of all its members, young and old, had
to be co-ordinated to achieve this end. Very often women were the
main money-earners, either by selling produce at market or by the
manufacture of goods (e.g. textiles) at home. In the late 20th century,
we are observing the rapid decline of the sole male breadwinner
engaged in stable, long-term, full-time employment. The era of the
full-time male in bureaucratic employment lasted for less than 200
years. We seem to be returning to an era of technological cottage
work, but without the informal social support networks that existed
in the 17th century.

As a species, we were never very good at managing big bureaucracies and we didn't have time to improve or perfect our practice.

In fact, we created organisational monsters which suited only the careerists who looked after themselves and who never gave a damn about useful purposes. The best formal organisations contained no more than about 300 people (remember the ABB optimum) because you could remember all the names and/or faces. Units of this size were, and are, both efficient and satisfying to work in. They are the natural *building blocks* of larger systems. I return to the question of *how* to build a coherent organisation on this foundation in Chapter 14. The late Gregory Bateson, in *Mind and Nature*, devised the perfect fable to illustrate the *naturalness* of this scale of organisation and to illustrate also the perils of unrestrained growth:

> They say the Nobel people are still embarrassed when anybody mentions polyploid horses. Anyhow, Dr P. U. Posif, the great Erewhonian geneticist, got his prize in the late 1980s for jiggling with the DNA of the common carthorse (*Equus caballus*). It was said that he made a great contribution to the then new science of transportology. At any rate, he got his prize for creating—no other word would be good enough for a piece of applied science so nearly usurping the role of deity—creating, I say, a horse precisely twice the size of an ordinary Clydesdale. It was twice as long, twice as high, and twice as thick. It was a polyploid, with four times the usual number of chromosomes.
>
> P. U. Posif always claimed that there was a time, when this wonderful animal was still a colt, when it was able to stand on its four legs. A wonderful sight it must have been! But anyhow, by the time the horse was shown to the public and recorded with all the communicational devices of modern civilisation, the horse was not doing any standing. In a word, it was too heavy. It weighed, of course, eight times as much as a normal Clydesdale.
>
> For a public showing and for the media, Dr Posif always insisted on turning off the hoses that were continuously necessary to keep the beast at normal mammalian temperature. But we were always afraid that the innermost parts would begin to cook. After all, the poor beast's skin and dermal fat were twice as thick as normal, and its surface area was only four times that of a normal horse, so it didn't cool properly.
>
> Every morning, the horse had to be raised to its feet with the aid of a small crane and hung in a sort of box on wheels, in which it was suspended on springs, adjusted to take half its weight off its legs.
>
> Dr Posif used to claim that the animal was outstandingly intelligent. It had, of course, eight times as much brain (by weight) as any other horse, but I could never see that it was concerned with any questions

more complex than those which interest other horses. It had very little free time, what with one thing and another—always panting, partly to keep cool and partly to oxygenate its eight-times body. Its windpipe, after all, had only four times the normal area of cross section.

And then there was eating. Somehow it had to eat, every day, eight times the amount that would satisfy a normal horse and had to push all that food down an oesophagus only four times the calibre of the normal. The blood vessels, too, were reduced in relative size, and this made circulation more difficult and put extra strain on the heart.

A sad beast.

The polyploid horse is an almost perfect metaphor for the over-blown corporation—a monstrosity which just grew, without adapting, from familiar and homely work systems. Big bureaucracies may have all the brains in the world but they can't bring them to bear. Peter Senge, in *The Fifth Discipline*, makes a similar point in reverse: if you cut an elephant in half, you don't get two small elephants—downsizers please note! The best thing about the small 'building block' organisation is that real talent is always visible and there is no place for the careerists to hide, or to plot. In the coherent organisation, you can't lead unless you are obviously *admirable*. In fact that is my simplest litmus test for successful leadership: is it possible to *admire* the boss? Nine times out of ten, if there is general admiration, there is practical *intelligence* at work.

THE PARABLE OF IMO, THE GENIUS MONKEY

Every act of imagination is the discovery of likenesses between two things which were thought unlike.

Jacob Bronowski

In Mexico, before the wheel was invented, gangs of slaves had to carry giant stones through the jungle and up the mountains, while their children pulled their toys on tiny rollers. The slaves made the toys, but for centuries failed to make the connection.

Peter Brook

This is the first story or cameo of the book, in the form of a parable. We have dealt, so far, with some of the variables concerning 'leadership'. We turn here to the link between leadership and intelligence in order to demonstrate how ingenuity can lead to widespread social change. Imo the monkey has become famous over the years, originally as a result of Robert Ardrey's wonderful work of science popularisation, *The Social Contract*, first published in 1970. Ardrey had learned of the trail-blazing work of Japanese scientists in studying the behaviour in the wild of large, self-contained and highly structured monkey societies. The scientists had established the practice of 'provisioning'—providing some of the monkey population's food needs but without distorting the natural pattern of foraging in their island habitat. This allowed the observers to study at first hand, and continuously, the patterns of social interaction amongst the monkeys and, above all, their *learning*—the way that intelligence diffused in the social systems.

Imo excited their attention from the start. When sweet potatoes, which monkeys love, were placed on the beach of the tiny islet of Koshima, all the monkeys laboriously picked the grains of sand from the food in order to eat it. It was Imo, just 18 months old, who made the mental connection with the little stream that crossed the beach not far way. Imo carried the sweet potatoes to the stream and allowed its fresh waters quickly to wash away the sand. After a while another youngster copied this method of food preparation and then, after a further period, Imo's mother did so. Very slowly the innovation diffused amongst the band, mainly amongst the young, and within families. The normal pattern was for the young to make the breakthrough, followed by their mothers, and then for new infants to copy their own mothers.

Imo was not this particular monkey's real name but the name attached to it by the Japanese scientists studying the colony ('Imo' means 'sweet potato' in Japanese). The monkey's real name is not known.

The point of the story, for observers of human behaviour in organisations, is that the clever new ideas never penetrated to the powerful males at the top of the social hierarchy. They never came into contact with the young. When caramels were introduced to another band, the pattern was repeated—it took a year and a half for the innovation to spread from the juniors to half the entire troop. But, in a parallel experiment, the 'alpha' (boss) monkey was induced to try another new and delicious food—wheat. The alpha female promptly copied him and the entire band of 700 monkeys took to the new food in just *four hours*. Why? Because everybody watches the leader. Nobody much attends to an Imo. By now a mature four-year-old, Imo devised a method for 'placer-mining' the wheat too. Interestingly, the youngest monkeys had figured out that it made sense to get downstream of Imo, so as to catch any floating grains that escaped the panning process. Something similar occurs near the smartest operators in big corporations.

There is, of course, a limit to the applicability of parables from the wild when it comes to human organisational systems. Nonetheless, all researchers and consultants understand the usefulness of 'soft research'—or time spent in the local pub after work talking informally to junior employees or suppliers. It always turns out that juniors understand things very well because they are close to the action that counts—at the front line. They are also invariably very sound on the *deficiencies* of their immediate and middle managers. But their overall understanding is likely to be fragmented because their picture of the system is partial. Those with the big picture, in the executive suite, usually see things clearly from an intellectual or analytical standpoint but they often lack the gut-feel understanding.

That is not to say that the human 'Imos' of this world could do the work of the 'alphas'. Those at the top of organisational systems always have years of accumulated learning about how to wield *power*. The most powerful people, almost invariably men, exude a kind of aura. Great actors have this same ability to receive the psychological projections of other people, and to feed off them in order to amplify their own projection of power. In the primate kingdom, it is sometimes referred to as 'low peripheral movement', as in the stately progress of the old silver-backed alpha gorilla at the heart of his band. He is surrounded by movement, but he demonstrates his power and his confident understanding of the total system (or, if you prefer, his authority) by his gravitas, and by his steely gaze. All the subordinate high-rank gorillas are in constant eye-contact with the source of power. Chief executives and chairmen who have not developed this skill always operate at a disadvantage and cannot transmit powerful messages quickly.

I frequently tell the story of Imo to executive audiences, in order to make a simple point about the unpredictability of real talent and the importance of getting clever people to the top of the system fast so that their impact is amplified. When I ask people to speculate as to *why* Imo's brilliant innovations diffused so slowly, it generally doesn't take long to establish that Imo's status must have been low. From there it is a short logical step to Imo's *youth*. But, even amongst all-female audiences, Imo goes on being referred to as 'he' right down to the wire.

This may tell us something useful about the way in which clever women think about cleverness. Imo was a political nonstarter not only because she was young but also because she lacked the 'attention structure' surrounding the high-status males. Lionel Tiger, in his remarkable book, *Men in Groups*, wrote: 'That females only rarely dominate authority structures may reflect the female's underlying inability—at the ethological level of "pattern-releasing behaviour"— to affect the behaviour of subordinates.' This is a contentious argument, to which we will return in Chapter 11. Imo's is a useful establishing story for this book, because it underlines the relationship between talent and structure. There is no use in having cleverness about the place unless it is tapped efficiently, and that is primarily a matter of organisational *structure*. There are many reasons other than femaleness for the neglect of talent, but it is without doubt the most spectacular cause of the waste of intelligence in organisations. This phenomenon is linked with another of Tiger's observations about the way that men's brainpower often seems to drain away when they get together in groups.

> The paragraph in the little boxed aside couple of pages back is a joke. It may not be a particularly clever or funny joke, but it is a joke just the same. The test for the reader is not whether it raises a chuckle but whether it is perceived as a joke at all. This is an oblique way of introducing the notion of *reframing*. To see the joke, you have to be able to connect two frames of reference or levels of abstraction. 'Intelligence' (however you define it) is linked with this capacity to think at two levels simultaneously. As Forster wrote: 'Only connect!' The model for this particular joke is the true story of a five-year-old girl interviewed on BBC

Radio. When asked the name of her dog, she replied: 'I don't know; *we* call him Rover!' This is a seriously bright kid, able to sustain a dynamic connection between the different societies of humanity and dogdom. As humans, we can't know for sure whether or not dogs assign themselves 'names'.

As we pass from reflections on 'leadership' to reflections on 'intelligence' we can see how Imo's story ties the two elements together. The Japanese monkey bands had clear, 'formal' and easily observable structures of leadership. Every monkey knew who the alpha was and, until eventually a new alpha supplanted him, he could rely on their subservience to him. Not too much energy was wasted in positional squabbling. And yet, Imo supplied another kind of 'leadership'—the kind that alters behaviour directly, because it offers a *better way* of performing operations that are important for societal and species survival. The way that those two forms of leadership interact probably determines the long-term success (survival) of the system. That is as true for modern corporations as it is for primate bands. The fundamental test of an organisation structure is whether the flow of ideas goes both ways—the flow of ideals and purpose from the top, and the flow of practical ingenuity from the bottom.

When Imo sat down to ponder the sweet potato problem, she did indeed look *thoughtful*, just like a small child facing a just hard enough puzzle. Stanley Kubrick famously captured that moment of primate concentration in his film *2001: A Space Odyssey*. Significantly, in the light of the examples to follow, both monkeys were holding an *object* in their hands at the moment of inspiration, and turning it over and over. Real intellectual power is never just academic or abstracted—there is always an element of the physical or the spatial. After all, it was solving practical problems in the real world that made us 'intelligent' (i.e. higher-order monkeys) in the first place. This aspect of intelligence is taken up in the work of Howard Gardner, discussed in Chapter 2.

2

Redefining intelligence

Why do we need to look at intelligence from a new angle? The answer is straightforward—we can see easily, just by reading the newspapers, that when 'intelligent' (i.e. highly trained and educationally certified) people come together in organisations they frequently make ridiculous mistakes. Even if they avoid glaring mistakes, they often proceed so cautiously as to miss the kind of opportunities that their juniors (like little Imo) can spot easily. When things go well continuously, over the years, you can be sure that the organisation is being led intelligently and that those at the top are intelligent *enough* to cope with the demands of their work. In making these judgements, it is always important to keep an eye on the longer term. A decision in the short term that seems to be intelligent (i.e. to have successful outcomes) may turn out to have bedded-in the seeds of long-term failure. Sometimes, intelligent people foresee such outcomes but are unable to *explain* their apprehensions to 'bright' but narrowly focused colleagues or bosses.

Sometimes those bosses are just dumb, but it is much more likely that they have taken their collective eyes off the ball. *Binary* bosses, who are concerned primarily with personal advantage, spend far too much time eyeing the internal competition, even though they may be quite bright when at home with the kids, or otherwise unthreatened. They are distracted—they lose focus and concentration. *Ternary* bosses, on the other hand, will be focused on the matter in hand, even though they risk a knife in the back by ignoring their competitors. They are much more likely to heed the ideas of a junior 'Imo' because they and the junior talk the same language. Seniority means nothing in the presence of a really fascinating possibility.

There are two particular aspects of intelligence which the next section deals with in detail, both of them crucial for successful leadership. The first is the concept of *broad-band* (or multiple) intelligence. The second is the concept of *systems thinking*. Both are involved in the exercise of *judgement*.

BROAD-BAND INTELLIGENCE

Chapter 9 contains the story of Allan Coman, until recently Director of Bradfield College in North Sydney. That is the logical point at which to deal with the nature of intelligence in young people just embarking on life's work. In that chapter (flick forward to it by all means) is to be found a fuller account of Howard Gardner's work on the nature of intelligence. Whilst Gardner was by no means the first to follow the path he took, he made an important contribution in extracting from brain-damage research some very interesting data about multiple 'intelligences'—capabilities located in different parts of the human brain. He reckons that there are at least seven distinctive intellectual capabilities (see Figure 5), and that traditional educationalists (and job selection panels) are inclined to ignore most of them. The effect of this is to overeducate and overpromote *narrow* people—those who are especially practised in (for example) the logical/mathematical and linguistic capabilities—whilst neglecting the *complementary* capabilities of other potentially valuable people. Sometimes the abilities, careers and *lives* of such people are blighted by this neglect.

One of the immediate applications of Gardner's ideas arises in relation to the 'glass ceiling' between women and the highest office. The point is that those who exclude women are not necessarily 'sexist' in the precise sense, merely ignorant about the nature of human intelligence. They may, in good faith, confuse a facility in one

- **Linguistic:** the sort shown in the extreme by poets

- **Logical/mathematical:** not only displayed in logic and mathematics but in science generally

- **Spatial:** the ability to hold in your head a model of the organisation of the world around you

- **Musical**

- **Bodily/kinaesthetic:** the sort shown by, say, dancers; the use of the whole or parts of the body to fashion some product or performance

- **Interpersonal:** the awareness of how to get along with others

- **Intrapersonal:** self-knowledge

Figure 5   Gardner's seven intelligences

or two intelligences with the real *broad-band* McCoy. In Chapter 11, I go into some depth on the differences between men's and women's *characteristic* areas of intellectual strength. The suggestion is that the challenge facing all organisations is not just a matter of being *fair* to women, or even of introducing a little compassion into the boardroom, but of shoring up a seriously *unbalanced* intellectual capability. One of the reasons why all-male decisions sometimes fail is that they arise from *half* a collective brain. Women, for example, are often very good at spotting humbug and stupidity in men. They are generally much better than men at this. It can be a very useful skill indeed if you want to avoid expensive blunders.

One of the currently fashionable ideas is that of 'emotional intelligence', as espoused in Daniel Goleman's recent book of the same name. Goleman, a science correspondent on the *New York Times*, draws heavily on Gardner's work. He argues that effectiveness has little to do with IQ scores (mostly based on logical reasoning) and much to do with 'self-awareness and impulse control, persistence, zeal and self-motivation, empathy and social deftness'. The 'intelligences' Goleman focuses on are the *interpersonal* and *intrapersonal* intelligences. He suggests that American society and education have succeeded in stunting these capacities and that women have been the principal victims of their scarcity. He also makes some sensible suggestions as to how schools might encourage their development.

Goleman has also helped to distinguish between the ability to think clearly about feelings and the more subtle ability to extract meaning from emotion. He quotes Gardner as follows:

> When I first wrote about personal intelligences I was talking about emotion, especially in my notion of intrapersonal intelligence—one component is emotionally tuning in to yourself. It's the visceral-feeling signals you get that are essential for interpersonal intelligence. But as it has developed in practice the theory of multiple intelligences has evolved to focus more on metacognition—that is, awareness of one's own mental processes—rather than on the full range of emotional abilities.

In my experience, it is often women who become terrified by the mob dynamic of male-dominated events. The point is that when you are frightened, or angry, or whatever, it means that you are participating in some kind of emotional interaction. If you can understand why, or how, you have a good chance of changing things for the better, either by shifting to calm rationality or, if need be, to another emotional state that suits you better. These questions are dealt with in more detail in Chapter 14 (Helpful Hint No. 2).

The marshmallow test

I go some way with Goleman but I think that his focus on these two particular 'intelligences'—the interpersonal and the intrapersonal—masks the importance of broad-band capability across the entire repertoire of multiple intelligences. However, there is one aspect of his argument that fits beautifully with the leaders described in this book. This is based on the well-known 'marshmallow experiment'. In this experiment, four-year-old children were offered a tantalising choice—a delicious marshmallow *now* or, if they were prepared to wait twenty minutes or so while the teacher ran an errand, *two* delicious marshmallows. Then they were left alone. Fourteen years later, when the children were re-examined, those who had succeeded in delaying gratification were the socially competent, academically successful and personally effective ones. The relative failures were invariably those who had cracked and grabbed the smaller prize sooner. My leaders, to a man and woman, have an outstanding ability to *persevere* with what grabs them as interesting and important. We can only speculate about what causes this but it must be soldered in very early in life. I don't believe it is entirely to do with the 'personal' intelligences.

The versatility of broad-banders

All the leaders described in this book are broad-banders. They are all 'bright' in the sense of logical thought and clear expression, as you would expect. But they are also *physical* people, in the sense that they have a *feel* for materials, for movement and for the physical world. Most of them, on the evidence, might have been outstanding exemplars of a *craft*, or an *art*, and they bring to their intellectual work a kind of earthiness about *real*, as well as symbolic, things. No matter how abstracted their work gets, they are impelled to plunge back into the nitty-gritty from time to time. They never lose touch with the basic materials of their endeavour. Furthermore, they all combine self-awareness with an acute empathy with other people's states. This means that, in Gardner's terms, they are masters and mistresses of the whole repertoire of 'intelligences'.

This versatility affords them two crucial leadership advantages:

1. *Versatility in work*
It is relatively easy for broad-banders to make *connections* because their minds have access to every possible way of thinking or doing. A good technician/boatbuilder may know how to build and continuously improve the design of big fast catamaran ferries. But, unless he also understands the psychology of passengers and ferry operators, he is unlikely to move beyond technical work. If in addition he understands that the real value to be added in a newly developing field lies in the logistics of construction, rather than in the more obvious area of design, then he may be able to *create* a niche, rather than struggle to compete in an overcrowded field. Bob Clifford, described in detail in Chapter 7, is a successful leader because he has made all these connections. His intelligence is broad as well as deep. As Jacob Bronowski said: 'Every act of imagination is the discovery of likenesses between two things which were thought unlike.'

2. *Social versatility*
It is relatively easy for the broad-bander to relate to all kinds of people and to understand what those people are trying to say. The person

gifted with broad-band intelligence can be inside the minds of others before they even open their mouths. Such a person can then easily *motivate* all kinds of people, for the same reason. It follows that such people have an advantage when it comes to leading multidisciplinary and international teams. Howard Gardner is not talking about national style as such, but it is clear that cultural differences simply reflect different *patterns* of thinking and intelligence. Charles Hampden-Turner points out that there is an important difference between the 'Anglo-Saxon' mindset (*universalistic* assumptions, *analytical* thinking habits, *individualised* social relations, and favouring *achieved* status—that is, rewarding people on the basis of measured, *recent* performance) and the Asian 'tiger economy' mindset (*particularistic* assumptions, *integrative* thinking habits, *communitarian* social relations, and favouring *ascribed* status—rewarding people for their holistic capability and general usefulness). He suggests that this reflects the domination of the logical/mathematical or formal science assumption in our culture and education. In that sense, the Asian cultures are more subtle, or more 'feminine'.

The intelligent leader, in my terms, is a versatile person with easy access to the entire repertoire of 'intelligences' (see Figure 5). It is not just that entrepreneurs like Bob Clifford tend to be physical but that great athletes tend to be cerebral, in the broadest sense. That great Australian, Sir Donald Bradman, was a gifted musician. At a young age, he could listen just once to a piece played by his sister (later a professional piano teacher) and immediately play it by ear. At school, he had an exceptionally early command of writing and excelled in languages. In maths, the twelve-year-old Don would 'race the teacher in his mind' in order to get to the answer first. (Bob Clifford was supposed to be hopeless at maths but he too could leap to the right answer in algebra, without knowing for sure how he got there.) My guess is that the *spatial* intelligence, neglected by Goleman, is crucial to the success of people like Clifford. Don Bradman always had what he called an 'X-ray picture' of all the field placements before he faced the first ball.

Later on, I will argue that broad-band development is natural for the human infant and only misguided parenting and schooling can create the imbalance we find in so many otherwise 'intelligent' people. If the parents fail, only really good schools can take up the slack (see Chapter 9).

Figure 6   Simple throughput model

SYSTEMS THINKING

Gardner suggests we are probably born with a broad-band mental potential. Any perceptive primary school teacher can point you to those children who are good at mathematics, and who also think logically and talk eloquently about quite complex ideas, and who can draw and sculpt, and who are gifted and graceful athletes or dancers, and who find musical expression easy and pleasurable, and who relate easily and assume leadership effortlessly in social settings, and who also possess composure and thoughtful self-awareness. Such children are obviously fortunate in their choice of parents. We can safely assume that, whatever their genetic endowment, they have been continuously stimulated throughout their young lives and that they also feel secure.

But, however precocious such children may be, you can't put them in charge of a big power station. It is not just a matter of their ignorance of technical detail; their capacity to handle complex information has to develop through many stages before anything so complicated comes within their range. The *capacity* for 'systems thinking', however, may be identified and encouraged quite young, and its development accelerated. Smart parents encourage this sort of thing; most schools don't do it at all. Let me illustrate this by describing a personal experience, in a class of about thirty seven- and eight-year-olds. My intention, with the nervous permission of the teacher, was to test the hypothesis that all kids are natural systems thinkers but most of their access to the subject is blocked by the forms and structures of 'education'.

I started with a very simple description of 'open-system' theory—how inputs get converted into useful outputs, illustrated by reference to the human body—food, energy, mobility, productive activity and waste products (see Figure 6). The last made the teacher a bit more nervous but, allowing a few giggles, it was very easy for the children to understand. We then shifted to the classroom TV set as an input–conversion–output system. The electricity input was easy—you could *see* the flex leading from the power point; the program input was trickier but somebody remembered the aerial outside. We then went *upstream* to the electric power station, via the grid, and ultimately to the mine, oil well or gas field feeding energy source material into the power station. It got really interesting at the TV output stage, because that was simultaneously the input to our consciousness as viewers. At one point the actress Joan Collins appeared on the screen. One little girl said: 'That's Joan Collins!' I said (touching the screen): 'It can't be—this is cool and she'd be *warm*!' We then all agreed that it wasn't *really* the actress but some kind of *representation* of her. It turned out that one of the little boys knew all about cathode-rays, so he gave us all a brief lecture which left me miles behind.

We also spent some time on how we could *know* that a pattern of lines and dots on a flat, two-dimensional surface was actually a three-dimensional actress. They figured out that we must have some kind of source material, on what actresses look like generally, stored in our memories, otherwise the image wouldn't *mean* anything to us. We also drew some pictures of the human eye as a gateway subsystem linked to the brain (where the files on what actresses look like must be kept). By this time we were getting, effortlessly, into the territory of first-year university psychology lectures on perception. The high point, speaking as a writer, occurred when we tracked upstream, via studios and producers, to the real sources of *programs*. Somebody has to *write* the material, so where do the ideas come from? Some of the boys were quite sophisticated about ideas churning about in heads and occasionally making creative connections. This was reminiscent of Bronowski's notion (cited above) of new ideas as connections between old ideas. But it was another little girl who took us even further upstream. *'The ideas come from God!'*, she announced, and that was regarded as good enough for our purposes. Starting with a simple, open-system view of a TV set, we had ended up, in about half an hour (and via a bit of physics and the psychology of perception) with theology. Not bad for seven-year-olds.

There are two particular things to be said about this demonstration of effortless *systems thinking* amongst the young. The following statements don't contradict; they *overlap*.

1. *Everybody is (potentially) good at systems thinking.*

All the children participated in this exploration. The teacher confessed that she could think of no other activity in the school year that so completely engrossed the entire class. Her conclusion was that *all* the children were quite good at this kind of thinking, but that the regular curriculum (chopped up into adult-logic boxes called *subjects*) left little room for this sort of thing. The point is that this capacity to understand *connections* in systems is widely dispersed. Given the chance, just about anybody can do it, preferably with friends. It is worth noting that this was an easy one-off for an outsider; teachers have to keep the show on the road day after day. It is also important to acknowledge that many teachers and many schools routinely do this sort of thing, especially in the nursery and primary sectors. It tends to peter out in the later stages of education, which is a tragedy. Einstein said: 'It is nothing short of a miracle that modern methods of instruction have not yet entirely extinguished the holy spirit of curiosity!'

2. *Some people are precociously good at systems thinking (right from the start).*

Having acknowledged that systems thinking is natural for humans, unless it is artificially stunted, it is also proper to point out that *some* of the children in this particular class were precocious in their ability to zoom backwards and forwards along chains of cause and effect, and to understand how some activities are subsystems of larger systems. All the kids were good but a few were *very* good. This sort of capacity, I believe, is the core of later, adult, ability to exercise judgement and leadership. I call it *intellectual firepower* (for want of a better description) because it involves handling and sorting *more* data, just like a computer with bigger capacity and greater speed. It is not the only skill or capability that leaders need, but it is the *sine qua non*—the bottom line, if you prefer. My assumption is that the precocious kids, given a good following wind, will be difficult to catch up with later in life, provided they continue to be stimulated by adults they respect, and provided they are not psychologically damaged by life. Precocity is self-feeding.

47

SYSTEMS THINKING AND JUDGEMENT

This excursion to the schoolroom has a purpose. We are trying to redefine 'intelligence' in a practical and useful way. We are not here concerned with the narrow forms of cleverness sometimes found in academic institutions, *unless* the cleverness involves systems thinking. As Professor R. W. Revans avers, that narrow sort of cleverness is good for solving *puzzles*, not for cracking *problems*. We are interested in the capacity for *judgement*. All the well-known books about leadership stress the importance of judgement, but they all have difficulty in saying what exactly it is. I share that difficulty. On the other hand, as Chapter 14 explains, some people are very good indeed at identifying other people with good judgement, as their track record over many years proves.

My working definition of judgement (adapted from my colleague Gillian Stamp's definition) is, my friends tell me, singularly unhelpful. On the other hand, all of the chief or very senior executives I have worked with over the years tell me that *they* understand it:

JUDGEMENT IS WHAT YOU DO WHEN YOU DON'T (AND CAN'T) KNOW WHAT TO DO (but you sense you have to do something—fast!)

The corollary is: If it is possible to assemble all the data required to make an absolutely cast-iron case for one particular decision, then there is obviously no need for an executive or manager to exercise authority at that point. If the data assemble themselves, the sooner the executive is replaced by a machine the better. A second corollary is that if all the data can be assembled, given all the time in the world, then there can't be any competitors breathing down corporate necks. The essence of sound decision-making is *timeliness*. If a thing is worth doing, it's worth doing badly (just well enough for the purpose)—but *in time*.

One of my acquaintances is a very clever Irish entrepreneur, a millionaire several times over, who is famed for moving fast in turbulent markets. I tried to pin him down once on the question of how he took so many decisions that turned out to be right in hindsight. He took me around the houses, with much talk of market research, staff work, strategy reviews, and all the rest of it. He confessed in the end that, after all the staff work was done and redone, '*I consult the leprechauns*'. He explained this in the following

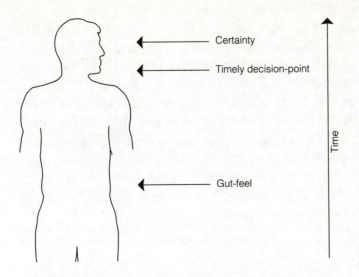

Figure 7   The anatomy of timely decision-making

Effective executives, at full stretch, *should* be under time pressure. Good judgement means that a sound decision can be taken *fast*, before the solution is obvious. The decision works its way up from 'gut-feel' to an intellectual rationalisation. It has usually reached about gullet level when the time comes for the *decisive* executive to decide.

terms. As a young man he had confronted many decision-points where his data were pointing in direction A and his instincts, or gut-feel, were pointing in direction B. Every time he had taken the A route it turned out to be wrong. Once he learned to run with his 'feel' for the situation, he began to make serious money.

We discussed this at length in order to try to understand what it was telling us about the exercise of judgement. The best we could do was that, at the point in time that the decision had to be taken, the rationale for the decision was still working its way up from the 'gut' to the prefrontal lobe of the brain, *but it wasn't there yet*. After the event, it was always possible to backtrack in order to unpick the *logic* of the decision. At the time, there was never the time. (For the anatomy of this process see Figure 7.) Other people saw the process as magic or 'intuition', or called him a 'genius'. People with good judgement simply move faster because they can compute *more* in a given time frame. In the chapter on Bob Clifford, boatbuilder extraordinary, he reveals an insight he grasped as a young helmsman: 'In sailing, every decision has a time-frame—in ten minutes, it's a different decision!' In real life, you can't go back and run it again the way you might at business school.

This ability to think quickly is a function of intellectual firepower. But we are not talking just about computing power. All the best leaders do things on the basis of 'feel' and by encompassing the *whole picture*, even though many of the necessary bits aren't yet in place. They are not just computing fast from one angle but making a kind of mosaic from a broad range of different views. Bob Clifford envisions each new ferry design long before the detailed donkey-work begins. He does it mostly sitting in aircraft. The link with the arts is obvious. Mozart described the act of composition as follows:

> First bits and crumbs of the piece come together and gradually join together in my mind; then, the soul getting warmed to the work, the thing grows more and more, and I spread it out broader and clearer, and at last it gets almost finished in my head, even when it is a long piece, so that I can see the whole of it at a single glance in my mind, as if it were a beautiful painting or a handsome human being; in which way I do not hear it in my imagination at all as a succession—the way it must come later—but all at once as it were. It is a rare feast. All the inventing and making goes on in me as in a beautiful strong dream. But the best of all is the hearing of it all at once.

It doesn't help us much to say that Mozart was a 'genius'. We do know that he was always precocious—performing at five years of age feats that most musicians struggle to attain in their maturity. We can argue instead that he was a person of extraordinary mental firepower, with a strong leaning towards the 'musical intelligence'. He was, in short, very *bright*.

In Chapter 6, I describe 'Stratified Systems Theory', Elliott Jaques' trailblazing analysis of the relationship of hierarchical structure to human judgement. Once you home in on 'judgement' as the core of the successful leader's skill, then you are forced to consider *structure*—the way in which people of different capacities and in different roles relate to each other. It doesn't matter how clever you are if you aren't *positioned* for effectiveness. Even Mozart needed positioning—in fact he was, like all my examples, an energetic and skilful self-promoter.

3

The frog and the bicycle: looking at systems

Before we move on to our first human leader, we need to pull together a few threads—in particular the linked concepts of *leadership, judgement, systems thinking* and *broad-band capability*. Leaders are responsible for pointing *systems* in *intelligent directions*. It is true that in order to achieve this they have to be persuasive, but this doesn't really distinguish the successful leader. We *all* need to be persuasive sometimes, especially when we are engaged in parenting, or in wheedling something we want out of parents. The *sine qua non* of leadership lies in the capacity to change and shift *systems*. That means, of course, *understanding* systems. The helpful thing about the metaphor of the frog and the bicycle is that it simultaneously addresses each of the aspects outlined above, and especially the connection between system leadership and intelligence. Bikes and frogs are different *kinds* of systems and the capacity to distinguish between them is the *kind* of intelligence that really matters. There is nothing new about this way of approaching systems thinking—it is merely a whimsical way of readdressing an old issue. However, children love it, which seems to be quite good enough a reason for airing it in these pages. The frog/bike metaphor is, however, directly linked with Professor Jaques' method of assessing levels of capacity to exercise judgement (referred to in Chapters 6 and 14).

51

Figure 8   The bicycle and the frog: a basic metaphor

All of the foregoing metaphors for leadership (the binary/ternary, the physics/chemistry, the rugby scrum, the polyploid horse) lead up to the bicycle and the frog (Figure 8). The reason for this is that, for some reason I don't fully understand, this particular metaphor seems to mean a great deal to Australian audiences. I refer to it from time to time in different places around the world, but only in Australia, and in the last three or four years, has it taken off as a powerful explanatory tool. That is why I give it pride of place here. It may be that the metaphor speaks directly to the sense of underdog rooted in Australian history (clever and resourceful people transported to the colonies for fighting back against thoughtless injustice) or to the perceived stranglehold of closely networked, but not necessarily clever, *men* over corporate life. Women in particular find the frog/bike idea enlightening, maybe because it makes systems thinking simpler and less convoluted—less like physics.

The essential difference between the frog and the bicycle, viewed as *systems*, lies in the relationship of the parts to the whole. You can take a bicycle completely to pieces on your garage floor, clean and oil every single part, and reassemble the lot, confident that the whole thing will work perfectly, as a bike, as before. The frog is different. Once you remove a single part, the entire system is affected instantaneously and unpredictably, for the *worse*. What's more, if you go on removing bits the frog will make a series of subtle, but still unpredictable, adjustments in order to survive. This sort of system, at a level beneath consciousness, *wants* to survive and will continue for an astonishing length of time to achieve a rough equilibrium as bits are excised—until it can do so no longer. At that point, again quite unpredictably, the whole system will tip over into collapse. The frog is dead and it won't help to sew the parts back on.

Why is this distinction important? There are a number of reasons why the metaphor is useful. Most big organisational systems contain bikish and frogish bits—that is, bikish parts which can be hived off and reattached in a new way without harming the overall system, and froggish parts which really are part of the core process. If you remove them, you damage the whole. A famous example is the British Minister of Transport Dr Beeching's decimation of British Rail, which closed down all the parts of the network that didn't (viewed as discrete systems) make money. The problem with this was that many of the smaller branch lines *fed* the big system. You couldn't understand their contribution in isolation. In fact some of the branch lines didn't feed the network *enough* traffic and were rightly closed down. Others really were froggish and their loss hurt not only the big railway frog but also the even bigger community frog served by those trains. The social and financial cost of that was enormous but, because that cost showed up elsewhere and later (on somebody else's balance sheet), Dr Beeching could ignore it. I apologise for the British example—it simply demonstrates the bike/frog distinction perfectly.

The use of the frog as metaphor reinforces the point that most complex systems, and all those containing and serving *people*, have 'natural' properties. Effective management aligns itself with natural flows and processes, and helps them along. Bad or dogmatic management tries to shoehorn the system into shape according to more or less crackpot management theories, and usually distorts and confuses things. Nowadays, many of the crackpot ideas encourage mindless competitiveness and limit the human instinct to collaborate across boundaries. The aim is always to 'drive out cost' from the various, and separate, bits of a bicycle. The problem is that separate cost-cutting exercises can weaken the integrity of the big frog. This won't be evident to the disembodied cost-cutters. If their minds are wired up in a bicycle sort of way, they can *see*, at the COMPONENT level of operation, that they are making an improvement. Usually it is the *customers*, as time passes, who begin to *sense* that, at the SYSTEM level of operation, the whole frog is weakening. That is the essence of the difference between the component and total system levels (see Figure 9). The bike approach is concerned only with the *what*—the

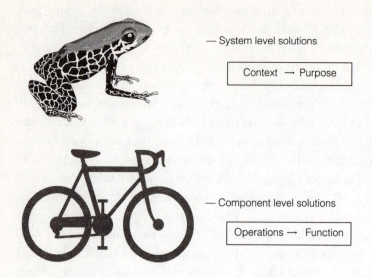

— System level solutions

Context → Purpose

— Component level solutions

Operations → Function

Figure 9   Improving systems operation

Intelligent leaders understand that complex systems are more like frogs than like bikes. You can disassemble a bicycle completely, clean and oil all the separate parts, and reassemble it confident that it will work as before. Frogs are different. The moment you remove any part, *all* the rest of the system is affected instantly, in unpredictable ways, for the *worse*. Binary 'leaders', and quite a few management consultants too, really do think that complex organisational systems will respond to the bicycle treatment. They think you can get a realistic picture of the total *system* by simply aggregating its *component* parts. They are not wicked, just dim.

functionality of internally consistent subsystems. Frogs are determined by their *environment*—the intelligent total systems question is not what or how, but *why*?

LIES, DAMNED LIES AND THE TYRANNY OF MEASUREMENT

'If you can't measure it, you can't manage it!' This has become a mantra of the bicycle approach to complex systems. It makes perfect sense if you have no feel for the whole frog. We are surrounded by 'performance measures' which break up systems into operational subsets, each of which has to be measured according to some yardstick or other. The yardsticks are usually dreamed up by the same bicycle thinkers

who believe that when you put it all together again it will make some kind of sense.

W. Edwards Deming, the arch apostle of statistical process control, must be turning in his grave. He understood better than anyone that the things that really matter, like love, generosity, trust, courage, integrity and happiness, resist calibration. For Deming, measurement of the key variables was always a servant of *learning*. In order to figure out what the key variables are you need wisdom and a good feel for the whole frog. Unfortunately for some economies, most economists are bicycle thinkers. The usual blunt tools like world market share, or the balance of payments, can't tell you if there has been a permanent improvement in growth prospects or economic welfare. Your personal trainer can measure if your diet/exercise regime has improved your general fitness and reduced your weight. He can't predict your actual performance in a competitive contest. In an economy characterised by distrust, the purpose of measurement is not to learn but to apportion responsibility and blame.

Spike Milligan once dreamed up a sketch which showed him sitting in a blizzard in his bathing costume. Somebody remonstrated with him: 'You'll freeze!' Spike: 'No I won't—look at the thermometer!' 'But you've got it in boiling water!' Spike: 'Of course—otherwise I'd freeze!' That isn't much sillier than some of the examples of daft measurement that have come to light around the world recently. Business schools, for example, are generally rated according to research standards. If the research assessments are to be made shortly, there is not much you can do to get existing staff to churn out papers fast. What you can do is hire people with enormous research CVs on generous short-term contracts, thus transforming your rating overnight. You may destabilise other schools' faculties, but that is their frog, not yours. The actual capability or usefulness of the new entrant is an irrelevance; the statistics have been satisfied.

When British Rail became subject to strict performance targets, its managers, who are not stupid, quietly lengthened journey times and redefined the word 'late' to mean more than five or ten minutes late. When performance measures entered the Health Service, hospitals started the waiting list clock ticking not from the first request for an appointment but from the much later appointment booking. The more intelligent the management the more devious will be the distortion of actual performance to make the statistics look good. The tail wags the dog. Once the performance measures are in place (pretending to be the same thing as actual performance), the operatives are relieved, to some extent, of the need to exercise judgement. Once that is achieved, you can start to hire cheap, low-capacity staff on part-time, short-term contracts and scrimp on the training. After a while, the passengers and the patients will find these people frustrating or infuriating, especially if they have have been given a spell in charm school, but the statistics are bound to 'prove' that there has been an 'improvement'.

This problem crops up in an acute form in the measurement of people. One senior government official, remarking on the drive for 'competencies' amongst senior staff, said: 'The problem is the people going for the MBAs are the no-hopers!' Any person possessed of good judgement will assess capability holistically, sizing up the whole person and relating that to the complex setting in which work has to be done. It is a good idea to have at least one of these people on selection panels, even if everybody else is selecting or promoting according to tick-sheet formulae. Deming saw measurement as the servant of intelligent leadership. We are in danger of installing measurement *instead* of leadership.

In 1995 the Kent police, subject to new performance measures, took things to their 'logical' conclusion. The 'clear-up rate' showed a rapid and startling improvement in the county of Kent. (Once you introduce 'performance pay' to a public service you really do motivate an improvement in the statistics.) The police had worked out that if you stop defining a whole range of misdemeanours (like mugging) as 'crimes' then the clear-up rate improves immediately. Actual convictions can be measured accurately; so the rate is improved if the number of crimes (versus convictions) diminishes. The real 'productivity gain' occurred when the police worked out that if you could persuade a cooperative villain (in the slammer for some crime or other and interested in remission of some of his sentence) to own up to another couple of hundred crimes, the ratio of crimes to 'clear-ups' could be transformed overnight. We are back to Spike Milligan.

The most spectacular recent example of the statistical tail wagging the dog (or the frog, if you insist) was *Il Sorpassa*—the exciting moment in the late 1980s when the Italian economy overtook the British, rendering Italy the fifth largest economy in the world. This was achieved by including estimates for the famous Italian 'black economy' in the official statistics. Overnight, the economy 'grew' by a sixth.

THE RAILWAY FROG

Railway systems, because they are complicated, always provide a good example of the way in which component parts relate to the whole. For example, there is no special problem in hiving off the maintenance and renewal of railway track to competing specialist engineering firms, provided you hang on to a core of expertise to protect yourself from exploitation. American railways did this a long time ago, and quite right too. Maintenance and renewal are components and therefore similar to parts of a bike. But the splitting of pathway provision (signalling) and train running into two separate organisations (to promote 'competition') merely creates the need for two sets of people to do the same job in order to ensure that neither cheats the other. This also tends to enrich lawyers, which is never a good idea. There are a number of quite simple ways of measuring the natural interconnections of system parts in order to arrive at sensible decisions about how to organise things. Train running and pathway provision can be shown to be inextricably connected, like the organs of a frog. People who understand this are usefully *intelligent*. Those who don't, however well qualified, are not safe to leave in charge of a model train set.

The British used to have very nearly the most efficient and cost-effective railway system in the world, even though its performance was distorted by chronic underinvestment from World War II onwards. Foreigners were astonished at how much was squeezed from so little, especially in the few years immediately prior to privatisation. By that time it had become remarkably competitive, internationally speaking. Most people who have any experience of what used to be called 'British Rail', even those with bad experience, sense that it is essentially a big frog. If you buy a ticket from 'the railway' at Land's End in the southwest corner, you expect to be able to entrain to John O'Groats at the northern tip of Scotland. You may be vaguely aware of passing through regional zones and you don't imagine that the same train or the same driver will take you all the way (he will probably have a wife and kids located somewhere or other). You do, however, assume that somebody will have given some thought to interconnections. But you would regard it as ludicrous, in the confines of such a small island, to have to buy a raft of tickets from a series of smallish *monopoly* railway journey suppliers up and down the country. But that is just what the British Government has achieved, in the interests of 'competition'.

The point is that transport in Britain is a function of scale and topography—the *natural* environmental system. The United States and, especially, Australia are another matter. If you weaken the frog by removing its parts (as if it were a bicycle), you merely strengthen its natural predators—private cars, buses and aircraft. The fantasy is that competition between smallish, route-based railway companies is feasible, as between airlines. If you submit the subject to *systems thinking*, it quickly becomes clear that the pathway systems are different in important ways—for example, if a train gets into the wrong place and keeps rolling, in the end it *must* bump into something. 'Near misses' in the air happen all the time but the truth is that it is very difficult for aircraft to collide, because there is so much *air* up there and pilots can change direction almost instantly. This is a great advantage. The parallel disadvantage is that you can't *stop* or *slow down* up there. From the economic standpoint, airlines have the huge advantage over railways that they are not obliged at great cost to *maintain* the air through which they travel. Once you dissect a railway *system*, the predators upon railway operators immediately get the upper hand. After that, the frog has had it. To survive, disembodied railway operators then have to cut services and raise prices, thus hastening their own demise.

However, there is still hope for the disembodied railway operator in a country like Britain. With luck, he may obtain the franchise to run trains in a heavily *loss-making* area. This franchise will normally involve a big public subsidy, for social reasons. This is a much more convenient arrangement than having to fight with bona fide competitors for customers. The money thus flows directly from the taxpayer to the operator, without the tiresome interposition of the railway traveller. The train operator, provided by gvernment with a (say) seven-year monopoly, has no incentive to invest in the longer term well-being of his disembodied bit of the system. The logical thing for him to do is sweat the assets he inherits and flog the rolling stock to death. Probably, somebody else will inherit his clapped-out equipment. All this is bad news for the local manufacturer of rolling stock, who could, in the meantime, be preserving local jobs and fostering local technology development. In truth, that train manufacturer was part of an international frog, sustained in the battle for export business (in a real market) by home sales.

BIKES, FROGS, COCKUPS AND CONSULTANTS

These are easily scored points and it would be wrong to deny that most big, centralised, public sector bureaucracies around the world desperately needed reforming. But most of them were bikes too, operating within rigidly bounded compartments and largely insulated from user experience. The frog/bike metaphor doesn't require us to *choose* between frog and bicycle—merely to recognise the essential nature of systems. Some systems really are bikish. Railways simply provide a near-perfect example of the frog/bike principle in action. But this is a book about intelligent leadership and we have to ask: what is going on in the minds of those politicians, executives and consultants who have spent the last ten years or so dismembering organisational *frogs* (in the name of 're-engineering' and privatisation) in the genuine but misguided belief that they are really *bicycles*? If we wish to act intelligently on the system, we need to decide early on whether we are dealing with cockup or conspiracy. Are these people mad, or bad, or just dumb? The fix, if there is one, has to depend on accurate diagnosis.

No systems analysis of modern leadership can neglect the impact of the worldwide management consultancy trade. In some systems (national railway systems may be a good example) it looks very much as though it is actually the consultants, rather than the government ministers, who are doing the governing. It is the consultancies that have a long-term and global perspective. Most politicians are not around for long and most have a narrow perspective on events. They are rarely a match for the consultancies. A conspiracy theory would suggest that the big consultancies that make so much money from promoting re-engineering and privatisation projects around the world know perfectly well that much of it makes no sense at all for consumers of services—or for the communities in which they live. It simply makes a great deal of commercial sense for the consultancies to persuade governments that the organisms they know to be frogs are really bicycles, and then to negotiate a contract to take them to pieces. The beauty of this is that the bicycle treatment is bound to make any complex (froggish) system *sicker*, thus ensuring even more therapeutic work for the consultants to do in the future. It would certainly be the intelligent thing for the international consultancy firms to get together in order to divide up the global spoils without too much messy competition. That would add up to a *global collusion* conspiracy theory.

There is an alternative theory which combines conspiracy and cockup theories. It might be that the top dog consultant/partners are old and wise enough to understand all this, but the junior consultants, who carry through the schemes and cope with the *angst* of the victims, are still naive enough to believe that the bicycle treatment will work. If they started their professional lives in accountancy, it is possible that they will go on believing that frogs are bikes indefinitely. Once signs of wisdom begin to manifest themselves (in the form of doubt) the younger consultants can be kicked upstairs into the partnership and manacled with gold. In the old days, before the big computer hardware firms got ruinously top-heavy, this was what happened to senior salesmen who learned, from repeated experiences, that the promised benefits of big schemes never materialised. They got kicked upstairs just as wisdom threatened to cut in.

SYSTEMS THINKING AND THE UNCONSCIOUS

The metaphor of the frog and the bicycle is essentially about intelligence—about ways of thinking about systems. But it has the uncomfortable effect of drawing in ethics. The sad truth is that, throughout history, human beings have demonstrated a terrifying capacity to believe almost *anything*, provided their motivation to do so (especially fear or greed) is strong enough. We have to remember that the broad mass of one of the most educated (but frightened and resentful) populaces in the world came to accept much of the Nazi gobbledegook. Robert Jay Lifton, in *The Nazi Doctors*, reminds us that nearly all the death camp doctors (professionals to a man) came to believe that *they* were being victimised by the very people upon whom they performed nauseating experimental operations.

You may say: 'That is crazy!' In truth, the other way madness lies. If you couldn't come to believe something of the kind, you really would go crazy with guilt and remorse. The victimisation fantasy is not only convenient but *necessary*. This is only an extreme example of the human being's almost limitless capacity for self-deception when the conditions are right. We can come to believe almost *anything*, in small progressive steps, and in empathy with likeminded others, when it suits us to do so. If we need to believe that a frog is a bike, then we are capable of doing so. It isn't a question of cockup or conspiracy, but a subtle blend of both. We get the conspiracy we unconsciously desire by remaining naive enough to participate in the cockup. True leadership is about clarity and truth. If you are brave enough to confront people with the truth, watch out—especially if they are collectively, but unconsciously, deluding themselves about something shameful. They will need to dispose of you in some way and, scarier still, they will effortlessly and quite unconsciously supply a justification for their actions. They have to.

Anybody in any doubt about this should read Gitta Sereny's magisterial account, *Albert Speer: His Battle With Truth*. This shows, with brutal clarity, how even the most intelligent of men may park uncomfortable mental material in the subconscious, especially when ambition is involved. Speer was clever, certainly, but he had been emotionally damaged by an otherwise privileged childhood. He craved attention and success to a pathological degree. Hitler supplied him with both. Speer understood sooner than any other member of the Hitler entourage that the war was lost but still he could not break the Faustian pact with Der Führer. That meant somehow not noticing the death camps and the genocide of the Jews. How can we describe such a man as 'intelligent', no matter how *clever*?

At a less cataclysmic level, I faced a morally equivalent challenge not long ago. I had the opportunity to sit in on the deliberations of some of the most senior tobacco barons in the world. I guess that if I had exercised 'leadership' by stating what I took to be the truth I might not have got out of the place alive. The worldwide tobacco business is very much an interconnected, and malevolent, frog—a sort of cane toad. However, in order for an individual to flourish within the system, and to live with himself, it is necessary to chop it up into mental compartments—like a bicycle sub-assembly. At this particular meeting, the executives' formulation of task took the following form: 'The timely exploitation of an eighteen-month window of marketing opportunity in the CIS and the Middle East.' Put like that, it sounds almost cosy. As I listened to the debate, I formulated the true primary task of the total system: *the timely replacement of deceased ex-consumers by young Third World women!* That is the kind of clear formulation you arrive at as a result of methodical systems thinking—not everybody wants to face the reality.

How then do we define 'intelligent leadership' in the tobacco trade these days—achieving higher and higher profits, or, in manageable steps, bringing about its demise? You could say that the characteristic of 'bicycle thinking' is to deal separately with the *components* of systems. The characteristic of 'frog thinking' is to embrace the entire system in all its subtlety and complexity. Frog thinkers can always handle bike thinking (about components) when they have to. Bike thinkers generally can't get their brains round the whole frog (system). Of course, they don't know that this is the case and you can't explain it to them. Some of them are politicians and government ministers.

PART II

A gallery of intelligent leaders

We move shortly to our major case studies. The story of Sir William Hudson of the Snowy Mountains Scheme, which comes next, pulls together some of the threads examined so far. The logic looks something like this: Successful LEADERSHIP depends on a variety of capacities but, above all, on the exercise of sound JUDGEMENT (getting it right most of the time). The exercise of judgement in complex circumstances depends absolutely on the capacity for SYSTEMS THINKING, something we can all do but at which certain people already excel at a young age. For the purposes of this book, we are defining INTELLIGENCE as this capacity to exercise judgement under pressure, in systems, not as the ability to pass exams or write clever memos. Those who prove successful in this turn out, for the most part, to be possessors of BROAD-BAND capability (remember Professor Gardner's taxonomy). They can not only think straight, they can *do* things well.

Sir William Hudson demonstrates the point beautifully, as do, in their own ways, the others presented. These leaders are a mixed bunch. Most of them are Australian, but I have included some magnificent non-Australians, or honorary Australians, where deserved. What they all have in common is the capacity to illustrate what I want to say about the connections between intelligence and leadership.

This does *not* mean that they cover the leadership waterfront, nor that they represent any kind of balanced picture.

Here is a *dramatis personae* arranged in overall order of appearance. Each character is listed under a heading that summarises his or her *role* in the narrative. We have met the first of them already.

1. INGENUITY AND POWER

The parable in the story of the monkey called 'Imo' demonstrates how important it is to have clever people at the *top* of pecking orders, and how very frustrating and wasteful it is to neglect, through incomprehension, talent at or near the bottom of systems. Imo stands for all those junior people who can *see* dangers or cockups looming but can't get it into the thick skulls of their superiors.

2. DIRECT LEADERSHIP AND NATIONAL PRIDE

The story of Sir William Hudson, first Commissioner of the Snowy Mountains Scheme, and my first proper 'boss', is an example of 'direct' leadership—where the leader's impact is felt mainly through his *actions*. The story illustrates the ternary principle rather well, both as to Hudson's approach to work and as to the importance of work that is actually *useful*. It also suggests that *maturity* and the *public service ethos* have something to be said for them in these times of greedy corporate juvenile delinquents.

3. JUDGEMENT AND THE MENTOR

Hudson's *alter ego* was the postwar Federal Minister of Works and Housing, Nelson Lemmon (introduced in the Hudson chapter). It was his capacity for *judgement*, exercised against the odds, that got Hudson for the nation. As the central theme of this book is the exercise of judgement, Lemmon is rightly included here as an unsung hero in the Australian story. He became Hudson's friend and mentor throughout the life of the Snowy Mountains Scheme, long after he left public life.

4. INDIRECT LEADERSHIP AND THE THREAT OF BRIGHT IDEAS

This is a companion story to Hudson's, but it concerns an *indirect* leader—one whose impact arises from ideas rather than from action. MARY PARKER FOLLETT, the great American management thinker, blazed like a comet in the 1920s and 1930s, then fell from view almost completely. Why? Her story demonstrates how difficult it is for a solitary woman in any field to exercise effective or *lasting* leadership. It also shows what happens when really penetrating insights threaten the established order.

The stories of Hudson and Follett are the main *establishing* stories for this book. Between them they exemplify some of the main themes. The reader should be warned that these first two accounts are *not* meant to be direct examples of the images and metaphors employed in Chapters 1–3. Leadership is more complicated than that. The later stories come closer to illustrating those themes.

5. THE MOST INTELLIGENT 'DUNCE' IN AUSTRALIA

The contemporary story of BOB CLIFFORD, founder and head of Incat, the Tasmanian manufacturer of big, fast aluminium ferries, shows clearly how formal education often fails to build on native intelligence. This story introduces one of the book's recurrent themes—the crucial importance for any nation to get its education system right. It is also an example of a direct leader whose indirect impact on an entire economy and society is profound.

6. RECOGNITION OF PATTERNS IN WAR AND BUSINESS

ROBERT KEEP is another contemporary Australian 'leader' whose story demonstrates the importance of perseverance when it comes to indirect leadership by ideas. If his enterprise, which concerns the patterns of currency market behaviour, fulfils its promise it will transform the character of those markets. This would be an example of *transformational* indirect leadership. In this case, we have a prior 'dry run' story of pattern-recognition under fire in the Vietnam war to show how broad-band intelligence is formed over time.

7. NURTURING LEADERSHIP AND INTELLIGENCE

ALLAN COMAN is an educator of genius—one of those rare people who not only understand the learning process but who also know how to mould institutions to make learning natural, useful and easy. His is the key leadership story for this book in the sense that all the other leaders described are people *not* stunted by their formal education. There would be many more such people if all the educators were like Allan Coman.

8. FIENDISH INGENUITY

'SPANSKY' and 'JAMIE' are pseudonyms for two real-life young tearaways, one British the other Australian, who demonstrated unusual managerial gifts. (They are introduced in the Coman chapter.) Unfortunately, both were forced to exercise their ingenuity *against* established authority. They provide an excellent illustration of Howard Gardner's theory of 'multiple intelligences'. They were clever all right, but not at the things their teachers and parents wanted. Their speciality was *subversion*.

9. THE 'INTRAPRENEUR'—OR BIG COMPANY 'IMO'

Inevitably, most of the characters in this book come across as 'mavericks'. This says less about the personalities involved than about the social *antibodies* manufactured by big organisations. JOHN LATHAM is an example of a maverick who stuck it out in one of the biggest corporations in the world—the once mighty IBM—and came close to saving the company's soul. He combines the talents of the foregoing—the derring-do of Clifford, the spymaster guile of Keep, and the almost paternal concern for juniors of Coman. But he was still an 'Imo'—able to perceive *patterns* where his seniors could not.

10. BUILDING VALUE OUT OF RELATIONSHIPS

LIZ O'SHAUGHNESSY is the first of two examples of 'relationship companies' led by women. The fact that her organisation makes (superb) airline puddings is neither here nor there. The point is that companies like hers show the way forward to a new kind of enterprise (characterised by *balance*) and a new model of leadership.

11. ART AND ENTREPRENEURSHIP—THE IMPORTANCE OF 'METHOD'

NOEL WAITE helped to release the energy and creativity of Liz O'Shaughnessy and hundreds like her. How this was achieved has as much to do with the disciplines of *art* and *craft* as with the orthodoxies of 'business management'. If it were the case that the key to all this lay in the infant Noel Waite watching, absorbed, as her father lovingly crafted men's suits, this would represent an important lesson for all teachers.

4

Sir William Hudson: an ideal role model

William Hudson was the first Commissioner of Australia's Snowy Mountains Scheme, a massive hydro-electricity project set in the Great Dividing Range, in southern New South Wales. Appointed in 1949 (at the ripe age of fifty-three), he saw the project through to its official completion ceremony in 1974, twenty-five years later. He had retired eight years before, in April 1967. Even that retirement, two days before his seventy-first birthday, had been postponed twice by Acts of Parliament. After the completion ceremony there were still five years' construction to go, and a further two years to the final installations. Hudson died on 12 September 1978, aged eighty-two, having very nearly seen the entire construction process through from beginning to end. He was knighted in 1955.

Why choose William Hudson as the ideal leadership role model? Those who worked closely with him may argue that he was not perfect, as man or technician—he had no need to be. The requirement was that he be exactly the right person, at the right time, with the right capabilities, to lead an enterprise of enormous value to Australia. For the purposes of this book, his remarkable story contains many of the elements necessary to appreciate the leadership requirements of today, from initial selection, through the years of endeavour, to the succession. He also represents a good example of what Howard Gardner describes as a 'direct' leader—one whose impact is felt through his daily work activity. (Mary Parker Follett, whose story comes next, is an example of 'indirect' leadership. In her case, it is the *ideas* that do the leading, long after the protagonist has passed from the scene.)

We are living through, some observers argue, a 'crisis of leadership'. Leading figures in politics, public life and business no longer command the respect accorded to their predecessors. Leaders are perceived to wield power without due responsibility or accountability. In countries like the United States, this cynicism has led to a serious challenge to democracy: those who feel disenfranchised—the young, the poor, the ethnic minorities—no longer go to the polls. Government, the apex of our system, is increasingly without a franchise. In the United States, some argue, leadership now comes from the *other* kind of poll—the opinion poll. At a time like this, we need inspiring leadership role models. Bill Hudson became my 'boss' just after my twentieth birthday. He also became, though I didn't know it then, one of the most important role models of my lifetime. The (autobiographical) story of how this came about can be found later in this chapter.

The most important thing about the Snowy Mountains project, in the drab years following World War II, is that it was big, exciting and important. It had the additional advantage of being remarkably comprehensible. You didn't have to be a genius to see the advantages of diverting water from the wet side of a dry continent to where the farmers most needed it (Figure 10). Nor did you need to be particularly clever to see that dropping enormous quantities of water a thousand feet and more added up to a simple, cheap and renewable way of making electricity (Figure 11). Even within a particular power station, the logic was easy to see. There are only a few moving parts in hydro-electric generation. They are impressively big but the list extends only to big pipework, big valves, big turbines, big generators, big electricity transformers, and more big pipes to flush the water out for re-use downstream. A child could understand it; indeed I use it occasionally to explain systems theory to children.

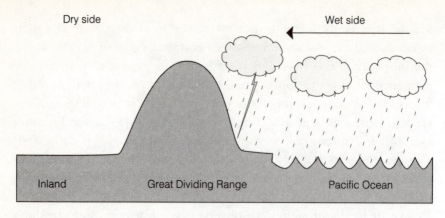

Figure 10 Southeast Australia (in section)

Figures 10 and 11 depict the purpose (logic) and process of the Snowy Mountains Scheme. Audiences all over the world love the simplicity of this demonstration of systems operation. They understand that the task of all leadership, wherever it is located, is to make useful purpose as comprehensible as this. (The big oil companies have always had the advantage that all operations are cast in 'upstream' and 'downstream' terms. This makes it obvious that the organisation's primary task is to *add value* along the way.) It is easy to see the need to dam up water on the wet side of the Great Dividing Range in order to tunnel it to the dry side for irrigation.

Running the Snowy was therefore a plum job, if you happened to have the capacity to handle the enormous complexity. The interesting thing about Hudson was that he never lost touch with the grassroots. I started work on the Scheme as a 'fitter's assistant'. This meant supporting a trained fitter (the redoubtable Robert Owen, then halfway through his marine engineering training). I don't think there can have been a lowlier job than mine, yet from the start I always understood my place in the scheme of things. Hudson understood that if the majority of the workers didn't speak much English it would be a very good idea to insist that engineers-on-the-job take the fitters and craftsmen through the construction flowcharts on a regular basis. Flowcharts are *graphical*—you can *see* the logic of the progression. That way, everybody was going to understand how he (hardly ever she in those days) fitted into the big picture. It was an equally good idea to ensure that everybody was accountable and useful. Hudson

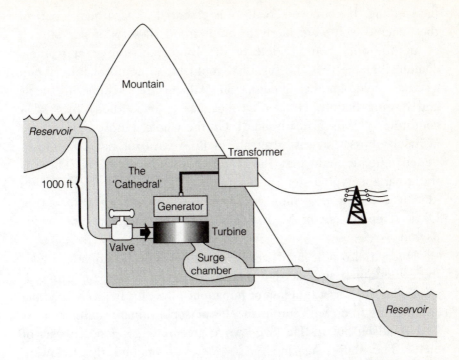

Figure 11   Tapping a cheap and renewable resource

> One can readily see how a lot of falling water can make electricity by spinning turbines fast. The Snowy Mountains Scheme is bigger but essentially no more complicated than the input–conversion–export system represented by a classroom TV set—which seven-year-olds can grasp easily. William Hudson's genius was to make all this comprehensible to the lowliest Snowy Mountains worker, even those with shaky English.

insisted that promotions should not be just a function of longevity of service, and that pay should be linked directly with performance. Remember that the Snowy Mountains Authority was a public service body—such ideas were revolutionary in those days. Hudson applied 'usefulness' to the scheme as a universal principle.

I never met Sir William but, as a humble Snowy employee, I benefited by the wisdom of the policies and practices he instituted. In my ignorance, I assumed that the sensible way things were arranged on the Snowy must be the way that all such enterprises were run. It took me years to learn that it wasn't so. Hudson took a personal interest in all the employees and was always direct and unassuming. If your work really was essential to a particular part of the Scheme, you were likely to be awarded all sorts of perks, such as an Authority house. Some of the European immigrant workers couldn't believe that the big boss could be so approachable. When a Czech hydrographer greeted Sir William by clicking his heels and bowing deeply, Hudson's colleagues enjoyed their chief's discomfiture—'Hudson nearly died!' On the whole, Hudson played the avuncular boss (he was, after all, in his sixties for the key growth period) but he could play the tyrant too, when necessary. There is the usual apocryphal story of his sacking a group of labourers sitting idly by the side of a Snowy road, only to discover that they were DMR (Department of Main Roads) staff and therefore not on his payroll.

Hudson also delegated wisely. True, he could be impatient with those less quick and incisive than himself, but most people understood that this was a function of impatience over his beloved Scheme, and nothing to do with intolerance or personal (binary) petulance. As Lady Hudson put it: 'He loved work, and he was a good chooser of men!' The staff magazine *Snowy Review* contained the following biblical parody in 1962:

> In the beginning God made a man and his name was Hudson. God saith unto Hudson: *'Go forth and take unto yourself disciples and the Snowy is yours.'* And it came to pass that Hudson recruited two who were named Lang and Merigan and together they went forth into the wilderness and recruited more disciples . . . to them was given a hard task with many privations . . . but they won through, and seeing this, Hudson said: *'These are my men in whom I am well pleased. Give them many increments.'*

Together these three, Hudson and his two Associate Commissioners, were the 'Holy Trinity'—they spent a total of forty-three years overseeing the scheme. This is a far cry from the short and sometimes meteoric 'careers' of modern-day executives.

There are a hundred aspects of the Hudson story which might be used to illustrate 'direct' leadership in action. The three aspects that best demonstrate his *intelligence* might be his mature wisdom at the time of his appointment, his preparedness to seek and accept good advice from wise sources, and his ability to juggle the contradictory demands of public sector responsibility and private sector urgency. Here is a review of each of these aspects.

1. THE LATE RUN

William Hudson embarked on the main achievement of his life's work at about the age that many senior executives now retire (fifty-three). By that time he had accumulated an enormous amount of *wisdom*, mainly as a result of supervising a string of hydro-electric schemes in France, Scotland, New Zealand and Australia, many of them on strict, fixed-price contracts. Hudson was born in Nelson, on New Zealand's South Island, the seventh of seven sons. His doctor father disapproved of the choice of an engineering career, adding in frustration: 'That's about all you're bloody well good for!' Times were not easy after his father died young. Hudson nonetheless graduated as an engineer with first-class honours from London University, having interrupted his studies to fight (and be wounded) in the First World War. Everybody I know who has been away to war has a pretty sound sense of *priorities*. Life continued difficult for Hudson. When the Depression interrupted work on the Nepean Dam in New South Wales, he was forced to find work overseas, initially in Scotland. His wife and young children followed later. By 1949 Hudson had crammed in more variety, disappointment and achievement than most corporate hacks in a lifetime. As a rule, a modicum of *humility* accompanies this kind of experience. The spoonfed graduate 'management trainee' often ducks the humility.

What, in its relentless search for youth, has the business community got against wisdom? The Japanese often keep the wisest old birds on their company boards until well into their eighties. The test, apart from wisdom, is not age but energy and enthusiasm. Hudson was a ferociously hard worker all his life. On the Snowy, he frequently worked until 3 a.m., seven days a week. The energy comes from caring about the outcome. How many senior executives today really care about the contribution their companies make to society (as opposed to caring about status and stock options)?

A favourite party trick

One of the best-respected and most successful executives in Europe, the late Sir Edward Choppen, previously joint chief executive of Esso Europe, had a similar mixed sort of career behind him. Ted Choppen's party trick was to know the name

and location of 'every pub in Britain'. I have seen him demonstrate this unlikely erudition. The explanation is that he spent
ten long years on the road hunting for service station sites on
street corners—and he possessed a photographic memory. This
is a good party trick to play on young featherbedded executives.
Choppen was another late runner and, somewhere out there on
the road, the modicum of humility, and wisdom, took root. By
the way, nobody would ever have described Ted Choppen as
tall or slim or beautiful or hirsute or youthful-looking or otherwise godlike in appearance. Yet those who recall him do so with
awe. He is recalled, it seems, as a *massive* figure, because (to
quote one colleague) he was possessed of a 'mind like a razor'.
Yet he also possessed another excellent party trick—he never
lost his humanity. The same goes for Hudson.

2. THE MENTOR

If you accept the argument that clever people are awkward by
definition, because they always see quickly how things could be done
better, or not at all, then protecting them from envious attacks from
peers becomes a necessity. This is where the (possibly) older, wiser
mentor comes in. In Hudson's case, the mentor was the man who got
him the Snowy job in the first place—Nelson Lemmon, Federal
Minister of Works and Housing in the postwar Chifley Government.
In some ways, the Snowy Mountains Scheme *made* Australia. Hudson,
more than anyone else, made the Snowy. Lemmon, largely unsung
to this day, made Hudson and created the conditions in which Hudson
and his team could flourish. Unusually, Lemmon got both to choose
his man and to support him over the years, long after he (Lemmon)
had passed from government office.

The claim that the Snowy made Australia may seem extreme from
the safe distance of the 1990s. But, fifty years ago, Australia was a
nation of just eight million people of overwhelmingly British stock,
emerging from a war in which it had finally become clear that the
country could not rely on anybody else, especially the British mother
nation. It was time to grow up and to take responsibility for rebuilding
national confidence and capability for the peace. Simultaneously, it
was time to absorb the necessary manpower for growth, at that time
from all over Europe. The Snowy, uniquely, did both. It stretched

Australian capability to the limit—the scheme was one of the biggest civil engineering projects in the world. It also soaked up huge numbers of immigrants in the best possible way—by giving them really important and challenging work to do, as they established themselves financially and culturally.

Nelson Lemmon, originally a wheatgrower from Western Australia, was the catalyst for all this, supported by other members of that government. Lemmon was smart enough to see that the Labor Government might lose office at the forthcoming (December 1949) federal election. His task therefore was to get the Snowy so well established that nobody could derail it. That meant ensuring its *national* bona fides, against the narrow parochialism of the State premiers. He achieved this by persuading H. V. 'Doc' Evatt, then Attorney General, that the Snowy should be secured as a Commonwealth project on *defence* grounds. His argument was that most of the east coast's power generation was located at the seaside. Memories of Japanese submarines in Sydney Harbour in 1942 were still vivid. In theory, a sneak naval attack could wipe out all power generation in one night. The argument was constitutionally shaky, but it did the trick.

When the time came to choose an overall boss for the scheme, Lemmon turned down quite a few eminent bidders, including very senior executives from the Mt Isa and BHP mining companies, on the grounds that they envisaged running things from Sydney as a kind of 'gentleman's job' (as Lemmon put it). Nor would Lemmon countenance an American as top man, even though the most obvious experience and talent were located in the United States. Lemmon saw the Scheme's *symbolic* importance for the nation, and the necessity therefore of having a local at its head. In the end, he settled for a New Zealander with a lot of Australian experience, who had the sense to milk American experience for all it was worth.

The first Lemmon heard of Hudson was literally scribbled on the back of an envelope, jotted down by a colleague of Hudson's at the Water Board. Lemmon liked the look of what he saw, especially Hudson's record with fixed-price contracts. His first step was to ring the 'trade union blokes'. The following account of the exchange is taken from Siobhan McHugh's excellent brief history of the Snowy Mountains Scheme (my italics throughout):

77

Trade union official: 'Hudson? We know him well!'

Nelson Lemmon: 'What's he like?'

TUO: 'Ah, he likes his *pound of flesh*—bit of a *slavedriver*.'

NL: 'That's good! But look, I'm thinking of him for a pretty big job, lot of contact with the unions . . .'

TUO: 'Ah, he'll listen to you. He won't be like some *tinpot boss*; if we've got any problems, he'll hear the story, no argument—he'll give you *a decision straight away*. You're in or you're out—*he's good!*'

This exchange needs careful study. Once we have made the assumption that the trade union official in question was a man of good judgement (Lemmon knew this), all we need to know is buried in the text. In the Introduction, I outlined the bare bones of a theory of leadership capability:

- the presence of intellectual firepower
- the absence of psychological damage

In a few short sentences, Lemmon was able to ascertain that Hudson was not 'tinpot' (selfish or overconcerned with status) and that he was decisive. The adjunct, 'He's good!', further suggested that the decisiveness was not precipitate, just sound (right most of the time). The 'pound of flesh', in other words, was a product of (ternary) need and purpose rather than an indication of (binary) tyrannical behaviour. Hudson, in other words, was both *bright* and *sane*. That may seem to the reader to be an oversimplification, but if you examine the history of spectacular cockups and blunders you generally find leaders who were not quite up to the job (in terms of its complexity) and whose psychological unsoundness was amplified by the resulting pressures on their intellectual resources.

It would be wrong to present Bill Hudson as a shrinking violet, however. Lemmon eventually got Hudson on the phone and suggested a discussion about the mooted scheme. The very next day Hudson travelled to Canberra and set out his ideas, even down to the location of the Scheme HQ next to the railway station in Cooma. He had worked it all out. Lemmon liked what he saw but expressed concern about Hudson's physical resilience at age fifty-three. Hudson responded: 'I've got a sleeping appendix and this is one of my real bad days . . . but if I'd told you I was crook, you probably wouldn't want to see me any more.' Lemmon suggested it might help if the appendix came out. Hudson had the operation the following day! His widow, Lady (Eileen) Hudson, recalled the day he finally got the job: 'He came home that night and said, "I've got that job". He had to ask Mr Chifley not to announce it until he got it cleared with the Water Board, because he'd just asked for the day off. He never did that—they must have wondered why he was going to Canberra, because he never took a day off.'

In these anecdotes we can see the unusual combination of modesty and ruthless determination that characterised Bill Hudson.

Lemmon, being a man of sound judgement, knew early on that Hudson was his man, but there was opposition to his choice at Cabinet level, especially from Jack Dedman, the Minister for Post-War Reconstruction. Dedman had objected, quite rightly, to the use of the *Defence Act* to smuggle the Snowy Scheme through Parliament. When Hudson's name came up, he reminded Cabinet that the rules demanded three nominations. So, Lemmon submitted another list, this time with three names on it—Hudson, Hudson and Hudson. In the end the Cabinet, prodded by Chifley (who trusted Lemmon's judgement), gave in and the rest is history. Having got his man, Lemmon had to create 'headroom' for the Scheme's management cadre. That meant paying Hudson 25 per cent more than the Prime Minister. He got that too. Chifley said to Lemmon: 'It's your baby, you've got to feed it!'

The art of judgement

In Chapter 6, we return to the question of judgement—what it is and how it develops. In the meantime, with Nelson Lemmon in mind, it is worth recalling Sir Geoffrey Vickers' dictum in his celebrated book *The Art of Judgement*:

> Selection boards . . . attach sometimes overriding importance to the capacity of rival candidates for 'good judgement'; yet their estimation of this is a matter for their own judgement and if they differ and fail to reach agreement by discussion, there is no means by which any of their judgements can be proved right or wrong—even, I shall suggest, after the event. Judgement, it seems, is an ultimate category, which can only be approved or condemned by a further exercise of the same ability.

Vickers was effectively arguing that the best and cheapest way to choose leaders of sound judgement is to find somebody else of sound judgement (like Nelson Lemmon, for example) and leave it to them. How do we find such people? Well, the obvious way is to use somebody with sound judgement to seek them out! . . . and so on. If the first Commissioner of the Snowy Mountains Scheme had been chosen by psychometric testing, or by a panel of youngish headhunters, or by a bombastic binary type, or by a panel of narrowly educated engineers, history might have been different. As Vickers points out, there is no way of knowing for sure. In this writer's judgement, Australia has much to be grateful for in Nelson Lemmon's exercise of judgement and in his resolution, having made up his mind. In any event, intelligent leadership is nine-tenths about judgement, so we will be returning to the subject. Lemmon died in 1989, not, in this writer's view, sufficiently honoured for his *catalytic* contribution to the making of Australian nationhood.

Once Hudson was installed he brought great organisational skills and enthusiasm to the task, but he was politically naive. As Lemmon commented: 'He didn't even know how to write a memo to a minister.' The Labor Government lost office in 1949, leaving Prime Minister Menzies, always lukewarm about the Snowy, to bask in the later glory of its success. Lemmon even lost his seat in Western Australia. He had been much too busy with his 'baby' to pay much attention to electioneering. This is a common fate of those who give all their energies to the (ternary) task and thereby neglect the (binary) political survival dimension. But he stayed in constant contact with Bill Hudson throughout the life of the Scheme. As McHugh says: 'They made a formidable pair.' It was, precisely, the relationship of a chairman (though an informal, private one) with a chief executive. Lemmon advised on the external positioning of the Scheme and Hudson made it happen.

As late as 1951, the Scheme came under threat of attack from Frank Packer's *Daily Telegraph*. Packer had got the idea that the Scheme was a sink for public money and that the New South Wales economy, then in mild, short-term recession, needed investment elsewhere. Packer induced Senator William Spooner, the new Minister for National Development, to visit the Snowy with an eye to closing the whole thing down. Lemmon advised Hudson to go on to the attack, getting the Prime Minister on side, explaining to Spooner the costs of the rumours for top management morale and, most important of all, organising a lobby of the powerful Murray and Murrumbidgee farmers. It worked. Never was a behind-the-scenes mentor so valuable for the longer-term, higher-order interest.

3. PUBLIC SECTOR VALUES AND PRIVATE SECTOR ENERGY

In the 1980s and 1990s, the name of the game has been 'privatisation'—a political and economic doctrine based on Darwinian principles: all human life is supposed to be driven by competition; survival is the right of the successful competitor, extinction the fate of the loser. The high priestess of the doctrine was Margaret Thatcher, a great battler herself, and inclined to intellectual confusion in the absence of a good fight. Thatcher, in and out of office, loathed consensus, and regarded public service institutions as the root of most social ills. She was, of course, a public servant, but that is to muddy conviction with logic. In a speech on 11 January 1996 she actually said: 'The very existence of the state, with its huge capacity for evil, is a potential threat to all the moral, cultural, social and economic benefits of freedom!' She wasn't joking. In her simpleminded view all public sector enterprise was pernicious and all private sector enterprise virtuous.

As a public/private hybrid, the Snowy Mountains Scheme is therefore an interesting, fifty-year-old, case. To provide a contemporary context, two developments are worth noting.

The rediscovery of trust

During the 1990s there has been a widespread, and overdue, recognition that successful human enterprise depends as much on (ternary) collaboration as it does on (binary) struggle. Both are important. School-level psychology studies teach us this. It seems that one of the reasons why some kinds of Asian businesses perform well is that the high energy levels stimulated by healthy competition are underpinned by *trust*. Even Francis Fukuyama, leading luminary of the American Right, now argues this way, calling it 'social capital' based on 'density of associations'. In the United States, if the ballooning numbers of lawyers are any guide, you can't trust anybody. The fun of the courtroom is only loosely connected with higher-order (ternary) principles like justice—the (binary) point is to fight and to *win*. It is very expensive, it drains away otherwise useful energy, it contributes nothing to common wealth and, worst of all, it enriches lawyers and encourages their proliferation. The natural concomitant of individualistic competition is distrust, which acts as a hidden tax on all economic activity.

Paying the long-term bills

Also in the 1990s, there has been the opportunity to assess the longer term track record of those public utilities (often natural monopolies) involved in the wave of privatisation in the 1980s. The United Kingdom privatisation project, which others around the world are in danger of mimicking, looked successful for a while, viewed from a narrow and short-term accounting perspective. It takes a few years for the wider picture (or the big frog) to become apparent to a broad range of people. Of course, at the outset, there were a small number of expert voices anticipating and predicting the wider costs to be absorbed, but nobody in government wanted (or was able) to hear them. Later in this chapter there is a brief, and depressing, review of the long-term outcomes of the privatisation of the British electricity supply industry. It is a signal lesson to any other country contemplating short-term, sectional economic gain at the risk of long-term degradation of the big system.

The intriguing thing about Hudson and the Snowy is that, right from the start, they hit on a mixed public/private modus operandi which worked well. That part of the Snowy that needed to belong to the people of Australia stayed under the aegis of the Snowy Mountains Authority. Because the SMA inherited all the bad bureaucratic habits of prewar public bodies, Hudson had to kick *it* in a binary direction—towards high performance, high reward, high punishment modes of work. Early in the life of the Scheme, the Department of Public Works had been given full rights to build the Eucumbene Dam. In the event, they were terribly slow; there was never the right plant in the right place and there was strike after strike. One senior Snowy engineer recalled: 'This wasn't good enough for old Bill. In 1956 he said, "I've had enough! You're going to take another seven or eight years at this rate . . . and you're going to cost a tremendous amount of money—it's not on and I'm going to get a contractor in." So he went down and was extremely rude to them—told them what he thought of them! Anyway, the contract was let to Kaisers.' The remainder of the dam works were completed in just twenty-two months.

In general, those parts of the Scheme that needed to move very fast, and nearer to acceptable risk thresholds, went to contractors. Still, most of them had to be hauled, sometimes reluctantly and resentfully, in the *opposite* direction—back towards civilised (ternary) employment practices. For example, after the death and injury toll began to mount, Hudson worked hard to install formal procedures to improve safety. He actually stated: 'This Scheme is not going to kill off as many men as big schemes usually do.' In 1959, when I arrived on the scene and by which time forty-eight workers had already died, the Snowy Mountains Joint Safety Council was set up and bonuses were offered to contractors on the basis of reduced actual costs, in terms of frequency and severity, of accidents. The chairman of the Council's working committee recalled that contractors' safety bonuses were related to what it cost to have a man off: 'It varied from 8 per cent to 18 per cent of their contract. You could see them all working it out—and then things really started to happen. Within two months the accident rate was lower!'

The point about this is that Hudson and his colleagues exercised pragmatic *judgement* when it came to these sorts of decisions. They were no more dogmatic in favour of public enterprise than they were for private ownership. *Balance* was the key value. Furthermore, if you could achieve worthy (ternary) outcomes, such as enhanced safety and an improved quality of working life, by binary means (tapping into contractor greed)—so be it. Of the 121 men who were killed in the course of construction, nearly all were in the employment of the contractors, who carried out the most dangerous underground work. In those days, death rates were calculated by the mile (for tunnelling) and by the million pounds (for other construction work). By those standards the Snowy was a 'safe' project—0.6 deaths per mile was pretty good by international standards, especially in granite. Robyn Williams, the distinguished science broadcaster, who nearly drowned on the Snowy (on a day off), recalls that the workers had a choice between the SMA, for fairly generous rewards and adequate safety, and the contractors (in his case the American Perini group), for really big money and serious risk. Williams, who is not stupid, lasted ten days with Perini and reverted to the Authority. I on the other hand (not brave; a bit stupid; only moderately greedy) never even considered the contractors and worked for the Authority throughout.

It was no bad thing that the first big contract went to the Norwegian firm Ingenior F. Selmer. The idea was to get something not too complicated built fast, to demonstrate success and progress to the public. In modern consultants' jargon this is called 'garnering the low-hanging fruit'. The Guthega project resembled most Norwegian high-head, long-tunnel installations and, more important, it offered the locals experience in all aspects of hydro-electric construction—a dam, a tunnel, a power station and a pipeline. The principle of the demonstrated early success is nothing new. Hudson grasped all this without management training or expensive management consultants. Culturally, the Norwegians were ideal, different from both the resident Australians and the southern European immigrants but not too different. They brought with them the typically pragmatic Scandinavian view of energetic commercial effort, together with strictly observed safety standards, in a publicly controlled enterprise.

Students of the privatisation process could do worse than study the success of the Snowy Mountains Scheme. It was a true hybrid of public and private, under intelligent leadership, quite unencumbered by political or economic dogma. Its purpose was manifestly useful. At its head was an engineer—a man who understood three-dimensional systems, materials and process flows, and the relationship of the spatial to the temporal. Above all, Hudson understood the complexities of the big 'frog'—not just the Scheme itself but the political and environmental context as well. He could give quick and sound decisions to do with any separate part of the 'bicycle' because he understood the big picture—the *context*.

How Bill Hudson became my 'boss'

This book isn't an autobiography, but two of its central features are the *nature of intelligence* and the *process of learning*. As I owe part of my learning and intelligence to my Snowy experience, it makes sense to set out the kind of impact that leaders like Hudson sometimes have on the young and confused. When I set off for the Snowy I was a student at law school, having spent the usual five or six years at secondary school and a further two at the university proper. To understand my confusion fully, it will be necessary to study Chapter 9, which concerns *education*, and in particular the story of Spansky, the genius subversive. That comes later. What I can say with complete conviction is that I had been puzzled throughout my years of secondary education as to why we did the things we did. Some of the 'subjects' were more interesting than others, but the *point* of the whole exercise never became clear to me. So far as I could tell, I was the only pupil in the place thus bewildered. We pupils certainly weren't the customers of the institution; if anything, our parents were. We were batch-produced *products* of the kind described by Charles Handy in *Understanding Schools as Organisations*.

Of course, I have given all this much thought since and I understand it better now. At the time, I was merely confused and far too lacking in confidence to query things or to mount a direct revolt. Instead, I just behaved badly, mainly to inject some amusement into a barren existence. If the school had a point, it was to get batches of pre-adolescent boys through the awkward years into successful careers. That required certification (Leaving Certificate, or similar) at around age seventeen and the passage to another kind of institution (e.g. university) for more of the same. The principal advantage of the university, when the time came, was the presence there of representatives of the other half of humankind—*women*. The advantage was intellectual too.

None of this required any connection with individual vocation. I know that many of my school colleagues were already embarked on a career trajectory that made perfect sense for their particular gifts and for their outside connections. They were the lucky ones. What you needed at school in those days was a good mastery of the linguistic and computational skills and, for successful socialisation, some skills in the 'bodily/kinaesthetic' arena (the path was smoother if you were terrific at rugby, cricket, running, etc.). What you didn't get then was any systematic individual analysis or assessment of capabilities, nor much experience in doing anything that felt *real*. (See Chapter 9 for Howard Gardner's stunning contribution to this problem.) By the way, in case this sounds churlish, this was a terrific school compared with most and my parents made sacrifices to pay for it all. It still didn't make much educational sense—that is, if you take education to be about enhancing capability by building on natural talents. Even in the 1990s, not much formal education takes account of individual (and idiosyncratic) ways of thinking and learning.

I can't say for sure what prompted me and a friend (another nineteen-year-old) to quit law school in order to hitchhike to Cooma in search of Snowy work. As they say, it made sense at the time. We were certainly both bored. Young men are supposed to seek danger and independence and it was much less risky than going away to a war. It was also an early lesson in perseverance and the importance of real capability because at that time (late in 1958) nobody in construction really *needed* unskilled students, however keen. We got signed up as a result of walking down a forbidden tunnel and making friends with a brilliant Czech engineer in charge of that shift. He wanted people around who were enthusiastic and quickwitted, and he fixed it. For me it was the start of a lifelong love affair with Czechoslovakia.

Almost overnight I went from being a medium-sized fish in a shallow (university) pond to being a tiny cog in a huge, but *comprehensible*, machine. For the next part of my life, I made a small contribution to the construction of a large underground hydro-electric power station. I still feel proprietorial about the power flowing from T1 (Tumut 1) station. Everybody else I know who made a contribution to the Scheme feels the same way— involved and proud. Robyn Williams felt, and feels, the same. The important point was that I began to learn again, for the first time since infancy, to exercise judgement in situations with real out-comes, and to believe that my contribution mattered. The irony was that by pulling out of schooling, I had engineered the *resumption of my education*. Anybody who attended a good technical school, or who studied any kind of practical engineering, would find this puzzling.

This is a very difficult thing to describe. If all your life you have been fed educational morsels in neatly differentiated boxes (called 'subjects'), you are likely to be unprepared for, and surprised by, the onset of any kind of *insight* about the interconnected workings of a big, complex *system*. To revert to the metaphor of the bicycle and the frog, it is as if all education had been designed to reveal to the student, one by one, the hundreds of different parts of a big bicycle. At the end, presumably, the complete bike would take shape, like a completed jigsaw puzzle. At that point, the process of education would be complete and, armed with a map of the whole bike, the student could go forth into adult life able to cope with anything. If problems arose, you could always go back to the morsels in order to plug any gaps or forgetfulness.

When Phil Sydney-Jones and I got to the Snowy two things

happened. Firstly, it was pretty obvious that *this* particular bike, in terms of all its details, was way beyond our comprehension. Even in the 1950s the Scheme had become very big and complicated. On the other hand, we quickly began to get a sense of the *frog*—the essential *interconnectedness* of the whole thing. That happened because Bill Hudson set out to make sure that everybody who worked on the Scheme, however lowly, had a feel for the totality. If you only understand systems as bits of bikes, you must be limited to doing what you are told, even if it doesn't seem to make sense. If you understand the *context* of your work, you are in a position to add value by *exercising judgement*—you understand the *why* as well as the *what*.

As a rule, these sorts of concepts are better expressed by creative artists than by a journeyman hack like me. William Golding, in his Nobel Prize-winning novel *Rites of Passage*, provides us with a beautiful description of how the *penny drops* when we move from book-learning to real-life experience. His 19th century hero, Edmund Talbot, is a few days into a sailing-ship passage to Australia. He has not sailed before and this is an old and uncomfortable tub. In his journal Talbot describes his first storm at sea, in the Bay of Biscay. He has been heartily seasick and has ventured up on deck just after dark and at the height of a storm:

> For some reason, though the water stung my face it put me in a good humour. Philosophy and religion—what are they when the wind blows and the water gets up in lumps? I stood there, holding on with one hand, and began positively to enjoy all this confusion, lit as it was by the last lees of light. Our huge old ship with her few and shortened sails from which the rain cascaded was beating into this sea and therefore shouldering the waves at an angle, like a bully forcing his way through a dense crowd. And as the bully might encounter here and there a like spirit, so she (our ship) was hindered now and then, or dropped or lifted or, it may be, struck a blow in the face that made all her forepart, then the waist and the afterdeck, to foam and wash with white water. I began, as Wheeler had put it, to *ride a ship*. Her masts leaned a little. The shrouds to windward were taut, those to leeward slack, or very near it. The huge cable of her *mainbrace* swung out to leeward between the masts; and now here is a point which I would wish to make. Comprehension of this vast engine is not to be come at gradually nor by poring over diagrams in Marine Dictionaries! It comes, when it comes, at a bound. In that semi-darkness between one wave and the next I found the ship and the sea comprehensible not merely in terms of her mechanical ingenuity but as a—a what? As a steed, a conveyance, a means working to an end. This was a pleasure I had not anticipated. It was, I thought with perhaps a touch of complacency, quite an addition to my understanding!

Golding captures for me the sense of awe and *partial* comprehension that overwhelmed me, once I began to get the hang of the Snowy.

I won't weary the reader with the rest of my story. I went back to law school for a while but my enthusiasm for the lawyers, and to a lesser extent for the law, had been fatally damaged. My head had been turned less by the *macho* aspect of the Snowy experience than by the insights and the intellectual challenges it afforded. I had got a whiff of the excitement of big, complex, living *systems*. I had also gained a glimpse of *real* leadership in action. I was lucky.

The reader is entitled to ask: *Isn't there some way that these natural processes of gaining insight and copying role models could be brought into the formal educational process, especially for those youngsters who are not 'academic'?* The answer to that question is a qualified *Yes, but with difficulty, provided you can find the educational leaders to parallel the Hudsons!* Chapter 9, about the remarkable Allan Coman, takes up this matter.

Hudson's story is that of a pragmatic engineer of high intellectual capacity. That was the particular combination needed at that time, in those postwar circumstances, to be a great leader. The Snowy Mountains Scheme itself was a pretty good example of non-dogmatic public/private integration and local/international collaboration. The Australian leader of today, if blessed with any intelligence at all, ought to be worried about the *long-term* costs of ballooning international debt and the creeping control of strategic national interests by unaccountable foreign corporations. Bill Hudson, we can be sure, would have understood the complex issues involved and wouldn't have been frightened of fighting about them. He would have made an excellent prime minister but, of course, he was much too busy to bother with politics.

FIFTY YEARS ON . . . WHAT *HAVE* WE LEARNED?

The Snowy Mountains story can now be considered from a safe historical distance. Not everything about it worked perfectly, of course, but it remains a pretty good example of public/private sector collaboration over the long term. It demonstrates that if you really want to understand the workings of complex systems, particularly those of national strategic importance, you need to do a great many sums over a substantial period—you need to take into account the whole 'frog'.

Let me further illustrate this with what might appear a digression. Again it is convenient to use an overseas example, although the subject is one that bears closely on Australian life too. It is the contemporary case of the British electricity supply industry, which suddenly moved from the public to the private sector. Countries all around the world, including Australian States, are imitating this example, without necessarily waiting for all the outcomes to become clear. In Britain, the privatisation of electricity is still hailed as a triumph by the bosses of the new private regional electricity companies, and by their wealthy shareholders. Not everybody else is impressed, except perhaps the *foreign* firms (mainly American and French) now buying up this strategically important industry.

The story demonstrates what happens when the accountants (who are always good at knowing the *cost* of everything—like the components of bicycles), rather than the engineers (who understand the *value* of integrating components into wholes), call the shots. Engineers know that complex technical systems need 'redundancy'—capacity held in reserve for dangerous peaks. The accountant mentality believes that you must 'sweat the asset'—squeeze every last drop of performance out of every element in the system. This goes for the people too—get rid of those whose contribution can't be measured precisely, and work the remainder till they drop. The costs of all this will be exported elsewhere; so long as they don't show up on your balance sheet you are ahead of the game. This is, of course, a crude piece of stereotyping designed to make a point. Naturally, there are saintly accountants and diabolical engineers.

The important thing to hang on to in examining the British electricity business is that nothing *real* has changed. It is still the same wires, the same overhead cables, the same generating stations, and the same customer care mistakes. The difference is in the money and it isn't until you have done all the attendant sums that you begin to understand what has happened. To take just a few aspects, the British Government gained an instant £8 billion from the one-off sale of the electricity businesses. (At the time of writing, the Victorian Government is getting the same kind of windfall profit in the same way.) But Britain still had to carry on paying the large, but unknown, interest on the stock used to buy the industry in the first place. After privatisation, the Exchequer also lost money that the electricity industry was forced to lend to the government in the last year before privatisation. This amounted to £1.8 billion. This 'public dividend' could easily have been much larger if the industry's capital structure had leaned towards equity and away from fixed interest capital. The government sold the assets and the British people were left with the liabilities forever.

There is much more to the story. Everybody now agrees that the new companies are making far too much money from what are still natural monopolies. How so? Firstly, the government encouraged very big price increases in the years leading up to privatisation in order to fatten up the corporations for private investors. This was really a covert form of taxation, displacing wealth from elsewhere in the economy. Secondly, the industry has been 'regulated' by a formula which obliges it to raise prices by less than the general rate of inflation. The firms were quick to realise that the best way to beat the regulator was by getting rid of ever more employees. The benefits flowed straight through to profits and the taxpayer picked up the bill for unemployment costs—another displacement of cost.

Of course, once the government had invented the pricing formula, there was no practical reason to privatise at all because the formula provided a continuing pressure towards increasing efficiency—the really useful outcome the economy and society required. Once in the private sector, the new companies set about reducing their corporation tax bills by every means at their disposal. The poor electricity industry regulator, with no right of access to the insider details of private firms, hasn't a chance. In the four years prior to privatisation, the publicly owned industry yielded £6 billion in tax revenues. In the four years after privatisation, with embarrassingly large profits flowing to the shareholders, the tax yield dropped to £3.1 billion. That is a shortfall in taxation revenues *in perpetuity!*

In the old days, the regional electricity suppliers were part of their local economies, making a community contribution—part of a complex local 'frog'. Nowadays, as disembodied components, they suck money out of the region. Before long, most of it will belong to foreigners, including American utility firms which have already crossed swords with the United States regulators over fraud and pollution. These kinds of pernicious costs, too, are incalculable but predictable. In Britain, as in Australia, the Americans are attracted by loose and inexperienced regulatory regimes. All this represents a loss of control over national strategic assets. The financial proceeds, likewise, will be sucked out of Britain.

By privatising electricity, the British Government got hold of a one-off bonanza (to finance income tax cuts) and lost a huge revenue base which might have come in handy at a time when the pressure to rescue the public welfare and support system is colliding with the reluctance of people and corporations to pay taxes. Embarrassingly, the much improved public corporations initially *not* privatised, such as the Railways and the Post Office, turned out to have much higher productivity than the privatised ones! When the Conservative Government tried to privatise the Post Office, after the electricity exercise had been absorbed, their own backbenchers voted it down. They could see, and so could their constituents, that sweating the Post Office asset would export unacceptable costs to the people.

The purpose of this story is not to make a political point about the ideology of privatisation. It merely draws attention to the complicated economic and social ramifications of major changes of this kind. There are a great many peripheral sums to be done, over many years, before any realistic assessment of benefit or disbenefit can be made. It has become clear in Britain that some of the supporters of privatisation simply aren't doing *enough sums*. They are neglecting the frog and focusing serially on disembodied parts of the supposed bike, either because they are implicated (like the newly very rich electricity bosses) or because the complexity is just too much for their bean-counting brains. The people at large sensed that the Post Office was a frog—not just a money-processing machine but (via local sub-offices in rural communities) part of the fabric of society. The value of that, people sensed, was incalculable.

The obvious question for the Australian citizen, anxious to *learn* from overseas example, is: *Can we be confident that our State legislatures actually understand the complicated long-term calculations needed to evaluate the public benefits of selling basic utilities to foreigners, even supposing we trust the motives of the buyers and/or the sellers?*

5

Mary Parker Follett:
a (nearly) lost leader

Sir William Hudson was a near-perfect example of what Howard Gardner calls a *direct* leader—somebody whose principal impact on events occurs through his actions and decisions from day to day. He might well require conceptual skills of a high order but his outputs are essentially *managerial*. Direct leadership always involves an element of role-modelling—demonstrating through behaviour the skills, attitudes and values that are consonant with the primary task. Gardner writes:

> I see both Churchill and Einstein as leaders—as individuals who significantly influence the thoughts, behaviours, and/or feelings of others. Churchill exerted his influence in a direct way, through the stories he communicated to various audiences; hence, I term him a *direct* leader. Einstein exerted his influence in an *indirect* way, through the ideas he developed and the ways that those ideas were captured in some kind of theory or treatise; hence, he qualifies as an *indirect* leader.

The Snowy Mountains Scheme was a very complex enterprise requiring no-nonsense management. Its leader therefore had to be a down-to-earth, no-nonsense person with the capacity to encompass great complexity.

The very intelligent *indirect* leader has an obvious problem. He or she is, by definition, ahead of the game. How then can the potential follower be expected to understand what the leader says or intends? It is not just that the *content* of the leader's utterances will be unfamiliar but also that the framing of the leader's mind is likely to be inaccessible. Leadership of a team at the front line is not so difficult; the objective may be nearly in view. The leader of a commando unit has a very simple, but dangerous, aim in view—to take out the enemy unit. The leadership is not exercised on the spot but in the weeks and months preceding, as moves are rehearsed and trust built up. The same goes for orchestral conductors—by the time the performance comes round, the whole orchestra ought to be almost on autopilot, so as to cope with the electric buzz generated by the big occasion. When Bill Hudson instructed his engineers-on-the-job to talk the men through the construction flowcharts, he was making sure that more distant objectives could be glimpsed in advance.

But, away from the front line, the leadership is *conceptual*; followers don't just have to see differently, they need to *think* differently. Leading artists always face this problem. Stravinsky's *Rite of Spring* is now familiar to us and so is its idiom. But it was composers like Stravinsky who *created* the idiom, over the years and around a succession of pieces of music that dragged public taste along. But the first performance of *Rite of Spring* in 1913 literally caused a riot in Paris. It wasn't just that the music was unfamiliar—it made people very *angry*. The feeling was that nobody should be *allowed* either to compose or to perform such music. It drove some people crazy. Creative artists often act as lightning conductors for deeper currents in society. In the following year, 1914, Europe really did go crazy. Perhaps it wasn't Stravinsky's music that introduced craziness to the scene, but that the ambient craziness found a target, or a sluice, in the music. This example indicates how bold leadership often involves more than blank incomprehension in potential followers—it can give rise to fury.

This is the context for the story of an extraordinary American, Mary Parker Follett. If the reader's reaction is '*Mary Parker who?*', I rest my case. My preferred path for readers of this book would be that they put it down now; beg, borrow or steal a copy of Follett's collected lectures (delivered just a decade or so after the *Rite of Spring* premiere); read them with care and wonderment; and then resume reading this volume, suitably chastened. (Failing that, that they go and read her works *after* they finish this book.)

The point is that virtually *all* the managerial-received wisdom (including all the works of the big gurus), over the sixty years since her death, was anticipated in her lectures and other writings. She was the Imo of them all. If her ideas could have been understood and acted upon, the world of organisations and management (and the United States economy) might have been spared much confusion, heartache and wasted time. If we accept that this is the case (and the evidence follows), then we ought to try to understand *why*. How is it possible for somebody who writes in clear and simple English, who speaks eloquently and forcefully, who provides a wealth of practical examples, and who reaches a wide and influential audience over a number of years, to virtually disappear from sight?

The obvious starting point is sex. Like Imo, Mary Parker Follett was female, but by no means of low social status. This might be connected with her impatience with the laborious protocols of formal research popular at the time, carried through by networks of male social science entrepreneurs. She just got on with it. 'Although her observations were based on a wealth of personal contacts with managers, her thought was not supported by formally designed research', Massie tells us in Pauline Graham's *Mary Parker Follett: Prophet of Management*. Follett was also the *only* woman prominent in organisational studies at the time.

Secondly, all her ideas were *inclusive* and *holistic*—always connected to parallel ideas—never narrow or rigidly bounded. This rendered them difficult for the narrowminded. You could say that she was one of the great 'frog' thinkers, surrounded by devotees of the 'scientific management' movement, most of whom viewed business organisations as 'bikes' to be tinkered with, using specialised tools. She said: 'We have to study a whole as a whole, not only through an analysis of its constituents.' Massie comments: '*Whereas most classicals* [classical organisational theorists] *viewed organizational developments as a series of discrete formal changes, Follett treated organization as a flowing and continuous process.*'

Thirdly, what Follett had to say must have been *threatening* to the conflict-dominated world of American business between the wars. History shows it to have been a 'binary' period, dominated by institutionalised warfare between owners and union bosses. Her arguments were pure 'ternary' in conception. Elton Mayo, that highly seductive Australian, and the other proponents of the 'human relations school' were much more acceptable to big business. They succeeded in repackaging binary conflict as highly persuasive (but still binary) 'human relations'. (Some commentators look on the human relations school as purveyors of 'cow psychology'—a way of 'tranquillising' the workers by seducing them away from a proper (ternary) concern with formal roles, authority and representation—all the subjects that concerned Follett.) Her colleagues hardly acknowledged Follett's work, though they all drew upon it. Follett, in the nicest possible way, really was subversive.

Her ideas are interesting in their own right but her real interest for us lies in the shortage of *followers* of her lead. Ironically, she seems to have anticipated this in her writing: 'Let us not think that we are either leaders or . . . nothing of much importance. As one of those led we have a part in leadership. In no aspect of our subject do we see a greater discrepancy between theory and practice than here!'

Warren Bennis, in commenting on Follett's work, suggested that the essence of successful followership lies in being prepared to tell the truth. It follows that effective leadership makes truth-telling possible. He illustrated the point as follows:

> Almost 35 years ago, when Nikita Khrushchev came to America, he met with reporters at the Washington Press Club. The first written question he received was: *'Today you talked about the hideous rule of your predecessor, Stalin. You were one of his closest aides and colleagues during those years you now denounce. What were you doing all that time?'* Khrushchev's face grew red. *'Who asked that?'*, he roared. No one answered. *'Who asked that?'*, he insisted. Again, silence. *'THAT'S what I was doing!'*, Mr Khrushchev said.

As Warren Bennis is one of the great gurus on leadership, it is well worth tuning in to his appreciation of Mary Parker Follett's contribution: 'Whether the subject is the shift in paradigms from a command-and-control, hierarchically driven organisation to a more empowered and democratic type or the significance of a shared vision or the importance of achieving an *"integrated picture of the situation"* or the need for *"expert"* rather than coercive power, Follett was there first.'

I can't do justice to her oeuvre here, but the following are a few of the themes she wrote about:

- *Constructive conflict*—the idea that differences are a necessary part of life and that difference is necessary for learning. *'We do not want to do away with difference, but to do away with muddle!'* In this, she pre-invented most of the standard conflict-resolution methods now in use in international and industrial relations. The problem, she knew, was that *'integration leaves no thrill of victory!'* In other words, if you are addicted to the binary (fight/flight) mode, you can never be satisfied with a compromise.

- *Management as a general function*—the idea that making things run properly is a complex *process* and cannot be reduced to a toolbox of techniques. It followed from this that managerial work had to be professionalised, so as to depersonalise the giving of orders. Once again, this is a ternary concept—the purpose of professional standards is to render interpersonal relations manageable.

- *The leader*—as someone who sees *'the whole situation'*, organises the experience of the group, offers a vision of the future, and trains followers. Follett was very clear, however, that the leader's power had to be earned through capability and commitment: *'Don't exploit your personality—learn your job!'* In this she anticipated the work of Elliott Jaques, and others, on levels of work complexity.

- *Horizontal authority*—a notion which prefigured today's focus on cross-functional collaboration in the radically flat organisation. GE's 'boundaryless organisation', as espoused by Jack Welch, might have been invented by Follett. She acknowledged the importance of the 'departmental' point of view but argued that department heads ought not to 'de-departmentalise themselves' but instead 'inter-departmentalise themselves'. Unlike many American theorists of the time, she understood that you cannot *dissolve* boundaries—you have to acknowledge them and make them manageably permeable.

- *Mutual problem-solving*—a practical process device which antic-ipated quality circles, participative management, employee involvement and other staples of the 'HR' trade.
- *Business as a social institution*—the idea that businesses are not merely economic units but that they interpenetrate society at every level. This concept is in the full flow of fashion as I write. The 'Tomorrow's Company' movement and the whole 'stakeholder society' idea are built around the centrality of business and its social obligations.

There is much more—but I would wish the reader, especially the female reader, to appreciate Mary Parker Follett at first hand. Her 1918 book, *The New State: Group Organisation the Solution of Popular Government*, is still ahead of its time, although the more farsighted thinktanks are now starting to catch up with her. In this book she dealt with the problem of governmental legitimacy in local communities—one of the hot topics of the 'stakeholder society' debate. Her last book, *Creative Experience*, brought together the fruits of all her consultancy experience in business. It might have been written yesterday.

If we can come to understand how Follett, of all people, came to be *todgeschwiegen* (Peter Drucker's term for her—the German for 'non-person'—in Pauline Graham's *Mary Parker Follett: Prophet of Management*), we might learn something about the challenge for lead-ership today. How can we know who today's Mary Parker Follett might be? Do we really expect it to be the next glib American male with a slick marketing organisation in the wings? If we could persuade ourselves that Follett was an impractical dreamer or (the standard male defence) 'emotional', we might have a part-explanation of her eclipse.

A BROAD-BAND LIFE

She came from solid Boston stock. Born in 1868, her childhood was not easy. Her mother was a nervous invalid throughout her life and, like Bill Hudson, Follett lost her father, whom she adored, when she was in her teens. Howard Gardner reminds us, in *Leading Minds*:

> Future leaders have often lost fathers at an early age . . . those who have early been deprived of a parent are stimulated (or feel pressured) to formulate their own precepts and practices in the social and moral domains. Their precocious dependence on themselves may place them

in a favourable position for directing the behaviours of others . . .
Jean-Paul Sartre claimed that in the absence of a father an individual is
forced to make his own choices. However, the pain associated with the
early loss seems to endure, and many of the once-bereaved leaders have
reported never having lost a pervasive feeling of loneliness.

Mary Parker Follett had to take charge of the family, no doubt a
salutary lesson in practical management. She went to Radcliffe College at Harvard and studied also at the other Cambridge (in England)
and in Paris. She graduated *summa cum laude* in economics, government, law and philosophy. Her student thesis, 'The Speaker of the
House of Representatives', published in 1896, became the standard
source on the workings of the Congress. By this time she was fluent
in French and German and already a considerable worldwide networ-
ker. Her circle included most of the forward-looking writers,
philosophers, lawyers and politicians, as well as the Boston aristocracy.

Everybody assumed she would pursue a brilliant, but cloistered,
academic career. That wasn't her way. When she came back from
Paris in 1900, she immediately got involved in the Roxbury Men's
Club, in the rougher part of downtown Boston. Coincidentally, she
took the same action as Allan Coman (see Chapter 9) by opening up
the school buildings for night-time use as recreation clubs and for
study. To provide special buildings when the school buildings were
there already *'would have been bad management on our part'*. Seeing the
need for employment placement bureaux, she set them up in the
evening centres. Later on, they were generally incorporated into the
Boston public school system, and widely copied elsewhere. During
this time she was well known for getting her hands well and truly
dirty, like all the leaders celebrated in this book. She characteristically
made a full technical study of the most economical way to bank
furnace fires before taking up the matter with the janitors.

Mary Parker Follett knew that true understanding arises only from
the fusion of practical experience and intellectual effort. Somewhere
in the middle lies effectiveness and practical intelligence. *'I do not
think we have psychological and ethical and economic problems. We have
human problems with psychological, ethical and economic aspects, and as
many more as you like, legal even.'* She was, in short, another broad-
bander, as comfortable and engrossed down in the boiler room as on
the most exalted lecture platform. The essence of 'frog' thinking is

to see that you don't have to use school buildings just for teaching lessons—not if there is a parallel need and an available timeslot.

Follett died in 1933, aged 65. Already her star was waning. Throughout the 1920s she had been a hugely visible figure as lecturer, writer and consultant to business and government leaders on both sides of the Atlantic. Yet Douglas McGregor's 1960 classic, *The Human Side of Enterprise*, in many respects a paraphrase of Follett's ideas, contains not a single reference to her work. Peter Drucker seems to have been the first to exhume her body of work. There is no printed reference to her throughout or after the war until Drucker's celebrated *The Practice of Management* in 1955. And even he was reminded of her existence by an Englishman—Lyndall Urwick.

It will come as no surprise to the reader that the Japanese always understood and appreciated her work. She was very much in tune with the consensual, thoughtful, careful and respectful approach to management which characterises the Japanese way. There is still a Mary Parker Follett Association in Japan, comprising business people and scholars; not in the United States, of course. My guess would be that she had to become a non-person precisely because she *wasn't* an academic dreamer. All her ideas arose from her experience as a no-nonsense manager at the tough end of town. The cynical view would be that the male-dominated American business Establishment between the wars simply wanted to go on doing what it had always done—screwing the workers. Because most of the bosses were good churchgoing folk, they needed an approach to human relations that made some sense but still allowed them to get their way without any real democratic obstruction. The 'human relations' school filled the bill. Follett had to go.

On the surface, Mary Parker Follett was quite different from William Hudson. He was a 'direct' leader; she an 'indirect' leader. He was an engineer; she a classicist. As a direct leader, Hudson left his monument behind him in the huge physical presence of the Snowy Mountains Scheme. Follett's legacy is buried in her writings; to extract the value, you have to sit down, read and marvel at her prescience. But both achieved their greatest eminence, and made their main contribution, in their fifties—in the prime of life, in the prime of wisdom. Both were clever, psychologically well-balanced, ternary broad-banders. In that important respect, they are like peas in a pod.

6

The intelligent
leader's qualities

The ternary approach to leadership takes the line that 'motivation' really flows from the 'third corner'—the objective or common ideal—discussed in the Introduction. If leadership succeeds, it means that the followers are *attached* to the objective. They are not following the leader so much as attaching themselves to a purpose which the leader exemplifies and embodies. This explains the awkward fact that successful leaders come in all shapes and sizes, and commonly lack the traits that classical leaders are supposed to have. Successful leaders are often decidedly uncharismatic. What matters is the bonding between the leader and the *good enough* purpose. The Australian leaders described in this book, if assembled in the same room (only two know each other already), would make a motley crew. The leadership, in each case, has flowed from the task rather than from the personality. Of course, interesting people conceive interesting tasks. If they are *good*, in terms of capability, pretty soon they will start to look like 'leaders'.

It is, however, fair to ask: What is the bottom line? What are the minimum requirements for successful leadership, expressed in terms that will be familiar both to lay people and to organisational selectors and trainers? What are the necessary qualities of less exotic leaders

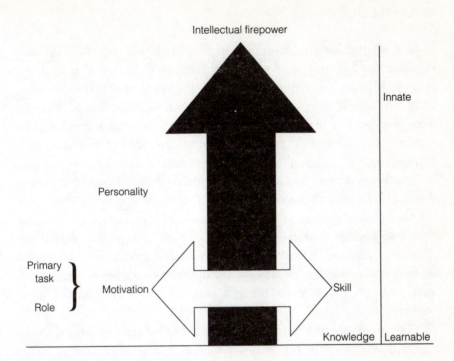

Figure 12   Hierarchy of talents

> The elements depicted are all potential *disqualifiers* for leadership
> roles, in the sense that a serious failing in any one is sufficient to
> rule out an individual for an important job. But the lower the point
> on the hierarchy the more 'fixable' the deficiency, via learning. By
> adulthood, the higher-order factors like personality quirks and intel-
> lectual firepower have become intractable. Most big blunders and
> cockups are caused by leaders who can't hack the complexity of
> top jobs, and can't hack the fact that they can't hack it.

than those we are considering? Figure 12 sets out the main variables.
They are arranged on a scale of learnability: from knowledge, at the
bottom (readily learnable or recoverable), to intellectual firepower, at
the top (very nearly immutable). It is useful to look at each of them
in turn. The point is that they are *all* important—a failure or short-
coming in any one of the elements may disqualify a person for effective
leadership. But when it comes to selecting for leadership capacity it is
the top two—the *presence* of intellectual firepower and the *absence* of
severe personality quirks or damage—that really count. When big
cockups and blunders do occur, this is where you look for the cause.

KNOWLEDGE

Almost all the leaders described in this book are 'experts'. William Hudson, for example, *had to be* a civil engineer in order to lead the Snowy Mountains enterprise. Mary Parker Follett *had to* have involved herself deeply in front-line operations and in the lives of front-line people in order to theorise about the wider employment systems that affected them. To anticipate stories yet to come, Bob Clifford *had to* know all about boat building and ferry operation, Robert Keep *had to* master model building (though not the arcane detail of currency trading), and Allan Coman *had to* understand the connection between educational process and learning. And the same principle applies to our other leaders. These people are unlike the 'company doctors' who come in from the outside with a general toolbox of knowledge about how organisations fail. Such fixers don't have to know much, if anything, about the ailing company's expert business.

The point about knowledge is that it can be acquired. Sometimes new appointments to big jobs fail due to the absence of key information, but this is unusual. The useful booklet *Taking Charge: Chief Executives Take up the Reins* (published by the search consultants Cordiner King) stresses the importance of newcomers learning the ropes. Here are the sentiments of a newly appointed managing director of a manufacturing company: '. . . *I thought I'd have a break, get my own personal affairs into order, but by the time I ended up darting here and there, back and forth, I only got a week. In hindsight I wouldn't have minded a few extra weeks, even a couple of months . . .*' The CEO of a not-for-profit organisation said: '*If I'd had my time over . . . I would have refused to get hooked into this thing of crisis management . . . and in a much more deliberate way gone around to all the centres and looked and absorbed.*'

These are both cases of the ultimately successful high-level transfer of an executive to a completely new and unfamiliar business. Acquiring knowledge quickly is not generally a problem for bright people, who know, or sense, where to go looking for useful knowledge. However, when new high-level appointments fail, it is sometimes attributable to a lack of understanding about the *politics* of the new organisation. What is significant about the leaders in this book is that they comfortably inhabit the spaces *between* fields. Their knowledge is not bounded by conventional disciplines or orthodoxies; they are connectors of fields of knowledge. As a result, each of them has created something quite new.

SKILL

Skills are learnable, up to a point. The infant ballet class makes the point perfectly—all the moppets, with much drilling, can learn the steps, but only a few were really meant by God to dance. Likewise, if God meant you to be an accountant, you are unlikely to succeed as a nurse. You could do it, but your areas of natural strength would be underdeployed. Sometimes miscasting can be a strength. Sir Colin Marshall, the Chairman of British Airways, would not claim to be a natural gladhander. Nearly everybody in BA knows he is officially an *introvert* (because BA takes psychometrics seriously and *everybody* gets tested). His skill-base is in cool analysis. But, coming from Avis to the airline business, he was smart enough to understand that British Airways *had to* learn to deal with its customers as friends rather than as inconvenient obstacles to flying aircraft about punctually. When BA instituted a company-wide program called *Putting People First*, Sir Colin assigned himself the obligation of appearing at every single session. If he couldn't make it, he would have the participants round to his office later on. Everyone could see that this shy, stiff man was out of his element but, of course, they understood and appreciated the *reason* that he so discomfited himself. Occasionally, great theatrical performances arise from *casting against type*, but it is unusual and difficult.

I normally place skill below motivation in the learnability hierarchy because I *think* that it is marginally more changeable by outside forces than at least the deeper motivations. In Figure 12, they are depicted on the same level, and as mutually reinforcing. If it turns out that you possess the gift of dance (the combination of the bodily/kinaesthetic and musical intelligences) then you may be powerfully *motivated* to spend a major part of your time dancing. The sense of growing mastery of the skill will be exhilarating, and an amplifier of motivation. On the other hand, if you start with the motivation, prompted for example by an older sibling's musical prowess, then your skills may grow out of that. Musicality is a good case in point because it is always held to be heritable. But new research suggests that, provided you start early enough, and you persist, almost anybody can become musically gifted—not, perhaps, to the level of a prodigy like Noel Waite (whose full story is in Chapter 12), but enough to fool a layperson. Even later in life (look at Colin Marshall) significant catching-up is possible, given strong enough motivation.

I noted above that one of the intriguing aspects of the leaders in this book is that they all appear to possess a broad skill repertoire. In terms of Howard Gardner's seven *multiple* intelligences they cover the territory. Noel Waite, for example, might have been a professional singer (she has perfect pitch and started playing tunes on the piano at three), a dress designer, or any kind of public affairs executive. She *was* an enormously successful commercial artist for many years, before tragic circumstances redirected her life.

Occupational psychopathology

Most people don't have the entire repertoire, as Gardner's researches indicate. This means that people who rise through the ranks to leadership positions are sometimes *unbalanced*, in the sense that their particular, narrow strengths continue to dominate their thinking. I call this *occupational psychopathology* or the way that natural strengths turn into weakness, given time and opportunity. It applies to all occupational fields but perhaps the most spectacular example is that of airline pilots. I know of no occupation where the vocational imperative is so strong, and so narrow. By and large, pilots-to-be *know*, by the age of about ten, that there is only one calling for them. For the most part, they will not contemplate the possibility of any other job and they will do almost anything to make sure that they *get to fly*. Why this is the case is mysterious. It is true that many pilots emerge from armed services families and quite a few grew up in sight of aeroplanes taking off and landing, but the only other variable I have been able to identify, as a result of working with hundreds of airline pilots, is that the *boys* (most pilots are male) often used to be tree-climbers. I remember well when I was young that there was a certain kind of nice but semi-solitary kid that you tended to forget about, until you heard the ambulance siren. An astonishing number of pilots come from the ranks of these children.

Of course, we are dealing here with an intermingling of special skills and strong motivation. It is the skill aspect that dominates the safety of air travel because more than 80 per cent of worldwide air crashes are caused by 'human error'. We can use this example to learn something about leadership generally. Pilots, in general, are fantastically good at certain useful skills but, being the particular self-selected folk they are, they carry compensating weaknesses. Probably no occupational group has been so exhaustively put through the psychometric hoops. Pilots are tested half to death before they are released into the cockpit. The overwhelming pattern is as follows. They are:

- Unusually good at complex data-crunching (if you have ever seen the array of information on a modern flight-deck, you will understand how important this skill is).
- Unusually dominated by cold, hard logic. Pilots find it virtually impossible to solve problems other than by the application of strict, technical logic. Happily, most of that logic is contained in standard operating procedures.
- Unusually decisive. Having taken the problem through the logical steps, the pilot is a courageous decision-maker. There are many occasions when that is exactly what the situation demands.

What this means is that the stereotypical pilot (there is virtually no other kind; we are talking about the ultimate monoculture) is ideally designed by nature to manage 99.9 per cent of what goes on in modern airline operations. At first blush, that is reassuring to the air traveller. The rub is that modern technology looks after the 99.9 per cent rather better than any human being can. It is the 0.1 per cent that presents the dangers, when something truly unpredictable crops up, often as the result of the simultaneous failure of two parallel systems. The stereotypical pilot is then probably the *worst* person in the world to take the necessary decisions under pressure. His pattern of strengths in pure logic incapacitate him for the totally ambiguous situation. He has had little practice, in life or in his technical training, in coping with *illogic*. This means that when things get *messy* he may be unable to:

- Absorb new information *intuitively*—by making *patterns*. The only exceptions to this are some female pilots and most ex-air force, fast-jet single-seater pilots. There isn't *time* for all the readouts under combat pressure—you absorb information in shapely chunks, not in orderly sequences.

- Share the problem with anybody else and put it to the test of opinion. If you think you know the facts and you have a foolproof logic for sorting them, why kick it around, even if you have an hour's flying time before you test your decision to destruction?

- Scan for new information 'outside the box'. If you have some time in hand, it makes sense to do a bit of 'what if . . . ?' brainstorming.

In the days when there was still a flight engineer in the cockpit, he was frequently the one who made the effort to interrogate the data banks for *more* information. He was also occasionally the person who saved the aircraft by so doing. In the older, three-person Jumbo cockpit, the engineer could physically take control of the aircraft, at a pinch. The engineers' mindsets were *similar* to pilots' but, happily, not identical. The engineer has now been replaced by technology, as a cost-saver. The two remaining pilots (as psychologically similar as peas in a pod) now have even more sophisticated data-crunching power separating them from 'seat of the pants' judgement. Happily, for the peace of mind of the air traveller, it is as possible to shore up the natural weaknesses of pilots as it is to shore up the natural weaknesses of their chairmen.

There are many other examples of the phenomenon of occupational psychopathology. Many of them parallel the case of the pilots—at the operational end what you need is routinised thinking, but at the executive end you need intuition. If you rise within the system, what was once a strength may become a weakness, unless the individual has a broad repertoire of skills to call on. This applies to accountancy, because routine auditing is no preparation for the detection of truly outstanding crookery. It applies to policing, because police operations often get in the way of inspired sleuthing. In the infamous case of the 'Yorkshire Ripper' there was a middle-ranking officer (an Imo) who *'knew'* the murderer was Peter Sutcliffe some years and seven *lives* before he was finally apprehended. Nobody would listen to him. Most of the police were thrown off the scent by a hoax audio tape (supposedly from the 'Ripper') with the *wrong regional accent*. Like the pilots, they had jumped too quickly to judgement.

Occupational psychopathology also occurs in the upper echelons of the law. Judges are generally drawn from the ranks of barristers. What barristers are good at is binary conflict. The best of them come to *believe in* their cases, however implausible, just as the great actors do. The two fields have much in common. David Marr's magisterial biography of Sir Garfield Barwick contains an acute analysis of this phenomenon:

> As an advocate he had a very great skill at solving his clients' problems, at getting them out of a fix, but as a judge he faced a different task: to set out the true position of all the parties, to identify and expound the truth. Few judicial ideas and principles emerged from the mass of his judgements. It was always easier to guess Barwick's response to a case than to predict what principles he would use to decide it.

Barwick was a king-sized *binary* who did not translate well to the necessarily *ternary* demands of the bench. You might argue that the quintessential barrister's skills are inimical to good judgement, except insofar as the barrister-promoted-to-judge will be able to see through the tricks deployed by counsel. Happily, most judges have broad-band abilities and manage the shift to ternary mode quite gracefully.

The most worrying case of all is that of the politicians. What it takes to fight your way through the alligators in the party political swamp is not necessarily what it takes to exercise *statesmanship*. You hope, in a democracy, that senior government ministers will be able to rise above the binary two-part battlefield in order to focus on the ternary end, the well-being of the *nation*. It doesn't always work out like that. In truth, politicians need both a strong binary instinct for survival *and* the capacity for detachment and statesmanship. It is an unusual combination.

MOTIVATION

I noted above that skill and motivation are bedfellows. The one can 'cause' the other. As with knowledge and skill, if you aren't motivated by the job in hand you are bound to fail in the end. Most of us have seen cases where enormously talented people have failed abjectly, solely because their heart wasn't really in it. In assessing this aspect, it helps to draw the distinction between two types, or levels, of motivation (see Figure 12):

- task motivation, where the individual derives satisfaction from doing work that gives intrinsic rewards
- primary task motivation, where the satisfaction derives mainly from identification with the organisation's purposes or outputs, rather than from the particular work tasks or role.

A good example might be the person who is fortunate to be working with figures, because he is very good at that (a professional accountant, for example)—but for an organisation whose purposes he deplores (a tobacco company, for example). Or another person might hold the wrong job in the right organisation. Liz O'Shaughnessy (see Chapter 12) loved her work in the speciality carpet business and had no quarrel at all with the outputs of the firm. Her demotivation flowed from the business practices employed. When we come to this level of the hierarchy we are dealing with quite deepseated aspects, linked with personal values. We can work our way through a demotivating experience but we can't easily relearn our basic motives.

KNOWLEDGE, SKILL AND MOTIVATION

Taken together, these three elements need to be more or less okay if an individual is to succeed in a job. They are important potential *disqualifiers* but they are at the malleable end of the occupational equation. You can do something about adapting each of them, at least for a while, if the current role incumbent really is the only available person. Training and development, if carefully targeted, can do something to enhance knowledge and skill. Money is a wonderful means of tweaking motivation in the short term, although it won't work indefinitely. What you can't do anything about is the next two elements in the hierarchy—personality quirks and what I call intellectual firepower. I focus on them now because it seems to me that they are generally misunderstood and that they are the primary cause of most big cockups and blunders.

PERSONALITY (TYRANNY, COWARDICE AND DECEIT)

This is a polite way of introducing the delicate subject of *psychological damage*. In the course of working for many years at high levels in big global organisations I have encountered, sometimes to my cost, a significant number of dangerous people. I mean, by that, people of tyrannical, cowardly and deceitful habits. These are generally people with the strongest possible 'binary' orientation, of the *survival* type. This means that their past experience, I suppose mainly in infancy, has predisposed them to approach all encounters as potentially threatening. These are the characters who aim to 'get their retaliation in first', on the assumption that you *must* have domination on your mind. Amanda Sinclair's descriptions (see Chapter 11) of the typical male-dominated, big-company, Australian-executive culture capture the essence very well.

In a fascinating three-year study of criminal psychopathy (based on interviews with long-term offenders in Scottish prisons), Lisa Marshall of Glasgow's Caledonian University discovered that an alarming proportion of successful stockbrokers and politicians turn out to have profiles very similar to those of the criminal psychopaths. They share the selfishness, callousness, exploitativeness, dishonesty, glib persuasiveness, shallowness, lack of remorse, instability, irresponsibility, social deviancy and promiscuity that are characteristic of the psychopathic personality. Both the convicted criminals and the successful professionals turned out to have had similar (hostile, authoritarian, inconsistent) upbringings. The 'successfuls' simply didn't kill anybody and probably had other, compensating, talents. The important point is that, in certain fields and organisational cultures, barmyness is no barrier to career progression.

Because we are dealing here with the executive suite, it follows that we are dealing mostly with *men*. Because behaviour of this kind is so prevalent, particularly around the boardrooms of some companies, it must follow that it is no barrier to career advancement. The probability is that the *best* way to get ahead in some organisations is precisely to behave in the way that damaged personalities behave. If there are sufficient other damaged souls around, it won't show. To be 'normal' in such a place is to seem odd. By contrast, other company cultures have ternary values and employ and promote notably sane people. Over the last thirty years I have had a good deal of exposure to ICI/Zeneca around the world and I have always regarded it as a relative oasis of calm and rational decision-making. This seems to be a deeply entrenched cultural tendency, constantly reinforced by the steady promotion of dedicated, low-key but highly intelligent executives—people like ICI Australia's current CEO, Warren Haynes. I don't, in other words, assume that *all* corporate cultures are as Amanda Sinclair describes—just a worryingly large minority of them.

The ICI case is worth examining briefly, if only to establish that this book's purpose is not to be rude about all big corporations. ICI Australia has always been a well-run organisation. There is a lively rivalry between the corporate HQ in London and the relatively autonomous Australian operation, but always in the context of an intelligent, *ternary* framework. The key is in the continuity. Sir John Harvey-Jones is one of the most famous, and successful, of all United Kingdom company chairmen. I have had the privilege, and the enormous fun, of spending some time with him. 'Larger than life' doesn't quite capture his personality. *He* makes the point that 'only ICI' would have hired him, aged 32 and straight from Royal Navy torpedo boats and Cold War espionage, without even a university degree, let alone in chemistry. How come? Probably only ICI would have had the confidence to post at the selection gateway the kinds of wise old birds with the intuition *plus* the authority to hire oddballs like Harvey-Jones on the basis of three fairly brief *chats* (not 'interviews'). As Geoffrey Vickers points out (I quoted him earlier), the capacity to exercise judgement, particularly when it comes to people, is rare and cannot be proved, except as a result of experience and 'track record'. ICI HQ simply posted smart cookies, without the benefit of psychometrics, at the gateway. The rest is history. Those who hired Harvey-Jones *knew* that they had probably just hired a future chairman of the company.

It isn't commonly known that Dick Beckhard, the doyen of the organisational development consultants, has acted as mentor and consultant to *all* the ICI HQ chairmen for nearly thirty years. If the chairman is there to provide context and continuity for the chief executive, who provides the context and continuity for the chairman? Typically, ICI has the long-term view. Even as the company has grappled with the short-term irritations of takeover bids from the likes of Hanson Industries, that calm long-term confidence and capability has persisted. It makes the company a tough target and a tough competitor. You could make the same argument about a well-founded corporation like BHP seeing off short-term 'financial engineer' predators. Anybody with experience of ICI Australia knows that that same low-key confidence and capability is built in. (In the conclusion to this book, I go into more depth on the subject of *mentoring* and the need for longer term, Beckhard-type relationships of trust as corporations get lean to the point of anorexia and executives get stressed to the point of madness.)

As evidence of the essential *sanity* of ICI, I cite a smallish piece of work I carried out some years ago. This was an enquiry into management development practices right across all the United Kingdom operating divisions. After a short period of informal research, I made a suggestion to the client which I suspected would be much too *simple* to be taken seriously. I had picked up what I thought was a gap between the rhetoric and the reality of management development. I proposed that our task force should fan out, in pairs, to test out in all the divisions whether there was a significant difference between the answers to these two questions:

- *What do you have to do round here to get things done?*
- *What do you have to do round here to get ahead?*

My presumption was that the bigger the difference, by company division, the bigger the problem in both practical and ethical terms. It would have been a very threatening exploration in many corporations, and especially in those that Amanda Sinclair describes. ICI ran with the idea, to very good effect, *because* it addressed its consistency and ethical culture. The offending divisions, where the gap was large, received tough and uncompromising attention from the 'Centre' as a result. The Australian company has the same outlook. This is the kind of corporate culture in which it is very *unlikely* that seriously damaged individuals will rise to high position. Once risen, such a person would stick out like a sore thumb in ICI.

Technology companies sometimes suffer from too *little* craziness when it comes to strategic thinking. That topic crops up in the section Intellectual firepower (below).

Damage out of adversity

Let me offer an example of the kind of psychological damage that often appears in the corporate world. I was once asked by a chief executive to 'counsel' a middle-level sales manager of an unnamed company on the eve of his planned promotion to senior management. The promotion looked pretty 'obvious' to everybody concerned, and the man himself—let us call him Keith—had been vigorously agitating for promotion. On the surface, in terms of seniority and proven success, his time had come. The *reason* why the chief executive involved me, it transpired, was that he had a bad feeling in his waters that Keith might not be up to the job, although he couldn't tell why. Call it *intuition*. I spent some time with Keith and played the major part in ensuring that subsequently some *other* kind of work was found for him. He was not promoted to the next level. I am quite sure to this day that I did both Keith and the company a big favour. Indeed, he passed on to other things elsewhere, but eventually caused a spectacular, and very expensive, disaster.

Let us be clear: Keith possessed all the mental agility he needed. The problem lay in a deeprooted binaryness. He had not had an easy life. He had been the youngest in a pretty tough family—very much the punchbag for all his big brothers. School was pretty rough too—a down-at-heel school in an underprivileged area. Being small of stature, Keith had been routinely bullied throughout his early years there. But, miraculously, on one memorable day, Keith experienced a remarkable conversion or insight. It dawned on him that his misery did not concern *whether* he would get beaten up but *when*! The certainty was that he would be beaten up yet again—the unbearable aspect was the terrible uncertainty about the timing of it. Keith wasn't stupid. He realised with a shock of insight that he could remove that awful anxiety by switching to the role of *aggressor*—by *controlling* the timing! From that moment on he took control of the uncertainty that mattered to him by hitting first. The surprise element worked well with potential aggressors.

When he grew up he became a salesman—and a very successful one. He combined a seductive and controlling personality with great gifts in the *interpersonal* intelligences—he could *read* the signs of weakening resolve and he closed mercilessly on his prey. In time, he was promoted to management and he drove his salesmen as hard as he drove himself. High-pressure selling is a tough, no-nonsense, *fight/flight* world. It suits the binary mindset admirably. When successful salespeople are promoted up the line, they don't always translate well to the demands of *dependence*. (The theory of the 'basic assumptions' of fight/flight and dependence is discussed fully in Chapter 14.) Any senior manager will sometimes need to take on important *fights*, but he or she also has to serve as a *dependable* figure for subordinates. Keith was fine on the fighting side. What his chief executive sensed was that Keith was not capable of accepting and amplifying the psychological projection of dependence. There is nothing wrong with *mature* dependence—it is a normal and healthy part of adult life. The problems arise with neurotic or *resourceless* dependence.

It doesn't follow that you can't become a successful leader if you have had a tough upbringing. Some of the very best leaders turn out to be those that have suffered adversity and overcome it through understanding and self-awareness. Such people *really* understand the underdog. Generally, these are people who have had a modicum of healthy *dependence* and *dependability* in their early caring relationships, no matter how adverse the material circumstances. If there has been *somebody* you can trust in childhood, the chances are that you will have the capacity to inspire trust when you achieve adulthood. Keith is one example of a naturally gifted person who may have been doubly unlucky in life's lottery—not only economically deprived but psychologically deprived as well. Whatever damage we may have suffered, there is always going to be some kind of work we can do well. Some occupations (arguably high-pressure sales among them) actually feed off psychological damage. But senior management is *not* a field for the too-damaged—not unless the organisation itself (the Nazi hierarchy would be a good example) is crazy.

There is a difference therefore between having *access* to binary combativeness and being *dominated* by survival needs. Most of us, save nuns and other reclusives, live in a naughty world. There will always be times when we need to have our wits about us and be prepared, if necessary, to see off a predator. To *always* shirk the fight is to display one form of psychological damage. People who *won't* fight often betray good causes. One of the well-known contributory factors in child abuse or murder is the *nice* social worker who empathises *too much* with errant parents/step-parents, who *knows* in her heart of hearts that disaster is possible but is unable to challenge less acute or more complacent colleagues in a crisis meeting or committee. But the really damaged people see *everything* in terms of dominance and submission. They can't help it and, without deep and painful therapy, they are unlikely to change much in adulthood. The presence of substantial numbers of people like this in high corporate position represents a long-term problem not only for the organisations concerned but for the country also.

If Keith had been promoted, he might well have survived for some time at that level, because the provision of support at the top tends to be generous and, sometimes, the operations are more opaque than at lower levels in the organisation. This is because the longer time-cycles involved can actually conceal substandard performance. At lower levels, cockups and blunders are likely to be exposed more quickly. As long as he lasted, he would have exported 'noise' into the surrounding system and, possibly, damaged other people as well.

Damage out of privilege

Keith's story deals with only one aspect of the damage-into-management scenario, though a common one. There is another kind of bad-news leader whose origins, by contrast, are generally privileged. Interestingly, the best writer on this phenomenon is the distinguished military historian/psychologist, Norman F. Dixon. His classic text *On the Psychology of Military Incompetence* points out that disastrous commanders are always *'careless—to say the least'* with the lives of their men. Some of these commanders are basically *'mild, courteous and peaceful'* men who have joined the peacetime military for, it might be argued, the wrong reasons—to shore up their masculine deficiencies and to satisfy an ideal of manhood. These leaders are generally reluctant to take tough and timely decisions. General Percival of Singapore drove his Australian colleagues to distraction by delaying crucial decisions about defending the island from the approaching Japanese army on the extraordinary grounds that mounting a defence might be *'bad for the morale of troops and civilians'*. The thousands of Australians who ended up in Changi detention camp did indeed encounter 'morale' problems—if they survived, that is.

But when it comes to wasting lives, there is another more dangerous psychological type which tends to rise spectacularly through the military hierarchy. This kind of commander, Dixon tells us, is characterised by 'overweening ambition coupled with a terrifying insensitivity to the suffering of others. These men, like Haig, Townshend, Walpole, Nixon and Joffre, seemed dedicated to one goal—self-advancement. Vain, devious, scheming and dishonest, they were certainly not inactive in the courses they pursued, nor of course were they necessarily without military talents'. Many of my readers, I suspect, will recognise at least a few contemporary corporate leaders in this chilling description. The awkward fact about the last ten to fifteen years of corporate life is that for many major organisations the period has involved *attrition* of people—just like the First World War.

The simplest and best way for senior executives to feed personal ambition in the modern corporation is to construct a rewards system based on stock options and then drive out cost through downsizing, so as to impress the stock market with the short-term 'improvements'. No new markets are created, no new technologies are developed, no competitive strengths are built. C. K. Prahalad has pointed out that something like 600 million new *consumers* have entered world markets in recent years, all of them hungry for new, useful products and services. The best that many Anglo-Saxon (American, British, Australian) firms have been able to do is to reduce the costs of existing business operations—just as with the generals at the Battle of the Somme, the response is more of the same. Of course, many senior executives have felt some *angst* about the spillage of loyal staff and about the shellshock of the survivors. But very few have devised a long-term way of holding the whole team together in order to conquer new fields.

The contrast: Asian stakeholding

At the time of writing, there is a persistent tendency on the part of Western binary thinkers to misunderstand the example of our Asian neighbour–competitors. If you are a fearful binary type, you will be motivated by short-term survival. You will have little trust and faith in a beneficent long-term well-being. If you observe the Asian 'tigers' to be doing well, you will want and need to believe that this is due to low government expenditures, less welfare, compliant workforces and an absence of regulations. You want to believe this because this is what you want for Australia and for your own corporation, because it fits in with the exploitative, short-term binary mindset. The person with access to ternary thinking is likely to view the causation differently. He, or more likely she, will observe that one of the reasons why Asian government does less is that corporations do *more* for their people. Moral debt looms large in these cultures. If the company lays on a free bus service, the workers are likely, on their own initiative, to repay the favour by devising a cost-cutting scheme. The company, in gratitude, then installs a day-care centre, and so the reciprocal cycle rolls forward.

Charles Hampden-Turner cites the example of Intel in Penang, where the Pentium processor is made:

> The managing director, a Chinese Malaysian, explained how he had started an in-house shop. Why? 'To save time', he explained, 'but also to generate profits, which we used to start the Credit Union. Now we have taken capital in the Credit Union and invested it in low- and medium-tech corporations in this area . . . it is so that any employee who has worked loyally for us but cannot learn the trigonometry needed for Pentium production can be outplaced in a company that our union partly owns. We find jobs for everyone.' We were standing in the middle of a flower garden, which was also the day nursery. The children were learning English. 'Good morning, visitor!', they chorused. Managers' children are educated at cost, technicians' at half-cost, workers' children are educated free.

Hampden-Turner is right. If you want to build a successful economy, you can't do it by wilfully misunderstanding what is happening amongst our neighbours and competitors.

This is a discussion about the psychological damage sometimes found in senior corporate executives. There is an obvious link with our next topic—intelligence. The binary mindset is partly caused by psychic damage and it also constrains thinking capacity. I will return to these general themes later but it is worth noting here that we are touching on the currently fashionable idea of the '*stakeholder society*'; that is, a society in which the various stakeholders—employees, shareholders, customers, community and government—achieve some kind of *harmony*. The government of Singapore proclaims *wa* or harmony between interests as their not-so-secret weapon. Things start to go wrong when one stakeholder gets into a position to dominate the others. There is not much argument any more that, in the 1970s, the most powerful organised workers gained advantage not by cooperating in improving the production process but by shaking down other stakeholders. In Britain, Margaret Thatcher orchestrated the necessary reaction against that trade union dominance. Unfortunately, she left behind a new dominance, this time on the part of the shareholders, the big pension funds and their stock option-motivated cohorts in the executive suite.

There is a growing acceptance that these 'socio-technical' questions are crucial to the long-term health of modern economies. Viewed in this light, Australia may be fortunate, as compared with the United Kingdom and New Zealand, to have enjoyed some kind of 'accord' with organised labour, brokered by government. The very idea of an *accord*, whatever its practical limitations, is ternary. It presupposes an agreement to limit one's binary *power* in support of a higher-order *collaborative* purpose. This ought to mean that, with a change in government complexion, there is no real need for a destabilising backlash against 'union power' in Australia. What is not generally accepted as part of the mix is that long-term economic decline may be *caused* by the cyclical and well-intentioned promotion of psychologically damaged people to high executive rank. If the out-turn really is a raft of damaged people at the top, it will be no surprise if questions of 'leadership' come into prominence.

The causation of damage

What are the other causes of the psychological quirks that produce such fearful, tyrannical, seductive or untrustworthy 'leaders'? One or two such causes are worth our attention before we consider the kind of beneficent environments that contribute to inclusiveness and harmony in society. One obvious cause is the failure of parents to provide a safe enough environment for the infant. Young children can ingest insecurity from their parents. Keith's parents, no doubt, were evidently unable to provide a secure and dependable passage through childhood for him. If a boy, in particular, is habitually beaten for no good reason by a father or stepfather, as Saddam Hussein and Josef Stalin were, then he is certain to be damaged by the experience and quite likely to grow up needing to feel overpowerful (because his inner sense of impotence is so overwhelming). We all now know the kinds of long-term damage that flow from the physical and sexual abuse of young girls, but in a male-dominated world few such girls, however undamaged, are likely to emerge in significant leadership roles. Damaged boys are another matter. Happily, these kinds of barbarism are relatively unusual.

Much more common, in the nicest of homes, is the phenomenon of so-called 'conditional love'. If a child grows up subject to conditional love, he or she is likely to need excessive doses of psychological reinforcement for the rest of life. This happens when parents, with the best will in the world, attempt to *manufacture* what they take to be the right or best kind of infant. The deal is: 'We'll love you, *provided* you behave in the approved way!' When children like this grow up to be bosses, they need *gratitude* the way addicts need drugs. It's not enough for subordinates and colleagues to work with them according to the dictates of formal (ternary) role relationships; they have to be personally *grateful* to the boss, in order to make up for the deeply embedded gratitude *deficit* in the boss's makeup. Such bosses will do anything to get you *in their gift*. It can get pretty claustrophobic.

This is not a book about child care and upbringing but, if you want your children to be clever, secure, inventive, independent and focused—like the entrepreneurs celebrated in these pages, then there is a right and wrong way to approach the matter. The trick seems to lie in accepting the child as he or she *is*, rather than trying to manufacture a particular kind of infant. This means waiting patiently to find out who this new person is and then giving thoughtful support to the development of *that* person. It is usually called *unconditional love* but you could just as well see it as a form of empirical scientific curiosity. The wise parent assumes that the child is *good enough* (i.e. perfect) and prepares to *learn* as well as to teach. The long-term payoff is in the psychological health of the child (a strong sense of identity) and in clarity of mind. Of course, like anything else, unconditional love can be overdone. People who cause a *lot of trouble*, like Nick Leeson of Barings infamy, or the occasional mass murderer, often turn out to have mums who still believe they can *do no wrong*—even after the whole world can see how naughty they have been.

The authoritarian personality

By far the most complained-about behaviour on the part of bosses concerns *bullying* of subordinates and kowtowing to higher authority. If effective leadership depends on respect and admirability, the bully or sucker-up can never assume true leadership because he or she cannot be admired by sane or decent people. Interestingly, there is a good deal of research evidence about the kind of parenting that produces such 'authoritarians'. Overwhelmingly, authoritarians emerge from households where parents are anxious about their status in society and where the values associated with this anxiety are imposed with a heavy hand.

First, we need to understand what is meant by the 'authoritarian' personality. The research that led to the concept arose directly from the Nazi holocaust. The question concerned how so many respectable God-fearing Germans became willing accomplices to mass murder. If the phenomenon was not *understood* properly, it might recur at any time, whenever the psychological soil was again fertile. At the end of the war, the task was given to a group of eminent psychologists and social anthropologists at the University of California, Berkeley, under the leadership of Erich Fromm and T. W. Adorno. Their starting assumption was that so remarkable was the pattern of amoral behaviour amongst prewar and wartime Germans that it *must* have been the case that a deepseated *personality type* was implicated. Some of these scientists had already been driven out of Germany in the 1930s.

The Berkeley team tested the attitudes and backgrounds of over 2000 Americans from many different walks of life. They were particularly interested in ethno-prejudice—the tendency of some people to locate all wickedness in outgroups. Those subjects that were the most anti-Semitic, rigid, intolerant of ambiguity and hostile to perceived outsiders were further subjected to open-ended projective tests and clinical interviews. All the evidence pointed to the existence of a particular and consistent constellation of attitudes and beliefs in the most prejudiced people. That constellation, famously, was dubbed the 'authoritarian personality'. There was an 'anti-type' too—those who were characteristically individualistic, tolerant, democratic, unprejudiced and egalitarian . . . all those characteristics to which most of us aspire.

When we consider leadership in modern organisations we are not, thankfully, concerned with homicidal racism or political repression, but we do see behaviour that evidently springs from similar sources. We certainly see plenty of aggressive bullying, intolerance, anti-intellectualism, and the projection of wickedness onto others. We see enough of this sort of thing to ask whether it is realistic to think of the *authoritarian personality* as an element in managerial and leadership failings. Most of us have encountered bosses who were apparently indifferent to the distress of others, especially subordinates. Stanley Milgram's famous experiments in the 1970s showed a direct link between managerial behaviour in institutional settings and the presence of the authoritarian pattern. These were the experiments where the subjects, *believing* themselves to be administering electric shocks to other subjects, were induced by the authoritative 'scientists' in charge to administer

119

increasingly severe 'shocks' to the actors playing the 'helpless victims', even when their physical struggles and screams could be seen and heard. The non-authoritarians, as predicted, quickly refused to continue administering the increased 'shocks', despite orders.

The authoritarian personality combines the following dispositions:

- a rigid adherence to conventional middle-class values
- an uncritical submission to the idealised moral authority of his or her chosen in-group
- a wish to identify, condemn, reject and punish people who violate conventional values
- a strong resistance to the subjective, the imaginative and the 'tenderminded'
- a tendency to superstition about 'fate' and a disposition to think in rigid categories
- a preoccupation with toughness, strength and identification with power-figures
- a generalised cynicism about, destructiveness towards and denigration of the human
- a belief in the dangerous forces at work 'out there' in the world
- an exaggerated and puritanical concern with sexual 'goings-on' on the part of others

The reader will see an obvious reflection of the *binary* mindset—but expressed here in psychological or psychoanalytic terms.

The followers of Pauline Hanson will certainly be people who deal with their fears and resentments by projecting their feelings onto outgroups.

The classic authoritarian grows up in a home where socially insecure parents teach their children to put personal success and the acquisition of power above all else. Children are encouraged to judge people for their usefulness, rather than for any intrinsic merit. They are taught to eschew weakness and passivity, to respect authority, and to despise those who have not made the socio-economic grade. Success is always equated with social esteem and material advantage. At the same time, the children are imbued with rigid views regarding sex and aggression. Childish transgressions are strictly punished and dissent is never tolerated. Sex is dirty and aggression is only permissible towards such outgroups as Jews or coloured people or law-breakers. Boys have to be masculine, tough and strong and girls have to be, under a frigid kind of feminine respectability, alive to the possibility of granting favours in the service of status-seeking.

A household *exactly* like this is probably uncommon. Households *quite* like this are not so uncommon. They may produce the kind of psychological damage that leads on to extreme ambition, ruthlessly manipulative behaviour, and the virtual absence of shame or guilt. In certain kinds of highly 'political' organisation, this is precisely the collection of traits that is likely to lead to career success and hence to 'leadership' position. When workers put together lists of the desirable characteristics of leaders, they invariably say that the good leader is prepared to 'stick up for' his or her staff when necessary. The authoritarian *always* sucks up to higher authority. Funnily enough, an almost identical behavioural type to this—the so-called 'J type'—had been identified by the Nazi psychologist Jaensch some ten years before Adorno and his colleagues did their research. The difference was that the J type was regarded by Jaensch and the Nazis as an *ideal* type—hard, unbending and, above all, *pure*.

INTELLECTUAL FIREPOWER

I have placed this element at the top of the pile in Figure 12 because I believe it to be the most intractable element of all, even compared with deepseated psychological damage. It is a very difficult subject with which to engage. With some trepidation, bearing in mind the 'gun lobby', I have chosen the term 'firepower' in order to emphasise the sense of *calibre*—the possibility of delivering more thoughtfulness and ingenuity per minute worked. I noted in the Introduction that we are all very unsure as to what intelligence *is*. Schoolteachers, who have a great deal to do with the emergent *capability* of children, sometimes regard intelligence as the capacity for book-learning and regurgitation of disembodied fact. Anti-intellectuals (like the delinquent Spansky in Chapter 9) usually look on real, useful intelligence as all practice and no theory at all. Cognitive psychologists are increasingly looking on it as a kind of data-processing, but they have an interesting problem with the *idiot savant* who is a brilliant processor but so narrow as to be unable to cope with ordinary life. Posh people in Britain still talk about a 'tremendously *able* chap' without specifying what exactly he is *able* to do, other than talk brilliantly. It is a tricky subject, but if we are serious about better leadership we have to tackle it.

I refer now to the trailblazing work of Professor Elliott Jaques, one of the founders of the Tavistock Institute in London. The Tavistock was set up to explore the ways in which the insights of psychology and psychoanalysis might be transferred to practical spheres like industrial relations and management. The idea made sense because anyone who has worked with industrial conflict will know it gets irrational fast and often. If you can determine the underlying *pattern* (if you like, the rationality beneath the irrational), you have at least a chance of resolving the conflict intelligently. Jaques cut his teeth on the long-running Glacier Metal Company project, which explored these questions for over thirty years continuously. Its principal aim was to devise and test ways of *constitutionalising* work relations. The chief executive, and one of the greatest postwar business leaders, was Wilfred (later Lord Wilfred) Brown. He had read his history. His conclusion was that the Germans had succeeded in taking the binary fight out of industrial relations by placing the key stakeholders in formal representational (ternary) roles. This, he reckoned, partly explained the German 'economic miracle'. Being a Scot, Brown was very reluctant to admit that the Germans might be better engineers.

Brown and Jaques worked as a complementary two-man team (in very much the same way as Hudson and Lemmon) until Brown's death in 1985. They took their cue from the wider system of society. The argument was that the British cracked the problem of political legitimacy in the 19th century, by gradually bringing everybody within the franchise—by giving them a *stake* in the democratic process. Prior to that the British were probably the most lawless and corrupt nation in Europe. People tend to forget how violent and widespread the civil unrest was in Britain in the first half of the 19th century. Once the institutions were fixed, the people magically turned into sober and virtuous late Victorians. The gene pool was unchanged; the institutional structures simply made it possible for people to behave calmly and sensibly. But, having got it right in society at large, the Brits never quite saw the connection with *industrial* democracy. Once the populace becomes sophisticated about civic rights and duties (and firms get as big as large towns), people will not put up with an absence of democratic participation in the occupational sphere—not willingly, at any rate. The Germans were the obverse. They went on having awful problems with civil democracy until 1945 but they grasped the *principle* of democracy in the workplace right from the start. The irony is that they *thought* they were copying English industrial practice, not realising that Robert Owen and the other pioneers of practice and thought were *Scots*.

As the Glacier project unfolded (it is still very much worth reading about) it made elbow room for outstanding people—'natural leaders'—to assume authority in the workplace, beyond their hierarchical rank. Because people were empowered by representative as well as operative and managerial roles, they got the hang of wearing multiple hats. It was a boon for any potential 'Imos'. When a visiting American tycoon visited the Glacier factory in Kilmarnock in Scotland, he found it impossible to understand how a convenor of union shop stewards could simultaneously be a junior manager. When the manager in question was asked about taking a particular decision, he could reply in all honesty: 'It depends whether I am wearing my hat as manager or shop steward!' The American, binary to the core, couldn't grasp it. By loosening up the authority structure, Brown and Jaques were making it possible for bright people to exercise task leadership in the spaces *between* formal structures.

After thirty years or so, they had become pretty good at assessing and predicting the ability of people to handle complex tasks and roles. This is the basis for assessment by 'intellectual firepower'. This means, in short, the ability to mentally process *complexity*, with particular reference to differing levels of *abstraction*. Currently, Jaques argues that this kind of capability can be gauged quickly by merely listening to an individual *talk* for a few minutes, firstly about a general subject, and then about something he or she really *cares* about. Buried in the use of language is the *structure of thought*—the way that superior and subordinate categories or classes are kept in tidy relationship; the way that different, but loosely related, subject areas are connected in order to pursue an argument. Over the years, Jaques' associate Gillian Stamp devised a formal protocol (sometimes called Career Path Appreciation) to make these assessments. They have been used all over the world and their predictive powers are startling (as measured by longitudinal studies of subsequent promotion). This formal method is described more fully in the final chapter. People with the gift of character and capability assessment simply do this intuitively. The people you want on selection panels are those who *never* make mistakes in this regard. They are much more reliable and cheaper than psychometric testing.

It is important to stress that intellectual firepower is only one of the capabilities a leader needs. I am stressing it here because years of experience have taught me that it is the most common and underrecognised cause of leadership failure. A lack in any of the other dimensions—knowledge, skill, motivation, or personality—*may* lead to failure. Human capability is *frog*-like—all the separate elements have to work well together in an *integrated* fashion. A lack in judgement *must* lead to failure eventually. When great blunders occur, the hunt is usually on for character weaknesses or political chicanery or conspiracy theories. More often than not the root cause has been the inability of the top person, over a continuous period, to hack the complexity of the situation at that particular level. He might have had the firepower to cope at the next job level down in the system. By definition, he won't know that this is the problem, except in terms of a vague sense of unease. If you can't hack it, you can't hack that you can't hack it! When the leader is out of his depth, what tends to happen is a slowing down of the corporate response to events. Important or urgent matters go to committee or on to 'the back burner'. When a leader is able to handle the complexity in a timely way, we generally call it 'judgement'. In my formulation, it is the presence of intellectual firepower that *brings about* the capacity for judgement.

The step-by-step development of judgement

Elliott Jaques suggests that there is a natural hierarchy of judgement—the capacity to cope with complexity in situations of ambiguity and pressure. This is intuitively observable as people grow up and extend their range of ability. Every schoolteacher knows that the average seventeen-year-old can perform mental operations way beyond the capacity of all but the most precocious primary school kids. The great Swiss epistemologist, Jean Piaget, demonstrated long ago how infants pass through *stages* in their capacity to make sense of complexity and ambiguity. Catherine Mant and Josef Perner provide a good example of this in their study of how children develop their capacity to comprehend *commitment*. Very young children understand commitment in terms of simple and inflexible *rules*. To tell a lie is always *wrong*, irrespective of the surrounding circumstances. The very young child will say that if you cannot fulfil a commitment, even though you were prevented from doing so by an act of God, the original commitment was a 'lie'. This looks absurd to an adult, but we forget how we ourselves have had to work through these conceptual steps towards a more complex and *realistic* understanding of when, why and how we become obligated to others.

The American psychologist Lawrence Kohlberg, building on Piaget's work, described no less than *six* stages of the development of 'moral' reasoning from childhood right through into adulthood. Controversially, he suggested that very few people achieve the highest levels of moral reasoning, which involve the processing of great complexity in the mind. When people behave badly or 'irresponsibly', unless they are deceiving themselves for personal advantage, they sometimes simply cannot comprehend how others see, and condemn, their behaviour—'*What did I do wrong?*' Jaques argues that managers similarly have to progress through stages in the mastery of greater and greater complexity. It is not just a matter of handling *more data* but of sifting and ordering information quickly—just as superior *software* squeezes more productivity out of a computer system with relatively low-level *hardware*. The effective leader knows what *not* to think about, and when not to think about it, so as to keep the central processing free for what is really important. The struggling manager out of his depth *loses the plot* and focuses on those matters that smart subordinates (Imos) can *see*, easily, are peripheral to the main plot—or he simply overloads his brain.

Jaques makes the connection between the stages of individual capacity, as they develop over time, and the levels of increasing complexity in organisational hierarchies. Furthermore, he suggests that the organisational levels are immutable, because they reflect the realities of human capacity. Organisations are made by people, and they can't escape the natural properties of their makers. In truth, when they work well they become like *organisms*—or, if you prefer, frogs. Figure 13 summarises Jaques' argument about the *kinds* of value added by each successive level, irrespective of whether the organisation concerned is a global manufacturer or a suburban solicitors' practice. If Jaques is right, no organisation, however big, needs more than seven or eight levels of hierarchy. On the other hand, a global firm absolutely needs every one of those incremental layers of authority. If you overdo the 'de-layering', it is the equivalent of cutting out a necessary *linkage* in a frog's nervous system. The system will lose the plot because part of it won't function properly. All this is explained in much greater depth in Chapter 14. At this stage we are concerned just with the data-crunching aspect of judgement.

Intelligent politicians (not an oxymoron)

Countries are very big systems and require very intelligent direction but it is not uncommon to find very smart (though sometimes narrow-band) public servants responding to intellectually-challenged politicians. Most politicians are hot stuff on the interpersonal intelligence but they don't always have mental staying-power. Their crowded schedules protect them from too much sustained thought. Also, their creativity may have been stunted since their teens by the perceived need to embrace just one side of every political argument.

If you compare, for example, the capabilities of national leaders like Paul Keating (gone now) and John Major (at the time of writing still clinging to power), a stark contrast is immediately visible. They are the same age and they come from comparable social backgrounds. Both have been educated mainly in the university of life. If we compare the immutable aspects of capability—the psychological and the intellectual—the differences show up. John Major is broadly accepted as a nice enough guy. He can be a tough politician, of course, but he lacks Keating's waspish bite. As Laurie Oakes put it succinctly: 'The trouble with Paul Keating is that if you give him a clip over the ear you get a thermonuclear attack back!' Keating clearly finds this tendency difficult to control; there is a strong streak of binary combativeness buried deep in his makeup. This is destructive—it was felt to be the main cause of his unpopularity amongst Australian women (half the voters) before the 1996 election. Many of them hated the idea of their sons growing up to behave in a similarly cruel, punitive and larrikinish way. It would be unthinkable for John Major to harangue a public servant for three-quarters of an hour for simply doing her job (stewardship of public funds in relation to a now infamous teak table intended for the Prime Minister's official residence). At that moment, Paul Keating *lost the plot*.

VII	Global corporate prescience	Sustaining long-term viability; defining values, moulding contexts	(25–50)
VI	(Group) corporate citizenship	Reading international contexts to support/alert level V strategic business units	(15–20)
V	Strategic intent	Overview of organisational purpose in context	(→ 10)
IV	Strategic development	Inventing/modelling new futures; positioning the organisation	(→ 5)
III	Good practice	Constructing, connecting and fine-tuning systems	(→ 2/3)
II	Service	Supporting/serving level 1 and customers/clients	(→ 1)
I	Quality	Hands-on skill	

Figure 13 Levels of work authority, complexity and talent

> This chart summarises Elliott Jaques' famous stratified systems theory. It depicts the natural and ineluctable steps from simple short-term work to the most demanding and complex work. The figures on the right refer to *years*—the 'time span of discretion' at that level of complexity. A serious error of judgement at (say) Level IV might take as long as five years to show through (by which time the culprit will almost certainly have shot through). Jaques argues that no organisation, however big or global, needs more than about seven hierarchical levels, because these strata reflect the natural increments of the human capacity to exercise discretion. On the other hand, 'delayering' *beyond* this minimal backbone of authority will inevitably weaken the organisation, because necessary *connections* will be severed. Nobody who works in an organisation is completely confined to his or her level of capacity—we all have to perform mundane chores sometimes and, perhaps, *over*stretch ourselves later the same day. But if we are *persistently* overstretched, without watchful supervision, we will eventually make a blunder.

Compare then the intellectual angle and there is a complete contrast. John Major's use of language is wooden and muddled. 'Majorisms' almost rival 'Bushisms' (George Bush's famous convoluted engagements with the English language) for obtuseness and meaninglessness. A favourite amongst British journalists is Major's statement to the Scott Inquiry into the illegal arming of Iraq: 'Something that I was not aware had happened suddenly turned out not to have happened!' This merely reflects his failure to grasp higher-order principles. Major is dull because he has no agility of mind. This means that when things get really complicated he closes down the discourse in order to keep it in control. Content analysis of his non-scripted utterances reveals their banality and lack of depth—a nice, dull guy in charge of a very big, complicated system. As a result, most of the big, important issues stay on the 'back burner' and the time spans of lower-level decision-making get shorter and shorter.

Keating, for all his bad binary habits, flipflops into ternary mode and is capable then of great depth and breadth. The 'big picture' may not have been the most important issue for the Australian electorate in 1996, but few Australians doubted Keating's capacity to comprehend it. Even his insults were poetic. They demonstrated a capacity to import earthy and emotional content to add impact—this was a waspish but *clever* guy in charge of a system just a third as big as the United Kingdom (in population terms)—a broad-bander. Take your pick. When it comes time to make choices (as between a Paul Keating and a John Howard, for example) people tend to factor in both of these aspects—the perception of *psychological damage* and the perception of *intellectual capability*. When the opinion pollsters get it wrong they often miss this intuitive aspect of popular perception. When people vote 'emotionally' (or intuitively) they remember what it is like to be bossed, or parented, by somebody punitive or out of his or her depth. The Australian people probably accept John Howard at his own estimation as a 'battler'. Whether he will seem *deep* enough, in the long term, for the more complicated challenges of leadership, we shall see.

The worldwide debate on political 'stakeholding' is connected with the stage theory of moral development and of judgement. Essentially, those who argue for explicit stakeholding for all elements in society and for the reining in of naked capitalistic competition are saying that society is a big frog and its multiple interconnections cannot be reduced to simple formulae. Their view is that 'the state' has to intervene in order to level the playing field, having taken democratic account of the public will. Their ideological opponents insist that 'the state' is a sinister and coercive enemy of individual 'freedom' and of the natural development of competition between 'free agents' in 'free markets'. Margaret Thatcher believes this and so do the huge numbers of Americans who positively hate 'big government'. These people combine laissez-faire economics with a doctrine of unbounded liberal individualism. The view is that *market relations*, regulated by contracts and lawyers, should determine the proper working of societies. All obligations and commitments can be traded or written down in contracts. It is not surprising that lawyer-politicians such as Margaret Thatcher see things in this way. The argument quickly becomes a *moral* argument. If we go back to Mant and Perner (above) we see that the understanding of mutual obligation and commitment is subject to stage development in infants. Maybe the free-marketeers have not yet developed to the point where they can comprehend higher-order societal obligations? Maybe we are really dealing with intelligence rather than ethics? Remember that Margaret Thatcher famously opined: *'There is no such thing as society!'*

SUMMARY OF THE ELEMENTS

When a leader fails, the failure can be caused by any one of the five elements I've outlined, or by any combination of them. Human beings are much more like frogs than like bicycles, so all the elements are interconnected all the time; and there are plenty of others (e.g sheer luck or variable physical energy levels) as well. My years of observing leaders and selecting people for big jobs has forced me to conclude that there is a symbiotic link between the two most important elements—the psychological damage factor and the intellectual firepower factor—hence the firepower UP and damage DOWN arrows in Figure 14. I noted earlier that Dr Wilfred Bion (one of the Tavistock founders and the fount of much of our understanding of group process) argued that arrogance and stupidity are virtually the same element, because the one always causes the other. In binary/ternary language, if an individual is strongly driven, or overwhelmed, by survival/control needs, then he or she will need to predetermine any uncertain situations. The only social justification for this is *being right* and *knowing what to do*. Eventually this will be perceived as arrogance, even though its wellsprings lie in weakness and insecurity. If you predetermine the local situation, you cannot be open to the wider 'law of the situation'—to use Mary Parker Follett's pungent term. This means you will never *learn*. If you never learn, you must get progressively more stupid.

The reader is entitled to wonder how anybody can rise to near the top of a large organisation and still be counted stupid or arrogant. This is all relative, according to the levels of work and complexity

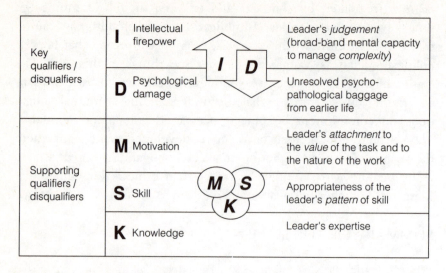

Key qualifiers / disqualifiers	**I**	Intellectual firepower	Leader's *judgement* (broad-band mental capacity to manage *complexity*)
	D	Psychological damage	Unresolved psycho-pathological baggage from earlier life
Supporting qualifiers / disqualifiers	**M**	Motivation	Leader's *attachment* to the *value* of the task and to the nature of the work
	S	Skill	Appropriateness of the leader's *pattern* of skill
	K	Knowledge	Leader's expertise

Figure 14 Leadership elements

The two most significant (because intractable) leadership disqualifiers are *poor judgement* and *psychological damage*, and they *interact*. When a leader is overexposed or overpromoted, his or her intellectual capacity becomes overburdened. At that point, any latent quirks are likely to emerge, under pressure, perhaps explosively. A previously equable boss may become tyrannical, secretive, impulsive, cowardly or deceitful. Suddenly, long-buried psychological damage from the dim past is painfully exposed. Decisions become erratic, or are delayed beyond reason.

(see Figure 13). Strongly binary people are *very* energetic, *very* controlling, *very* demanding, *very* seductive and, of course, *very* ambitious. They can hold it all together with remarkable facility, like one of those circus jugglers with multiple plates spinning on sticks, but there is no time or space for serious thought. The weakness generally shows up in argument. The failing leader, in the eyes of bright subordinates, 'misses the point' or cuts off the debate (in the interests of 'getting on') just at the point it is getting complicated (i.e. interesting and demanding). Stanley Baldwin, one of the dimmest of British prime ministers, was well known for sucking blotting paper when he 'went out of gear' mentally (Neville Chamberlain's description). You can be quite sure that the failing leader's spouse, if any, will know the truth.

The story moves on now to the rest of my intelligent leaders. The reader can take it as read that they earn their place here thanks to their broad-band mental capacities and their *lack* of any of the crucial disqualifiers listed. Above all, they combine practical intelligence with my definition of sanity. All of them are a bit *eccentric*, but that is another matter. All Imos are eccentric by statistical definition.

7

Bob Clifford:
the ingenious 'dunce'

Every organisation needs one core competence—innovation!

Peter Drucker

Bob Clifford, AO, boatbuilder extraordinary, is beginning to be a
well-known figure in Australia. In the global ferry world, he is already
a very well-known figure—the man to watch. There aren't very many
Bob Cliffords in Australia, or anywhere. Part of the argument of this
book is that there could, and should, be many more, if only we
understood 'intelligence' better, in order to give it the chance to
flourish. To think or write about Clifford is to question what we *mean*
by 'intelligence'. He is also another example (like Sir William
Hudson) of *direct* leadership, in the sense that he personally com-
mands the Incat (International Catamarans) empire. But he also
illustrates a number of the other elements dealt with above:

- The crucial importance of broad-band intelligence, with particular reference to the *physical*, the *spatial* and the *interpersonal*. Being a broad-bander means that Clifford can easily work with anybody, whatever his or her pattern of intelligence. This is important in the rough world of boat-building. Part of the delight of Bob Clifford is that he was famously 'dumb' at school.
- The capacity for holistic 'frog' thinking. Clifford has always worked things out in the round before getting down to the bikish details. The similarity to Mozart's account of the creative process (in Chapter 2) is striking. This capacity to visualise the totality *speeds up* the cycle of design and manufacture and promotes market leadership.
- The passage over time through the levels of complexity, from a relatively simple fishing boat, built to solve a local commercial/technical problem, to the creation of a global enterprise to solve large-scale marketing problems for international shipping firms. Clifford's story reveals the points at which *he* sensed it was time to move on to bigger and better things.
- The crucial importance in leadership of the *ternary* principle. The real motivator for all Clifford's dedicated staff (despite his undoubted charisma) is the big, beautiful craft they slip out of the Hobart shed every few weeks. They sense that the boats are his true love, so they love them too.

At the time of writing, Incat churns out about four very big, very fast, aluminium car-carrying ferries per annum, on a 12-week cycle, alongside the manufacture of smaller and more conventional craft. The business is bursting at the seams of its big yard near Hobart, and expanding fast. About 700 Tasmanians currently work round the clock at the yard and a network of licensing arrangements around the world extends Incat's range of influence. Clifford's (current) biggest cat is a 91 metre craft with capacity for up to 1000 passengers and 240 cars. Its top speed of over 40 knots means that it has the capability of transforming the economics of certain kinds of ferry routes. In the Baltic Sea or around the Far East, there are many calm-water routes where quick turnaround is much more important to operators than huge payloads. This is the maritime equivalent of developments in the computer world (see Chapter 10)—where local speed and flexibility become more attractive than reliance on big, cumbersome centralised systems.

To exploit the quickly growing fast-ferry market requires at least four particular kinds of operational intelligence:

- The psychological capacity to get inside the minds of ferry operators from many different cultures and to foresee for years ahead the constraints and opportunities that confront them.
- The technical capacity to combine aluminium fabrication with constantly developing design principles to devise better and better solutions to a particular kind of transportation challenge.
- The intellectual curiosity to innovate; to leap ahead of conventional assumptions in order to see what can be made to happen.
- The managerial capacity to nurture, and renew, a big workforce under conditions of constant change.

This is called in the trade a 'socio-technical system'—a combination of psychology with leading edge technology. One expert puts it this way: 'You see, Robert Clifford *understands* aluminium!' But that is not enough; you have to understand the operational setting as well. Clifford says: 'I've been a yachtsman *and* a ferry operator. I know that *weight is a state of mind*, and I understand customers!' The statement, WEIGHT IS A STATE OF MIND, is pure Clifford—as much philosophy as technology!

ASPECTS OF LIFE

The inventive dunce

We are jumping ahead. We need to recall that this remarkable entrepreneur 'felt inadequate' throughout his schooldays, failed the ability test to get into high school, was therefore sent to (the private) Hutchings School in Hobart by his ambitious parents, and failed everything there too (in the 'B' class, of course). He 'even failed woodwork!'—apparently quite an achievement, and deeply ironic for a man who would subsequently sculpt some of the most beautiful and efficient craft on the seas. Clifford cheerfully copied most of his homework (and usually got caught doing it) and failed his Schools Board Examinations. He didn't even try to pass.

But, significantly, his first serious reading began at around thirteen or fourteen years of age, as a direct result of a new passion for sailing. His actual 'homework' at this time (despite the teachers) was voracious reading, of a very focused kind, about the technology and techniques of sailing. Clifford began to read when reading had a serious purpose for him personally. Howard Gardner (Chapter 9) calls this the 'crystallising experience'—the first moment when a child really connects with the educational experience in such a way as to engage curiosity and stimulate further exploration. This is when the young person senses: 'This is me!' If we accept that God made Bob Clifford to make boats, then it is fortunate for the Tasmanian economy that he had privileged access to sailing as a teenager (in his case via school), because the sailing unlocked the intellect. That sort of access even ten years later would have been too late to kickstart what was to follow (because creating a major international enterprise usually takes most of a lifetime).

But this was a happy childhood. The young Clifford would actually turn up an hour early for school, so much did he enjoy all the companionship and activity. His main pursuits were swimming and sailing. Water, it seems, was his true medium. Somewhere outside the curriculum, some important learning was going on inside the 'beanhead'—Clifford's standard nickname to this day. For example, take this insight on market positioning and technology development: 'In sailing, every decision has a time-frame. In ten minutes, it's a *different* decision!' It sounds like a simple statement, but it illustrates the importance of any executive's capacity for decisiveness in a turbulent environment. Clifford did not need to be taught this principle at a business school—he learned it through the seat of his pants as a teenager at the helm.

The reader will know by now that Bob Clifford was a 'bright' kid, but obviously not bright in the way that schoolteachers generally recognise. Chapter 9, which describes the schooldays of the young subversive, Spansky, deals in some detail with all the facets of brightness. Spansky, who didn't get to go to an expensive private school, ended up in a reform school for fiendishly inventive delinquents.

Before we leave Clifford's schooldays (and in the hope that some of his ex-teachers may happen on this book) it is worth noting that he was usually able to get to the correct answer in algebra, but without working through the formal, sequential process. No doubt, the other pupils were picking their way serially through all the formal steps of an algebraic 'bicycle'. Clifford already had the 'frog' in his head, but not the mental means to unpack it. As Howard Gardner comments: 'IQ tests would be completely different if they were designed by entrepreneurs!'

Even now, Clifford knows that if a design works 'on the back of an envelope' it will work in practice, though somebody else will have to sit down and carry through all the detailed calculations: 'There's an awful lot you can't put into the drawings!' When Incat made its first cat (an unsatisfactory design, as it turned out), Clifford took enormous pride that his rough and ready speed calculation of 26 knots was within 0.1 knots of the detailed calculation of Australia's foremost naval architect.

The young boatbuilder

It is an arbitrary matter to split anyone's life into compartments, but necessary if you want to extract some learning. Anyone who fails at school, like Bob Clifford, needs to start feeling capable, about something, soon. Too much continuous failure seems to be corrosive (cf. Spansky). There is likely to be a big element of luck in all this. After leaving school early, Clifford spent three years as an apprentice compositor in a small printing works, in the days of old-fashioned mechanical printing. The saving grace of the job, which had no long-term career prospects, was that it called for compositional (hence spatial) skills, which are essentially creative. From this vantage point he also got to watch a small-scale entrepreneur—the owner—build up a business from nothing much to twenty employees. Once you have *seen* how relatively easy it can be, entrepreneurship holds few terrors. Even as a teenager, Clifford also saw the technological revolution in printing coming over the horizon. That was *really* interesting.

Matters were taken out of his hands. His father, who owned and operated three butcher's shops, retired and decided to go into fishing. For the next ten years Bob Clifford became a fisherman. The family bought two boats and spent five years making no money at all with basically inferior resources. In those days there were still plenty of fish about but you needed the right sort of all-weather boat to get at them in order to make some money. Clifford could already 'see' in his mind's eye how you could transform the cost vs performance equation and he had a plan in mind for the *right* boat. He set about building it 'on overdraft'. It was done through an established boat-builder but most of the donkey work, including all the materials purchasing, was carried out by Clifford and his father. The reader can imagine the learning to be got by a young man at the age of twenty-three in carrying through every operation, from conceptualisation to construction, of a project like this. One of the interesting things you learn is 'how to keep people waiting (for payment) *nicely*'— but 'always pay the bank!'

They made a good boat. 'We launched her on the Wednesday, went to sea on the Sunday, and twelve days later we had a full load of lobsters.' Two years later another boat was built and the business boomed. By the age of twenty-five, Bob Clifford knew how to design and build for commercial operation. He also understood, in a relatively simple form, how to juggle parallel resources over time while a project comes slowly to fruition; a useful lesson. (In Chapter 9 I refer to the ways in which this particular lesson might be learned by *lots* of youngsters in education.) By his mid-twenties, Clifford had worked in close harness with two older role models—one a classic entrepreneur (though on a small scale) and the other a *craftmaster* in the solution of technical (fishing) problems. He soon outstripped them both, but the experience told.

The turning point

Most successful entrepreneurs can point you to a significant moment when historical developments coincided with personal readiness to exploit an opportunity or create something exciting. For Bob Clifford, that defining moment probably came on Sunday night, 7 January 1975, when he was just thirty-two years of age. On that day a 10 000 ton freighter ploughed into the Tasman Bridge over the River Derwent. In a few seconds, Hobart's only fixed river crossing disappeared into the water. It was a good time to be the Tasmanian capital's only ferry operator.

How had this come about—the shift from fisherman to ferryman?

By his late twenties Clifford had realised that he required more than fishing as a life's work: 'My mind was too active; I wanted to get into the ferryboat business.' To the detached observer, it looks as though Clifford might really have wanted, and needed, to *build more boats*. There was one false start in the ferry business, and no financial help at all from the State Government for the young entrepreneur. The hero of the hour and an early begetter of the Incat achievement was Tony Travers, then manager of the ANZ Bank at Sandy Bay. Bank managers come in for a lot of stick, so it is important to celebrate the occasional one who has both judgement and the courage to act on it. He underwrote what was to become the Sullivan's Cove Ferry Company, an association of Clifford's accountant, ex-wife, father and doctor—a fairly typical entrepreneur's first company.

The company was posited on the idea that there was still a ferry market in Hobart, even though the construction of the bridge ten years before had killed off the existing passenger ferry. Crucially, Clifford succeeded in acquiring a liquor licence, in order to back up the passenger trade with charters and tourism. At this point, connections became important. Ex-fishermen always know how to get hold of terrific fresh crayfish, scallops and so on. Clifford invented the weekday lunchtime restaurant cruise, an instant source of healthy profit. With the construction of a second boat, the company could run five lunchtime cruises every day. As things turned out, possession of the liquor licence was more than useful.

When the bridge bash came, Clifford was ready. 'It was the first bit of government assistance we ever got. I knew what to do—I had fantasised about it happening!' Clifford was at a party that night and did not learn of the accident until some hours later. But by the following morning all his plans were laid and his twenty-five staff fully briefed. The history of the next few days and weeks is fascinating for the catastrophe theorist but too detailed for our purposes here. In hindsight, it can be seen that it took the authorities a long time to come to grips with the problem facing the city. Clifford moved smoothly into action and not without friction with those authorities; it was a time for assertiveness.

This is a book about intelligence—that is, the capacity to operate effectively in complex and demanding situations. What is interesting about the Clifford response is, once again, the mental connections. He understood straightaway that passengers need a user-friendly frequency on the way to and from work. He could see, and empathise with, the commuter's state of mind. That meant a walk-on service. He built three new small-to-medium-size, monohull, 300-passenger ferries fast, all named after bushrangers. The government, effectively in competition with Clifford by now, made the mistake of going for big 600/700-passenger ferries imported from Sydney, which necessitated building a huge terminal infrastructure, which meant the deployment of piledrivers for the construction of new jetties, and so on. Clifford quickly achieved a five-minute-cycle timetable, utilising the existing infrastructure. On top of that, he had the sole liquor licence.

'For three years, I had the biggest hotel in Australia!' It was, in fact, the publican's dream—the captive and thirsty customer you 'kick out in twenty minutes time'. Late each day, when the other ferries' loads thinned, the Clifford boats still set off with full loads: their customers were enjoying more than a journey—it was an *experience*! By moving fast, with an eye to the consumers' needs, Clifford had created that most valuable asset—*customer loyalty*.

The big idea

It took three years to construct the new bridge over the Derwent. Long before the ferry bonanza came to an end, Bob Clifford was engaged on the next enterprise. In fact, International Catamarans, set up with the distinguished naval architect Philip Hercus, was formed as early as 1977. The Sullivan's Cove Ferry Company was wound down, selling its ships at a profit.

The origin of the Incat business is interesting. It perfectly reflects Jacob Bronowski's dictum: 'Every act of imagination is the discovery of likenesses between two things which were thought unlike.' In the scramble to solve the Derwent crossing problem, Clifford had hired a hovercraft from Sydney. This craft was number 34 from the Hovermarine boatyard in the United Kingdom. Two things became apparent immediately:

- It was of fundamentally poor design and hardly ever worked properly. The maintenance load was therefore huge. Like a lot of British inventions, it was ingenious but silly. Clifford and his colleagues found it hard to credit that well over thirty-four of these ugly ducklings had been sold around the world.

- The travelling public loved it, to the point where it was possible to charge double the usual ticket price. It offered a stylish and *interesting* way to travel and, despite all the disadvantages, it was *fast*.

It was really at this point that Bob Clifford earned his spurs as an *intellectual*. I use the word deliberately. When he is not globetrotting you are likely to find him in the evening sinking a few beers with friends, at the Shipwright's Arms on Battery Point in Hobart, as he has always done. 'Intellectual' is probably the last word most people would use to describe this amiable, bearlike figure. There is no pretension about Clifford. But what makes him stand out is the kind of intellectual curiosity shared by all good minds. Bright people have to know how things work, and they have to find out what might happen if . . . That Clifford is a successful entrepreneur and leader is commonplace. That he is, at base, the possessor of a formidable intellect is much more important, and the point of this book.

Bob Clifford had to understand *why* the hovercraft worked at all and what stopped it working optimally. Essentially it was merely a 'cat with a skirt'—a device for cutting down friction. But its shape was inefficiently high and square and its propulsion, by high-speed diesel driving small propellors through an inefficient 'vee' gearbox, was wasteful. The challenge was to take the *principle* of the catamaran down a different path by redirecting the forces. Catamarans have certain fundamental advantages over monohulls—they require less power for a given speed and the large available deck space is ideal for the carriage of passengers. If you can make them big and stable enough, they can also transport motor vehicles over longish distances in ocean seas.

At the outset of Incat, Clifford and Hercus were working on these technical problems in parallel with Scandinavian designers, though they did not know it at the time. Clifford now takes the view that this isolation was a help rather than a hindrance: he and Hercus were forced to confront all the problems from first principles. That meant that all the solutions would be fundamentally innovative. For example, one of the reasons that Incat has been able to see off *shipyards* all round the world is that its approach to manufacturing owes more to aircraft assembly than to traditional shipbuilding methods. Later on we examine the work of another Australian innovator (Robert Keep) in a different field. He takes the view that Australians have a *combined* advantage: easy connection to a networked world, together with easy *dis*connection, in order to *think*.

With catamarans, the big technical problems cut in with increased size. The history of Incat, from the first commercial design (18 metre) in 1977, to the current 91 metre craft, is a story of problem-solving—how to make a big, fast boat with the inherent advantages of catamaran design but none of the disadvantages. The solution was the 'wave-piercer'—a compromise between the simplicity of a conventional catamaran and the SWATH (small waterplane area twin hull) type of vessel. The characteristic of the modern wave-piercer is the central hull which rides above the surface in calm conditions but picks up buoyancy in heavy seas, thus preventing nosediving. Bob Clifford has an interesting scar on his forehead—the result of the entire *bar* of a prototype vessel hitting him (rather than vice versa) when the craft 'stuck its snout in'. Immediately before this happened, Clifford sensed that the boat, which was actually *surfing* in high seas at the time, was near its limit of safety. 'I'm really a test pilot for these boats!'

Along the way, the shift from steel to aluminium construction occurred (delivering crucial weight savings) and the move from propellor to water-jet propulsion. The boats also require highly sophisticated ride control systems, which are still under continuous development. Because Incat was in the vanguard of this technology, the company had to suffer and solve the problems that always accompany innovation. That is the downside; the upside is to be continuously some years ahead of the competition. There is much more to come—very fast, very big, custombuilt freight carriers, for example, maybe powered by gas turbines. The Incat kind of boat could now go much faster but the problems that then arise are different kinds of problems—nearer to the world of aircraft than to maritime technology. Bob Clifford is there already, constantly trying out new possibilities on the backs of envelopes. The word around Incat is that the senior managers dread the return of the boss from his constant visits to customers and prospects around the world, because sitting on long-haul aircraft gives him time to *think*—and that means even more ideas to be processed.

Positioning

The world is full of inventors with good ideas. Most of them remain obscure figures and many get ripped off by smart businessmen. This means that their intelligence, though formidable, operates across a narrow range. Many of them have been narrowly absorbed in scientific endeavour since childhood (see the reference to Sulloway in Chapter 1). Bob Clifford, we must remember, had been an amiable, highly sociable, physically active and popular 'dunce' who wore his intelligence lightly. Right from the start of Incat, he seems to have had a good feel for what the marketing people call 'positioning'. As one famous marketer puts it: 'There is only so much room at eye-level at the checkout—the trick is to *be there*!' Clifford knew from the start that these new kinds of boats could not be sold on paper. Incat's third catamaran, and its first aluminium boat, barnstormed its way from Hobart to Cairns on its delivery voyage. *Six* had been sold by the time of arrival. Clifford had also grasped that the wave-piercer catamaran technology also delivers a terrific-*looking* boat—ideal for the flashy Great Barrier Reef trade.

That was only the beginning. It was also at Clifford's suggestion that James Sherwood, the proprietor of Sea Containers (one of Incat's first big international customers), should go for the Hales Trophy— the 'Blue Riband' for the fastest crossing of the Atlantic by a passenger craft. Hoverspeed Great Britain, the first 74 metre catamaran, broke the record in 1990, completing the crossing at an average 36.6 knots. Bob Clifford was the captain for the record-breaking voyage but handed the vessel over to its new owner on arrival. This was a mighty useful public relations exercise but it also underlined one of the key sales features of these boats—their capacity to flit quickly round the world to wherever the business is. Some of them migrate annually between the hemispheres in order to serve seasonal markets. Even back in 1986 the very first fast 30 metre ferry, *Our Lady Pamela*, took her delivery voyage from Hobart to Portsmouth under her own power (in order to ply the fifteen-minute crossing between Portsmouth and the Isle of Wight).

Since then, Clifford has succeeded in positioning himself and the company in spectacular fashion. Firstly, his syndicate won line honours in the fiftieth Sydney–Hobart yacht race in 1994. This meant acquiring the maxi *New Zealand Endeavour*, renaming it *Tasmania*, and assembling the right crew, quickly, to carry out the job. It was the first Tasmanian boat to win the most famous race to Tasmania. The announcement of the challenge had taken place just three months before, on 8 October 1994, just twelve days after another canny exercise in positioning—a visit to the Incat yard by the Prime Minister, Paul Keating, to officially open a new construction shed and slipway.

Nine hours after the announcement Bob Clifford ran the $40 million *Condor II*, at high speed, on to Black Jack Rocks near the entrance to the Derwent River, during her sea-trials. Forty-eight people were on board at the time, many from the purchaser's organisation. Of course this was a catastrophe, but as an exercise in attention-grabbing it takes some beating. The huge craft sat on the rocks for forty days, an unavoidable topic of conversation in Hobart, as the salvage effort got under way. Many theories about causation were canvassed, some of them salacious, all of them engaging. The real cause was technical and quite dull, but Hobartians had a wonderful time with the story.

It would not be quite accurate to say that Bob Clifford enjoyed the outcome of the grounding. In some ways it reinforced his cavalier reputation. But the disaster did present an absolutely gripping technical problem—*not* how to get the ferry off the rocks *but* how to get the ferry off the rocks *undamaged*. After many unsuccessful attempts, the problem was solved by creating 'the biggest hovercraft in the world'—by virtually floating it off, largely undamaged, on a cushion of air. It wasn't a bad advertisement for the resilience of the design, nor for the ingenuity of the Incat team. *Condor II* is now at work on the Western Channel run between Guernsey and the United Kingdom port Weymouth and is making money for an operator who must have experienced one of the most exciting sea trials on record.

There is more to be said, later, about the development of Incat over the years. The point here is that there is an element of *theatre* in all this. Listening to an entrepreneur like Bob Clifford is not unlike talking to theatre directors. They of all people understand the relationship between substance and illusion. Everyone in the theatre knows that terrible things can, and will, go wrong. You could even argue that all the most intelligent leaders are basically hams—but acting in the cause of a worthwhile text. From a technical standpoint, the main thing to do after the grounding was to manage the public relations outfall. From the emotional, or theatrical, standpoint, Bob Clifford (the helmsman) knew immediately what had to be done: go back to the yard, to the people who really matter—those who had built the beautiful vessel—and *confess*. Clifford assembled the entire workforce and, prefacing his short speech with the obvious remark, 'We fucked up!', explained and apologised. That's leadership. That's also intelligent.

BOB CLIFFORD AS INTELLIGENT LEADER

This book posits that if we want better (smarter) leadership in all walks of life, we are going to have to improve on most of the current crop of leaders. This means examining what we *mean* by leadership and intelligence. Having established Hudson and Follett as a *direct* and an *indirect* leader respectively, we've resumed the individual stories with Bob Clifford because he demonstrates the difference between conventional views of 'leadership' and a possibly more useful view for the future. As I noted in the Introduction, most studies of leadership are concerned with the capacity of 'leaders' to get people to do things, especially difficult or unappealing things. The focus is usually on the *process* of influence that underpins the leadership. Accordingly, many of the most compelling leadership stories concern people who very much *wanted*, or even *needed*, to *be* a leader.

Bob Clifford is interesting because there is little evidence from his observed career, or his account of it, that *being* a leader was ever of any importance whatsoever to him. He seems to enjoy the role immensely, but that isn't the point. What matters most is that he is in the process of *transforming* a substantial chunk of the Tasmanian economy and society. That was never his intention; it is the by-product of his following his *vocation*. As the aftermath of the Port Arthur catastrophe demonstrates, Tasmanian society has been desperately dependent on *too few* sources of economic sustenance. In the course of creating a system to build terrific boats, Clifford has created, amongst many other things, a voracious demand for highly trained apprentice craftworkers. This demand is reverberating *upstream* in the Tasmanian educational system. If it causes a transformation there, then it is highly likely that Tasmania will begin to look like one of those places around the world where major inward-investors like to place their bets. A really effective technical education infrastructure always bulks large on their wish lists.

Michael Porter, in his hugely influential book *The Competitive Advantage of Nations*, explains how economic *clusters* gather around entrepreneurial activity, *provided* that the research and educational infrastructures are in place and there is a pragmatic approach to government subsidy. There is already a big cluster of suppliers around Incat, and most of them are under pressure (from Incat) to raise their game to the very best international standards. This *ought* to put the heat on both State and federal governments, especially as the latter (at the time of writing) is in the process of withdrawing the ship-building 'bounty' which has accelerated the development of this strategically important industry. All this is the transformational impact of one man's 'leadership'. Paradoxically, Clifford never set out to be a leader but he did *make something happen*! If I were a new prime minister of Australia, I am pretty sure I would make it my business to understand how this particular entrepreneur got to be a *leader*, and to see whether, over the long term (long after I passed from office), it could be made to happen again wherever in Australia the soil seemed to be fertile.

Above all, if I had anything at all to do with the education business, I would want to understand how the possessor of a prodigious intelligence like Bob Clifford could have been regarded as a dunce at school. As prime minister, I would require my education ministers to get to the bottom of this conundrum—just to make sure that, in the future, not too much native Australian wit was junked for want of recognition.

8

Robert Keep:
from spy to guru

Robert Keep is less well known than Bob Clifford, because he inhabits the arcane world of international currency trading. Not many people know very much about this world, and most assume that it is peopled by fiercely clever troglodytes. Robert Keep will tell you that most of the 'experts' haven't got the faintest idea what they are doing. In most cases, you would do better to take investment decisions by throwing dice rather than by taking advice. His breakthrough (the creation of an *algorithm* for tracking market movements over time) is described in general terms later on. It cannot be understood properly without an understanding of the person behind it. This doesn't mean that all creative people have to lead a life as eccentric as Keep's, but it does mean that big achievements require many years of gestation, a lot of prior variety, and a healthy start in life (from the mental standpoint).

This is a tricky subject. The world of currency speculation is littered with crackpot schemes and snake-oil salesmen and there are always plenty of gullible punters avid for new 'systems'. There are authenticated stories of punters being prepared to back such investments as 'Iguana Gold' or even 'Underwater Airlines'. In telling Keep's story I am not underwriting the method, merely demonstrating how *indirect* leadership operates. At the time of writing, Keep's algorithm is already changing the practice of big currency players, especially in Australia. If the claims made for the method turn out to have validity, the entire basis of market prediction will be altered. This is the notion behind Howard Gardner's *indirect* leadership—an *idea-driven* revolution in practice. The kind of leadership referred to here is *intellectual leadership*. Of course, Bob Clifford's leadership is intellectual too, but the visible part of it involves big, fast boats and an adoring workforce of several hundreds. Keep has very few followers, thus far. They are rich, thoughtful and very discreet. What the two have in common is very little interest in *being* a leader. This is another story about ternary focus on the *object*.

It can certainly be argued that international currency, bond and commodity trading are becoming more, not less, predictable, because so many automatic protocols now trigger trading 'decisions'. There is also the presence of large-scale market-rigging activity, as in the Sumitomo case (in copper), or of 'rogue' trading by unscrupulous loners, as in the Barings collapse. These influential players reduce variety at one level whilst increasing it at another. A player as influential as George Soros has the worldwide market clout to say (effectively): 'The ice is brittle—let's put $3 billion on top to break it!' In other words, new conditions, mostly caused by information technology, are in place. It is a time to keep an open mind about new ways of understanding the big international market 'frog'.

I must declare an interest. I was at school with Bob Keep, so I know him pretty well. The other Australian 'geniuses' herein I have had to study more quickly than I would have wished. Because Keep went to very much the same kind of school as Clifford, a word on all-male private schools may be in order. In 1995 I travelled around Australia with my daughter, who was preparing a thesis on the policy and practice of teaching in Australian schools. I owe to her the insight that, whilst no more than 7–8 per cent of British schoolchildren are educated privately, more than a *quarter* of Australian children go to private schools. The figures are not directly comparable, because of the disproportionate impact of the Catholic education system in Australia; but it is a fact worth bearing in mind when we come, later on, to consider how both Australia and Britain can set about 'mining'—i.e. *not wasting*—all the national talent. It is hard to say whether or not the relatively large numbers of former private school pupils in Australia (some of them described here) make it even harder than in Britain for talent to emerge from the state school sector.

Here the Clifford and Keep stories diverge slightly because Keep was always regarded as clever and he effortlessly excelled in almost everything. But even then he was one of Jacob Bronowski's 'contrary men'. The best way that I can describe it is that in a school almost exclusively comprising *canines* (big, bouncy, amiable, mostly harmless boys) Keep stood out as a *feline*. Smooth of countenance, sallow of complexion, graceful of movement, subtle of mind, he was always socially accepted by the other boys, but he was definitely different. 'Louche' is the term favoured these days for this slightly dangerous quality. The mothers of debutantes in the United Kingdom used to call it NSIT or Not Safe In Taxis.

To illustrate this, what I remember most vividly about Robert Keep was that he was almost unhealthily good at *acting*. It didn't seem natural for a seventeen-year-old to know how to upstage everybody else, to use silence to shattering effect, to phrase long Shakespearian passages with perfect timing, and so on. In my naivety, I took that kind of histrionic skill to be something emotive. With the benefit of hindsight, I reckon now that Keep was a terrific actor because he really *understood the text*; he was in the play but he was also, simultaneously, *surfing* the play. The rest of us were binary actors, doing our best to please the audience. Keep was engaged in a private communion with William Shakespeare *about* the play, the ultimate ternary position. We never did a *Midsummer Night's Dream* but, if you did, you would cast Keep as Oberon and Clifford as a superb Bottom. Both men have that theatrical capacity to be mentally in two places at once. In the leadership literature it is called 'presence' and regarded as a histrionic trick. My guess is that it is also a function of intelligence—the ability to rise mentally above a system whilst still physically *in* it. The Shell Company calls it 'helicoptering'.

I lost track of Bob Keep after school. He ought to have gone on to university, and he did—for a few months—until boredom set in.

At least I lasted a couple of years before I repaired to the Snowy Mountains. Keep astonished most of his friends by going into the Army as an officer cadet. He reckoned he needed a firm surrounding discipline to stop his mind wandering about. Just like Clifford, he knew his mind was 'too active'. The Army knew what it was getting; the canny psychologist who conducted the last selection interview remarked that it might turn out disastrously, because Keep was so much cleverer than the existing officer corps, but it would be no bad thing for the Army to find out if it could tolerate such brightness, or even put it to use. He knew (see Norman Dixon on military incompetence, as mentioned in Chapter 6) that the Army was dangerously monocultural. He also sensed that the Army might be dangerous for Keep.

Wisely, after a tempestuous period of training at Duntroon, the Army posted Keep to Military Intelligence. Here he experienced a meteoric rise through the ranks. Effectively, he became the military version of a *spy* and he did well at it. After all, espionage and acting have a good deal in common. Things were going well generally. Not long after, Keep was appointed Aide-de-Camp to the Governor-General, Lord Casey, and posted to Government House at Yarralumla. I will draw a discreet veil over the next, lubricious, part of this story, to protect the innocent. The psychologist turned out to be right: Keep was too ebullient for the *peacetime* army. Clever intelligence officers really come into their own in war and there happened to be a war on at the time. He was dispatched, not quite in disgrace, to Vietnam.

The next part of this story is now well known and has been the subject of a series of studies and a celebrated television documentary—*Long Tan: The True Story*. It is an account of 'one of the biggest intelligence blunders of the war' in Vietnam and it concerns Robert Keep centrally. It is a re-run of the Imo story—that of a young but very bright member of the band or system who sees clearly what is the case but cannot penetrate the sensibilities of the elders. By July of 1966 Keep was Intelligence Officer at Nui Dat in Phuoc Tuy Province, the base for the Australian Task Force.

Keep, like any good intelligence officer, made sure that he had the best possible understanding of his environment. The Australians had proved an unexpectedly effective irritant to the North Vietnamese Army. Keep, thinking like the enemy (the mind in two places at once, just like a good competition analyst in business), knew that some kind of test of Australian capability was likely. Soon he began to sense that something wasn't quite right about the Viet Cong movements in the area. Various fragments of information, all an intelligence officer ever gets to process, were coming together in his mind to make a disturbing pattern.

Keep, as a wise intelligence specialist must, stayed close to the wireless operators. They are Imos by definition, close to the environment but lowly of rank. Their leader was another Imo. The most experienced wireless operators had learned to identify their individual Viet Cong counterparts by their Morse Code *touch*—they even assigned them names. It is the same trick that allows a discerning music critic to tell you whether it is Horowitz or Ashkenazy playing Chopin. The Australians never cracked the enemy's code, but the operators could tell *where* their counterparts were—even when they changed their call signs. Using this information, Keep realised that some of the enemy's detachments were in the *wrong place* (according to the official intelligence briefings) and in dangerously large concentrations. Simultaneously, he was receiving from the SAS sketches of the clothing worn by the enemy in the vicinity which suggested that some of them were not local guerrillas but new detachments of crack troops. The pattern of enemy fire (in short controlled bursts rather than amateurish sniping) supported this view. Keep began to formulate a *hunch*.

The hunch, in brief, was that the enemy must be massing for a major attack on the Australian position. The longer Keep sifted the information at his disposal the more convinced he became. His problem was to persuade those above him that there was a real danger of the Australian forces being overwhelmed. Potentially, the two Australian battalions were outnumbered four to one. Some of his superiors had become dependent on the Americans' intelligence and that, in Keep's view, leaned to the complacent. As it turned out later, the Americans actually *wanted* the Viet Cong flushed from cover by attacking the Australian position. In late July the Viet Cong forces made a strong feint at the Australian lines, to test their defences. After their withdrawal, the top brass convinced themselves that the enemy had quit the immediate area. This was reassuring (for them, not for Keep).

It was said of the commanders at Pearl Harbor in World War II: 'They were disinclined to be attacked!' As we have noted, people (and especially those in high positions) can persuade themselves of *anything* if their motivation is strong enough. The senior officers preferred to believe that the Australians had pacified the entire area. Keep's conclusion was exactly the opposite.

After the feint the enemy 'starved' the Australians of action, in order to persuade them that the threat had gone away. This redoubled Keep's suspicions. By now convinced of the Viet Cong intentions, Keep travelled to Saigon to alert Major Peter Young, the Assistant Australian Military Attache and an old friend. Young pulled out all the stops to re-examine the evidence, but turned up nothing concrete to support Keep's theory. There was little he could achieve at long range—the real ostriches were back in Phuoc Tuy Province. In fairness to the Army hierarchy, a number of extra patrols were sent out specifically to gather evidence for or against Keep's hypothesis—there were, in other words, a number of thoughtful senior officers who sensed that Keep *might* be right. Obtaining hard evidence was seen to be the problem.

Fate then took a hand. Keep, under serious strain, fell seriously ill with encephalitis and was evacuated back to Australia. Within a few days of his departure the big attack came, just as predicted. The Battle of Long Tan was the most significant Australian engagement of the entire war. In the event, the Australian troops were very lucky. Casualties were severe but the force was not annihilated, as it might have been. In its way it was a classic of military incompetence. As Norman Dixon points out, the kinds of people who generally wish to go into the Army in peacetime are precisely the kinds of people likely to blunder in this way when there is a war on. It is another example of the *psychopathology of occupational choice*. The Army found it difficult to contain Robert Keep, just as the selection panel psychologist had predicted, but it almost made proper use of him. Almost, but not quite.

A NEW FORCE IN THE MARKET

The story moves forward twenty-five years now. The old school ran a thirty-five-year reunion in Sydney, which I could not attend. They did, however, send me a printout of all the members of my cohort, together with addresses and phone numbers. By this time, after a long gap, I was revisiting Australia regularly. I resolved, just out of curiosity, to see what had happened to the handful of school colleagues I recalled as especially interesting. Bob Keep, for obvious reasons, was top of the list. I was warned by one or two other former school chums that Keep was barking mad—promoting a crackpot scheme to second-guess international currency trading. As those warning me were essentially in the senior officer mould, and canine, I decided to see for myself.

Right from the start I found the logic of Keep's product—'Market Reality'—persuasive. Essentially, it is a safety device for serious long players in international currencies, commodities and bonds. It identifies trends and flags up more or less strong buy/sell signals. It is in fact a simple algorithm, based on the principles of quantum mechanics, which took Keep more than ten years to refine—he won't say perfect. The symbolic language is so simple that his eleven-year-old son can understand it. The system now has a proven track record. It accurately anticipated the 1994 bond crisis, the rally in the United States market in the first half of 1995, and the subsequent dollar downturn. Clients of Market Reality depend absolutely on their daily bulletins from Keep. The system, however, does not make extravagant claims—it is merely a sophisticated way of tracking market events. It provides, for example, the reassurance needed by big players to stay *in* the market (i.e. to do nothing) when others are needlessly, and expensively, bailing out.

Its worldwide distributors say (the financially illiterate may safely skip this quote):

> The product enables the picking of individual trends and confirms that those trends are real and not merely counterbumps . . . For example, related trends similar to the long bond market's relationship and immediate impact on the stock market can be identified before they occur. Market Reality allows a sensible judgement to be made before the turn in a market occurs.

Dr Marc Faber, one of the world's leading market economists, describes Keep as 'kind of a genius'. He writes:

> What I like about Robert's work is that it is very simple to understand and most suited to the busy executive whose reading time is limited. Every morning I get a fax on my desk (in Hong Kong) with the . . . symbols for a variety of financial futures, commodities and currencies and within a few minutes I have an idea of the state of the market and any changes which might have taken place.

These are impressive enough testimonials but there are also plenty of wise old birds around the markets prepared to pooh-pooh any such fancy method.

Keep works mostly at night, as the data flow in from (say) the North American futures market. By 10.30 each morning his bulletins are dispatched to his very few very rich and very discreet clients and his work is done. He spends much of the rest of the day wandering around the Sydney foreshore, *thinking*. In every way, Market Reality is a very Australian invention. In fact, its origins lie in Australian *horse racing*. When Keep was invalided home from Vietnam it took a long time for him to get strong enough to resume normal life. After Vietnam he needed something undemanding and, above all, Australian to take his mind off recent events. Looked after by a medical orderly, he started his convalescence by going to the races. That very first race meeting got his creative juices flowing again. It was a small meet; just eight races with quite small fields and dry going. This reduced the number of variables involved. Bob Keep, like any intelligence officer and like all bright people, is *observant*—almost obsessively so. He also takes notes incessantly, as naturalists and writers do.

He observed the *pattern* of the bookmakers' odds as the day progressed, taking notes the while. Just as in Vietnam, he was searching for the *meaning* behind the public data. Back at the hospital he began to analyse the information and discovered, with some excitement, that there was indeed a pattern which could not be explained by chance. It looked as though what was happening was some kind of combination of more or less predictable human behaviour (on the part of punters and bookies) with elements of specialised insider knowledge (possibly possessed by owners). What it all meant wasn't clear. What was clear was that it must mean *something*—the pattern was inescapable! The really interesting thing was that if you could understand the pattern, as it developed over the course of the day, then you wouldn't *need* insider information. What the insiders knew would show up, alongside any other important variables, incorporated in the figures—and you might be able to devise a higher-order interpretative system.

At this point Keep was in the same openminded mental state as Bob Clifford when he began to work out what a hovercraft *was*. The thing existed, but what did it mean? It is a state not unlike that of the young child trying to figure out how something works. In *The*

Unschooled Mind, Howard Gardner argues that this is a pure state that most of us grow out of. If we are lucky, we may retain this kind of enthusiastic curiosity into our adulthood. Both Clifford and Keep were in their thirties when these puzzles engaged their minds. You can argue that these two must be especially 'clever' people. Alternatively, you can argue that all children are like this but that, without meaning to, we train it out of them. If you desire a coherent national education strategy, it is a very good argument to follow up.

Robert Keep's convalescence was slow. He spent a very long time working on the horse racing system—too long, he now admits. It was not until the mid-1980s that a colleague pointed out to him that the way punters approach their task has similarities to the way that speculators operate in financial markets. (Remember Bronowski's dictum!) Markets, like the selling of high-tech catamarans to ferry operators, are 'socio-technical systems'. There is a lot of technology involved (most of which is taken for granted and the impact of which is usually forgotten) but there is also a huge psychological element to it. Markets are based not just on perceived 'realities' out there but on people's *assumptions* about other people's assumptions about reality. It is one thing to try to understand the psychology of the individual punter or speculator. It is quite another thing to understand the *collective psychology* of the whole market. In fact, Keep doesn't pretend to be a psychologist—merely an observer and analyst of repetitive *system patterns*. The fact that unconscious human behaviour causes the patterns is neither here nor there. The important thing is that fifteen years of dedicated, some might say obsessive, work appears to have produced a scientific principle with some predictive power. The elegance of the thing lies in its simplicity.

In one of Bronowski's lectures, 'Knowledge as Algorithm and as Metaphor', he cited Newton and Einstein as scientists who always imagined how the world works in terms of simple, or childlike, images such as balls, clocks or trains. Keep will argue that most financial analysts have lost the capacity to understand the big 'frog' (another simple metaphor) because they have become mired in their own complexity. Dealers, on the other hand, only ever deal with *bits of the 'bicycle'* because the average time span of a trade is just a few minutes. They are close to the frenetic action, and likely to formulate good hunches, but rarely have time to stop, think, and see *patterns*. Analysts, on the other hand, are generally buried under their computer systems and nobody can understand their arcane language. They are disconnected from the dealers who have the 'feel' of the frog but not the means to understand it fully. No one has an algorithm that draws together the day-to-day workings of the 'bike' (the mechanical aspect of trading) with the 'frog' (the socio-technical supersystem).

ROBERT KEEP AS INTELLIGENT LEADER

Let me repeat: on the surface Bob Keep is a different *kind* of leader from Bob Clifford. Clifford is the quintessential *direct* leader, leading the troops from the front. Keep's leadership (however Market Reality and the algorithm turn out) is *indirect*, from the shadows. Clifford's direct influence is on the Tasmanian economy, not just in the short term but in driving technology development, design principles and education in the long term. Keep's direct, short-term influence is narrow but, if he turns out to be right, he will *revolutionise* his field—it will never be the same again. If the algorithm fulfils its promise and goes public, it has the potential to dampen the volatility of markets generally. That would be an extraordinary achievement for one man who started out as a soldier. But, under the skin, what Clifford and Keep *do*, and what intellectual resources they mobilise, are remarkably similar. Both are driven by a *big idea*, both pursue it obsessively and both have been prepared to devote many years to its fulfilment. Clifford, always at full stretch, has sailed perilously close to failure along the way. It is too early to say whether Keep is an 'Imo' all over again—too far ahead of the game to be comprehended by the big boys—or certain to be wrongfooted in the end by the big *system* changing.

I doubt it is a coincidence that both of them were outstanding sportsmen, and in sports that call on highly developed *spatial* skills as well as the *bodily kinaesthetic* intelligence. The core skill that links them together is the capacity, driven by curiosity, to make meaningful *patterns* out of very complicated and messy fragments of information. It is this ability which allows them to ascend the levels of work (see Figure 13, earlier) so as to take on more complexity more quickly than their peers do. There are other people around who might be able (given the motivation) to achieve similar feats, *but not so soon*.

Behind the scenes

Tom Stoppard, the playwright, started to become a millionaire when his most famous play, *Rosencrantz and Guildenstern Are Dead*, first opened in 1967. In this play, Hamlet and the court of Denmark represent the *subplot*, glimpsed dimly off-stage. Stoppard is taking the audience behind the proscenium arch to explore events just beyond the boundary of the familiar Shakespeare play. Here the bit-part players, Rosencrantz and Guildenstern, find themselves centre-stage. To achieve this, the playwright has first to imagine the world beyond, then begin to explore the connections between the two worlds. Clever people like Robert Keep are always impelled to find out what is *behind* the obvious and the superficial. Playwrights and business innovators ought to talk to each other more often than they do; their work is fundamentally similar. In the next chapter, Allan Coman shows how theatre and business both demand the capacity to cope with, and positively enjoy, ambiguity and *mess*.

The nice thing about Stoppard's play is that it wasn't his idea in the first place. His agent had always wondered about these two odd, misfit-like characters lurking in the Hamlet subplot and put forward the idea of building a play around them. Only Stoppard could have written it, however. Keep's breakthrough depended to some extent on his habit of spending time with oddball people *outside* his immediate circle. His focus shifted from horse racing to financial markets because a friend and drinking companion from the finance world (about which he knew nothing) made the essential connection between punters and currency speculators. From then on the intelligence officer and obsessive observer became just the right person to do all the donkey work. People who stick to their own narrow profession or society rarely achieve this sort of thing because their fundamental assumptions are rarely challenged. This is where the *interpersonal* intelligence comes in; it *creates* curiosity about other people and their ideas.

9

Allan Coman: an educator of genius

There was so much talent there that it was all fuckin' wasted. I mean, 'Spansky', he was thick as pigshit really, but if someone had took him and tutored him . . . He'd got so much imagination!

Any examination of people who have 'made it', like Hudson, Follett, Clifford and Keep, prompts curiosity about those who *might have* made it but didn't. Talent is randomly distributed in populations so it is unrealistic to expect everybody to shine. On the other hand, it is perfectly clear that an awful lot of native talent is underused or just wasted. The society that squeezes *most* from *all* of its populace will be the society with the greatest *energy* and *purpose*. Any prison visitor will tell you that a remarkable proportion of those inmates who are not just mad or otherwise psychologically incapacitated turn out to be rather bright. In these internationally competitive times, no society can afford this sort of waste on a big scale. What does 'bright' mean?

Let us turn to Professor Gardner's admirably practical definition of intelligence: *'The ability to solve a problem or fashion a product that is valued in at least one culture or community'*.

Many psychologists and educationists would quibble with this definition, focusing as it does on *output* and *usefulness*. If our concern is with intelligent *leadership*, not just with book-learning or eloquence, then it fits the bill. If we are interested in the intelligent leadership of *education*, then the test of success lies in the resourcefulness of the output—educated young people fit for general capability and active citizenship. Because education has the power to shape a nation's future capability, no area of leadership is more important. If we discover educational leaders who are consistently successful in these output terms, we need to cherish them.

The reader will be aware that the examples of leadership described so far are not exactly drawn from the ranks of the under-privileged. True, Bob Clifford's father was 'only' a butcher, but he did have three establishments. The point is that all of the foregoing examples were privately educated. Both contemporary examples (Clifford and Keep) are *men* of a certain *age* and the only woman so far was an American; that deficiency is rectified later in Chapter 12. The purpose of the present chapter, apart from the telling of an inspiring story, is to explore how the talents of the *young* and the relatively underprivileged can be developed and exploited. This involves three elements:

- revisiting Howard Gardner's important work (briefly mentioned in Chapter 2) on the multiple nature of intelligence (or *intelligences*, as he argues)
- meeting two further 'inventive dunces' (here called Spansky and Jamie) who were not quite so lucky in formal education as Robert Clifford was
- examining how Allan Coman, the hero of this chapter, has *persistently* turned schools round so as to produce confident, resourceful and stylish young Australians, fit for anything

Allan Coman was, until recently, Director of Bradfield College at Crows Nest on Sydney's North Shore. In the space of three years Coman transformed the College from a 'sink' institution for about 150 awkward, difficult educational failures into a thriving and much sought after centre of excellence for over 500 very successful students, nearly all of whom now get into some kind of work or employment upon graduation from the College.

In order to understand Coman's achievement, we have to understand something about the *materials* with which he works. Bob Clifford works with aluminium, Robert Keep works with data. Coman works with, and transforms, the intellectual effectiveness of young people aged between sixteen and twenty. The important thing about Coman's graduates is the word 'effectiveness'. They may well be able to negotiate their way around formal examinations, but the main thing is that they have become the kinds of young adults you can safely employ, confident that they will work resourcefully and purposively.

So, in order to appreciate what Allan Coman has achieved we are going to 'reverse-engineer' the process, by examining some exceptionally bright school failures, amongst whom were 'natural leaders'. We'll begin in Britain and then move back to Australia. Spansky, a fiendishly inventive subversive, was the archetypal clever failure. Jamie was much the same. Coman's achievement was to create (in Australia) a college fit for 'Spanskys'.

But first, in order to understand Spansky and his like, we will further 'reverse-engineer' the argument by taking a little more of a look at Howard Gardner's theory of multiple intelligences.

WHAT IS INTELLIGENCE?

As the reader will be aware, the concept 'intelligence' resists definition. We know that IQ tests are good predictors of performance in formal education, but we also know that formal education is a lousy predictor of adult capability, except in those fields (like academia) built on the same assumptions. If you work as researcher or consultant, as I do, you learn very quickly that high formal rank is no guarantee of practical intelligence. The people I meet in corporate boardrooms are a bewildering mix of the very bright and the amazingly dim. That's only my opinion—another observer might take the opposite view. I do know that when I sit, as the outsider, on selection and promotion panels, my casting vote is often decisive. The panel is apparently about to appoint an obvious dimwit; they turn to me and say: 'What do you think, Alistair?' I reply: 'This bloke is an obvious dimwit (and maybe a nasty piece of work as well)!' It then turns out that they all *knew* this was the case, at gut level, but were prepared to be swept along by 'groupthink' towards a ghastly and expensive mistake.

In order to make sense of Spansky and Coman, the most helpful view of intelligence is that put forward by Professor Howard Gardner of Harvard in his 1983 book, *Frames of Mind*. Not all academic psychologists agree with Gardner's formulation, but then again, not all psychologists are very bright. Some in my experience teeter on the fringe of sanity. The attractive thing about Gardner's work is that it flows from a *connection* (remember Bronowski's dictum). Gardner was one of the founding researchers on Project Zero—a major effort to address the failings of the United States education system. Simultaneously, he was carrying out comparative work on brain damage. He started to remap the way that human *capability* (the output of intelligence) is highly localised in the brain. Severe damage in one particular place leads to severe curtailment of particular capabilities. If Gardner had buried himself in *either* of those fields—the medical or the educational—rather than connecting them, we might not have benefited from his important contribution to education practice.

That contribution was the theory of 'multiple intelligences'—a theory which involves the suggestion that IQ assessments, for example, tended to sample only a couple of the many thinking capabilities of the human being. The other capabilities, in certain circumstances just as useful, were generally ignored by the huge American psychometric measurement industry. Gardner argued that people who are good at things in the real world are in fact calling upon a very wide repertoire of intellectual skills. He took a stab at describing that repertoire, basing his argument on the tasks that different parts of the brain perform. He reckoned that there were at least seven distinctive forms of intelligence. These were (elaborating on Figure 5, earlier):

- linguistic (the ability to manipulate language effectively, the archetype being, perhaps, the poet)
- logical mathematical (the ability to manipulate symbols, typical of the successful scientist)
- spatial (the ability to process information continuously in three dimensions, like a sailor or a sculptor)

- musical (the ability to manipulate sound in a complex way, like a composer or, combined with the following, a performer)
- bodily kinaesthetic (the ability for physical coordination, as found at the highest levels in athletes and dancers)
- interpersonal (the ability to know what is happening between people and to mobilise it, as good teachers and salespeople do)
- intrapersonal (the ability for self-understanding, without which all the others may be distorted in use)

The multiple intelligences idea was *dynamite* for education theory and teaching practice. The theory behind most schooling in the West has long been that with the process of measuring 'intelligence' (usually reduced to an IQ), and grading schoolwork, schools were rendered 'fair'—i.e. geared to children's natural capacities. Gardner argued that the opposite had been achieved—we had created the 'uniform school'. If natural capacity is not uniform, then the uniform school is by definition unfair to those who don't fit the mould. If you happen to be strong in the logical mathematical and linguistic intelligences, you are bound to be defined as 'bright' by conventional schoolteachers, because that is how they got to pass *their* exams and get into the teaching profession. Confronted by a Spansky or a young Bob Clifford (who cheerfully fails everything), such a teacher has no way of identifying and appreciating a different *kind* of intelligence.

The point about the seven intelligences (if you accept the argument) is that they crop up in an infinite number of combinations. Gardner is hardly dogmatic about the intelligences themselves; since the original book was published his colleagues have noticed what seems to them to be an eighth distinctive capability—to do with the understanding of natural phenomena, as demonstrated by the great naturalists. My favourite illustration of the idea (and of the bodily/kinaesthetic intelligence in particular—see Chapter 6) is the infant ballet class, which many parents enjoy or endure. Confronted by a long line of scrubbed moppets in identical tutus, every one of them trained to the hilt, you don't have to be a dancer yourself to be able to see, instantly, which one of those children God meant to be a dancer.

That child herself cannot explain her gift to you; she is barely aware of her skill, apart from the sheer enjoyment it affords. The music seems to flow through the young body and the body seems to 'know' how to move beautifully. This grace is not, of course, located in the limbs, but in the feedback loops between limbs and *brain*—it is an aspect of *intelligence*. Gardner could tell you exactly which part of the brain to go for if you wished to affect this capacity. The dancer is pre-eminent in the bodily/kinaesthetic intelligence, but will also need musical intelligence. If she takes up choreography later on, she will also need spatial intelligence. If she graduates to management of a ballet company, she will need most of the others (especially the interpersonal) and enough logic and self-knowledge to delegate wisely. Some people, irritatingly, seem to be strong in the entire repertoire. Gifted primary school teachers can point these 'broad-band' children out to you.

Before we move on to Spansky, a notably knockabout character, it is worth recalling that many successful people are very *physical*. The psychologist Liam Hudson (himself an ex-rugby player of note) reckons that a disproportionate number of the really outstanding thinkers in his field are, or were, outstanding athletes of one kind or another. Bob Clifford came alive when sailing captured his imagination but he was also an outstanding swimmer and hockey player. I remember with absolute clarity the way in which confronting physical problems (most of them potentially dangerous) concentrated our minds on the Snowy Mountains Scheme. Because I believe that the best 'systems thinking' is partly spatial, I have always held that civil engineers are the intellectual aristocrats of the engineering world. You can't help but learn something if a bridge falls down.

The logical outcome of Gardner's ideas is the 'individual-centred school'—a school which attempts to meet the incoming pupil at least halfway by adapting its curricula and methods to reflect any particular combination of abilities. Devotees of process re-engineering will see that Gardner's approach is just this—a re-examination of the through-put (pupils) in terms of the dominant transformations in process. Gardner argues that schools need three new roles: an *'assessment specialist'* (to identify, so far as possible, each student's repertoire of intelligences, preferably not by the use of formal tests); a *'student-curriculum broker'* (to find a sensible match between what can realistically be adapted to individual need and what must remain standard fare); and a *'school-community broker'* (to carry out an analogous matching of school resources to community needs).

SPANSKY AND 'THE LADS'

Spansky was one of the subjects of an intensive study of a tough boys school in the British Midlands, carried out by the sociologist Paul Willis in the 1970s. Willis's book, *Learning to Labour—How Working Class Kids Get Working Class Jobs*, is a delightful read, partly because he taped and lovingly transcribed (verbatim) the fifteen- and sixteen-year-old boys' language—profane, obscene, witty and always vigorous. If I knew of an Australian study of the same pungency I would have drawn on it. There will certainly be schools like 'Hammertown Boys School' (a pseudonym) in Australia. Happily (see *Jamie* below) I have succeeded in finding an Australian Spansky.

Spansky and his mate Joey were the ringleaders (the teachers' description) or the natural leaders of 'the lads'—an informal group of twelve non-academic, working class boys. This group was the primary subject of the study; it had cohered much earlier on, in the junior years. The group as a whole acted as leader of the school's *counter-culture*. There is little doubt, on Willis's evidence, that these kids were *bright*, even though they were the despair of their teachers. There is also no doubt that, viewed from the outside, they were very destructive—violent, anarchic, racist, sexist and shamelessly dishonest. Although most of their energies were devoted to having a 'laff', there is ultimately a sad quality about their lives. Having a 'laff' necessarily involved fighting (usually with pupils of Pakistani or West Indian extraction), vandalism, exhibitionistic drunkenness and smoking, affectionless sex, thieving and endless opportunistic disruption of others' tranquillity.

The point about the delinquent activity of 'the lads' was that it involved *teamwork* and was endlessly *inventive*. All those interested in staff and managerial development prick up their ears when those two ideas (teamwork and inventiveness) are touched on. Willis comments:

> . . . 'the lads' develop the ability of moving about the school at their own will to a remarkable degree. They construct virtually their own day from what is offered by the school. Truancy is only one relatively unimportant and crude variant of this principle of self-direction which ranges across vast chunks of the syllabus and covers many diverse activities: being free out of class, being in class and doing no work, being in the wrong class, roaming the corridors looking for excitement, being asleep in private. The core skill which articulates these possibilities is

being able to get out of any given class: the preservation of personal mobility . . . The common complaint about 'the lads' from staff and the 'ear-oles' (conformist pupils) is that they 'waste valuable time'. Time for 'the lads' is not something you carefully husband and thoughtfully spend on the achievement of desired objectives in the future. For 'the lads' time is something they want to claim for themselves now as an aspect of their immediate identity and self-direction. Time is used for the preservation of a state—being with 'the lads'—not for the achievement of a goal—qualifications.

Sometimes 'the lads' act like directors of a theatre of the absurd:

Joey: Gates are the latest crack. Swopping gates over. Get a gate, lift it off, put it on somebody else's.

Bill: That's what we done . . . there was an 'ouse there for sale. We took the 'For Sale' sign out of the one, put it in next door, then we took the milk carrier from the next one, put it in next door . . . we took a sort of window box on legs from the porch and stuck that next door. We swapped stacks of things.

Spansky: And dustbins! [laughter] . . . every night, go into one garden, tek a dwarf out, and in the end there was a dwarf, a sundial, a bridge, a dwarf fishing, all in this one garden, and there's a big sundial up the road. He got one end of it, I got the other, and carried it all the way and put it in.

In all this, the *content* of schoolwork has no interest for these boys but they are endlessly fascinated by the possibilities of the *process*. Once again the theatrical metaphor springs to mind. One of the few curricular options taken up by 'the lads' was a film option, where they could make their own short films—invariably, in their case, films about bank robberies, muggings and violent chases. Willis notes:

Joey gets more worked up than at any time in class during the whole year when he is directing a fight sequence and Spansky will not challenge his assailant realistically. 'Call him out properly, call him out properly—you'd say "I'll have you, you fucking bastard" not "Right, let's fight".' Later on he is disgusted when Eddie dives on top of somebody to finish a fight. 'You wouldn't do that, you'd just kick him, save you getting your clothes dirty.'

When it comes to artistic authenticity—to getting it right—Joey's veneer of not giving a damn falls away.

Joey, by the way, comes from a big family, known as a fighting family. His father is a foundryman. Joey leaves school without any qualifications and is universally identified by teachers as a trouble-maker—the more so as 'he has something about him'. Joey has 'presence', like most natural leaders. Willis points out that 'Joey walks a very careful tightrope in English between "laffing" with "the lads" and doing the occasional "brilliant" essay'. Spansky, the most charis-matic of all, recalls:

> In the first and second years I used to be brilliant really. I was in 2A, 3A, you know, and when I used to get home, I used to lie in bed thinking, 'Ah, school tomorrow', you know, I hadn't done that homework, you know . . . 'Got to do it' . . . But now when I go home, it's quiet, I ain't got nothing to think about. I say, 'Oh great, school tomorrow, it'll be a laff', you know.

I suppose that any ex-teacher reading about 'the lads' in these pages might experience a shudder of painful recognition. The point is that these kids were 'bright', but in ways that spread eccentrically over Gardner's seven intelligences. The ringleaders, Spansky and Joey, were even good at the linguistic skill; they simply didn't bother much with it after they turned thirteen. But, above all, these boys were skilful in the interpersonal intelligence. They knew exactly how far you can push a teacher, just short of boiling point. Willis put it this way: 'The soul of wit for them is disparaging relevance: the persistent searching out of weakness. It takes some skill and cultural know-how to mount such attacks, and more to resist them.' All the evidence suggests that the other key intelligence of these boys was the spatial. Their ability to conceptualise the school *system*, so as to dissolve its boundaries, borders on the inspired. They evidently had a feel for the big 'frog'; not so the conformist 'ear-oles'. Not only could 'the lads' push teachers to the limit; they pushed the school system as a whole to the limit. They did it for a 'laff', but you could see it as a form of continuous, empirical, scientific experimentation.

'The lads' knew that they were clever, despite the teachers' occasional insults, and they also knew that what they did with (or to) the school was difficult to pull off. After 'the lads' left school (I will pass over the drunken binge on the last day) they read drafts of Willis's book and met him a few months later to discuss it. Joey, returning to the theatrical/creative theme, put it beautifully:

I thought that we were the *artists* of the school, because of the things we did, I thought definitely we had our own sort of *art form*, the things we used to get up to. And we were definitely the *leaders* of the school . . . if we were all separated and placed amongst groups of the ear-oles we could have been leaders in our own right . . . something should have been done with us!

Joey, on top of everything else, had a pretty good grasp of the principles of group dynamics.

If I am right that the leading 'lads' were pretty good at the *interpersonal* and the *spatial* intelligences, then this ought to give us pause. The best managers are always good at reading systems, and 'see' them in their mind's eye as processes. They also have to be hot stuff on the 'people side'. 'The lads', you could argue, possessed the core *managerial* skills. The problem for them, and therefore also for the teachers, was that Hammertown Boys School had nothing for them to *manage*. The creative urge to take charge was there but it was displaced—they managed subversion of the entire system instead—for a 'laff'. Most of the teachers, hooked on the logical/mathematical and linguistic intelligences, just took the boys to be dim but infuriating. (Willis took it that confusion observed in the staff room between the terms 'corporal punishment' and 'capital punishment' simply meant that, subconsciously, some of the teachers itched to *kill* 'the lads'.) I noted at the outset that a surprising proportion of prison inmates turn out to be very bright (ingenious) people who have simply got into resentful, anti-authoritarian bad habits. Teachers please note.

JAMIE: A HOMEGROWN 'SPANSKY'

It has always seemed a pity to me that the most carefully documented case I could find of fiendish teenage ingenuity unregarded by adult educationists should be the *British* story of Spansky. I am indebted to Sue Shegog and her colleagues at CBT (Competency Based Trainers) in Launceston for the account of Jamie—as we'll call him—a boy possibly even more fiendish and ingenious than Spansky and his chums. It's nice to think that Australia can still outstrip the Old Country when it comes to high-class delinquency.

By the age of fourteen, Jamie had been expelled from a 'priorities' high school and had lived rough on the streets of Launceston for two years. He was the eldest of nine children and the family just didn't have room for a teenager in a three-bedroom Housing Commission home. Somehow, he had learned to survive, and even prosper, without being made a ward of the state or being placed in a youth correction centre.

At school his first great entrepreneurial achievement was the covert takeover of the school's 'certificate of merit' system. These certificates were awarded on a weekly basis to the 'ear-oles' who had most closely conformed to the school's behavioural and disciplinary code. Jamie could see, easily, that the wrong sort of (boring) pupils were getting these awards. His point of observation was his semi-permanent spot between the Principal's door and the administrative staff office. Because Jamie was always in some kind of trouble, he became a familiar 'piece of office furniture' in that strategic point at the heart of the school system. That spot became his virtual classroom. For most of the pupils, it was a place to be avoided at all costs; for Jamie, it was a vantage point from which he was able to study the *process* by which the merit certificates were awarded and distributed.

Access to the store of certificates and mastery of the Principal's signature were the easy bit, once that strategic bridgehead had been achieved. From that point on, the number of merit awards increased steadily and a great many parents were rendered very happy indeed by the documentary evidence of their children's progress. Jamie was supplying a kind of unofficial *social service;* and he was learning, fast, about managing dynamic systems. The key to that was the *spatial* awareness of the power system—the importance, as in military tactics, of occupying the high ground and making judicious use of strategic intelligence, covertly obtained. Robert Keep (Chapter 8) has read this account of Jamie's tactical nous and looks on him as a natural intelligence officer.

But Jamie's greatest entrepreneurial achievement concerned his first love—motor cars. Jamie had been driving illegally since the age of ten. Scaling the security fences of petrol depots, emptying detergent drums, cutting petrol tank hoses and filling the drums was easy enough, provided you understood the terrain and the security check frequencies. Once again, the core skill was *spatial,* reinforced by a good grasp of human nature.

By the age of fifteen, Jamie had befriended a single mother and taken on the responsibility for looking after her and her baby. Whatever else Jamie was, he was a *responsible* person. In order to hang on to his social security benefits, he enrolled in a six-month automotive course, part of a government program for unemployed youths, school refusers and other young people thought to be at risk. Let Sue Shegog take over the story at this point:

> I was contracted to teach the non-vocational section of Jamie's course, which included a subject called 'Enterprise Learning for Self-Development'. I was soon to learn that the enterprise skills I wished to nurture were well developed and thriving amongst my group of Auto boys. Who was educating who? The challenge for me was to channel these highly developed skills into activities which were socially acceptable while still meeting the boys' needs.

This statement is quite a good example of the humility needed in approaching the 'education' of those who are both gifted and underprivileged. Anything more patronising is doomed to ignominious failure. Sue Shegog decided that the boys' idea of an Easter egg raffle might be a safe sort of project for them to cut their teeth on. The idea felt a bit 'wossy' to some of the boys (I am not up on Tasmanian slang but I take it that 'ear-oles' are always wossy), but after a round of brainstorming, discussion and group problem-solving they decided to give it a go. Easter was looming at the time, so it represented an intelligent use of timing, a crucial success factor in any business.

The first great surprise for Jamie was how *easy* it was to obtain goods *honestly*. He was 'blown away' by this discovery, seeing in it a whole world of possible high-level, and highly creative, scams. I can picture Jamie carving his way through that den of (perfectly legal) thieves in the City of London, inventing devilishly creative 'financial products' designed for gullible punters. Back in Launceston, Cadburys donated a washing basket full of Easter eggs and a range of other local firms gave soft toys, baskets, cellophane and so on. Once Jamie was committed to the enterprise, he was seriously 'pissed off' by the misuse of the takings by another member of the team. Poacher had become gamekeeper, almost overnight.

But the Easter egg initiative was merely the dry run for the major project—the complete restoration of an old car which the group had negotiated to purchase from TAFE (the Technical and Further Education body) for a nominal $1. The boys spent virtually *all* their time at college working on the vehicle. Jamie blossomed as a natural leader, demonstrating *by example* the perseverance, dedication and technical capability required to manage a highly complex task under time pressure. Of course, the project had a list of desired 'learning outcomes' which were wildly outreached by the reality. 'Learning outcomes' are for young students; the work done was, in a word, *adult*.

Suddenly, well into the project, Jamie didn't show up for a whole week. After an exhaustive 'tracking' exercise it was discovered that Jamie (the 'irresponsible' delinquent) had been obliged to look after one of his brothers for the two weeks of school holiday. Omnicompetent Jamie thought he would be expelled from the course for having to miss two weeks and lacked the confidence to ask for support during this period of family need. Naturally, Sue Shegog, together with the course coordinator and the rest of the teaching staff, rallied around to look after the nine-year-old brother for the remainder of the holiday. Kids like Jamie are so 'adult' in some ways that it can be difficult to recall that they are still kids, with the same dependent needs as the rest of us. Teachers, driven to distraction by the ingenuity of the 'Jamies' and the 'Spanskys', sometimes forget this.

The eighteen-week course ended in triumph with the group and their project featuring in the local newspaper. As the car wasn't quite ready, the boys organised with their vocational trainer to return to college to complete the few remaining tasks. After that, it was time to sell the car, finalise the P&L statement and set out the final report on the project. (Like the Bradfield projects, this one was designed to let the boys see the process through from conception to the final conclusion—the sale.) The TAFE personnel chose that moment to revert to type, deciding at the last moment that the car should remain in the college, to be disposed of at their discretion. Furthermore, as the 'unemployed' had completed their course, they had no right to remain on campus.

The alert reader will anticipate the next step in this saga. In an unanticipated way, the TAFE officials were merely ratcheting up the scale of challenge for Jamie and his confederates. By that time, Jamie had the local knowledge: getting the keys from the college storeman (so as to 'complete' a few final touches) was easy enough. Within the day, the car was driven out through the front gate and sold, with just a few illegal changes for good measure. Six weeks later, all hell broke loose in the college. Where was the car? What might happen if it was involved in an accident (it was still, notionally, registered in the college name)? There was a great urgency to speak with 'these troublemakers'.

There was to be one further betrayal by the system. Sue Shegog takes up the story:

> Discussions between Jamie, the college, the course coordinator and myself resulted in an agreement that, if the car was returned to the college, Jamie could purchase it for $10, prior to the government auction to be held within the week. The car was duly returned with the original pieces restored to the appropriate places. Jamie faced the music only to have the system let him down again. Once the car was back on college turf, Jamie was told in no uncertain terms by senior TAFE staff to clear off—the deal was off! The incoming group of long-term 'unemployed youth at risk' trashed the car as part of their learning over the following eighteen weeks!

When last heard of, Jamie was nineteen. He had become a father just before his seventeenth birthday and was working part-time, in a very flexible way, to support his young family. I like the idea of a meeting between Jamie and Spansky, supervised by Sue Shegog and the main figure in this story, to whom we now return, Allan Coman. That quartet of natural 'Imos' could reinvent *useful* education for all Australian under-twenties.

ALLAN COMAN AND THE BRADFIELD COLLEGE STORY

Allan Coman took kids into Bradfield College at about the same age as Spansky's Hammertown Boys school spewed them out. When Bradfield College was established in 1993—as a joint venture between New South Wales Technical and Further Education (TAFE) and the Department of School Education (DSE)—its original intake included a high proportion of 'difficult' students who had failed elsewhere, or dropped out, or who had a record of indiscipline. At the beginning, the College was obliged to accept most of the students who presented themselves. Now that the College has 'come of age', something that Coman dates to mid-1995, it can afford to be more choosy, but it is still finding space for the 'Spanskys'—quirky characters who seem to have 'something about them'.

The proof of the success of Bradfield lies in the demand. The College is experiencing exponential growth and the enrolment is expected to continue to rise. This is being achieved by expanding part-time numbers and accumulating student numbers by running the College Monday to Friday 8.00 a.m. to 9.30 p.m. on weekdays and 8.00 a.m. to 4.00 p.m. on Saturdays, and by expanding the existing facilities.

I have to say that my experience of Bradfield College is limited so far to three visits. Whenever I have given lectures in Australia about the Spansky phenomenon, informed observers have instructed me to head for Crows Nest. A great many people in the education world are now looking at Bradfield and some of them helped me gather the information I needed. Let us begin with the College mission, a statement to warm the heart of Howard Gardner:

> To be a centre of educational excellence providing students with *many pathways* and *relevant experiences* leading to *rewarding career* opportunities through curriculum, industry training, and *life skills* in an independent and innovative *learning environment*.

The italics are mine. This mission statement at least makes the right noises. It suggests that book learning is important but it makes it quite clear that this is not enough. More important, it gives the hint of a college adapting to the diversity of students. Finally, it establishes the educational process and responsibility as something that extends well beyond the college gates into the outside world. Now consider the key words in the 'Core Values' statement:

1 Our core business is learning with a vocational focus.
2 We are client-centred and service-oriented.
3 Our emphasis is on development of the whole person.
4 Our learning occurs in an environment of change.
5 We work in teams to achieve quality learning.
6 We create connections by doing as we have agreed.

The students say that the special atmosphere of Bradfield lies in the friendly and supportive relationships between students. That is to be expected in an institution that sets out to encourage team working. I would suggest that this is, at base, a function of the special relationship that has been established between staff and students. The College is an almost pure expression of the 'ternary' principle (see the Introduction) because it is *firm but fair* (firm on standards, explicit about rights and duties). There is no slacking at Bradfield. If you don't fulfil yourself you can expect close, watchful, supportive and expert supervision, probably involving your family as well. Yet you must take responsibility for your own work.

Allan Coman says that the strongly vocational approach accounts for about two-thirds of the students' enthusiasm, commitment and success after leaving. But he insists: 'What really captivates the students is the *enterprising streak*!' Industry-based learning is based on business planning. The process is sophisticated, involving a broad sweep of trend data, utilising newspapers and other data sources. The students are being encouraged to carry out the same process as Robert Keep did when he started to scan the horse racing odds—taking a step backwards and allowing the data to wash over you. Coman is absolutely insistent that the students should experience the essential *messiness* of 'right-brain thinking'. Then comes Bronowski's *connecting*—clustering the information gathered into meaningful clumps, using imagination. Next comes the building of potential projects around the clumps. These are then subjected to feasibility studies and, if need be, tested to destruction. If the project looks as though it will run, you set it up and run it, with just the right amount of hand-holding from College staff.

How to use a brick

The Bradfield practice of putting students together in enterprise industry teams and encouraging them to see the whole task process through, from conception to fruition, brings together a number of this book's themes so far. If the culture is one of working together in groups, then students have to learn to appreciate different kinds of contributions—or, if you prefer, different combinations across the Gardner repertoire. The *scanning* (messy) phase of the Bradfield projects is particularly important because it permits the 'divergers' to shine. The psychologist Liam Hudson used to conduct experiments based on 'uses of objects' tests. These tests ask people to think of as many possible uses as they can for everyday objects like milk bottles, bricks, shoes, suitcases and so on. Divergent thinking seems to be an independent variable (in relation to formal examinations, IQ tests and the like). Very bright convergent thinkers (as tested) can usually think of just a few different uses for a brick, then their inventiveness quickly peters out. A diverger, on the other hand, will go on and on for hours in leaps of imagination and fantasy, until the need for food or rest cuts in. (For the brick, 'tombstone for a mouse' is my favourite amongst the suggestions.) The diverger may not be the most useful member of the group when the business plan is being put to bed, but he or she is *crucial* in the scanning phase.

Interestingly, Liam Hudson found that when boys aged around sixteen to twenty years were asked to do the uses of objects test under examination conditions, but *as if they were somebody else*, their imaginations ran riot. Doing the test as 'Robert Higgins, the successful but sober computer engineer', the boys brought forth *twice* as many unusual or creative uses as when they answered in their own right. Doing the test as 'John McMice, the well-known, uninhibited Bohemian artist', brought forth an avalanche of ideas of 'staggering violence and obscenity'. Once again, we can see the releasing power of the theatrical metaphor and its uncomfortable proximity to the unacceptable. Spansky and Joey (those surreal rearrangers of other people's front gates) would undoubtedly be dab hands at uses of objects tests, especially in an assumed role (and more especially as McMice). I find myself wishing, wistfully, that Spansky and Joey could have been transported to Australia upon leaving school, placed in Bradfield College and engaged immediately in purposive, managerial group work demanding creativity.

Turning things round

On the occasion of my second-last visit to Bradfield, four of the students had just come second in the Internet category of the World Skill Olympics, competing with university teams from Finland, the United States, France, Malaysia, Hong Kong, the United Kingdom and other countries. The Finnish team (all graduates) beat them by just *one point*. Not bad going for a group of students from the 'recovery group' who had been kicked out of other schools. It looks like the revenge of the 'Spanskys'! The four had run a global multimedia demonstration for the Prime Minister three weeks before; even the hardheaded media applauded their chutzpah. How can these kids get so smart so fast? Well, Bradfield is now producing information workers—a kind of talent feedstock for the participating firms. Allan Coman says: 'We're creating a new kind of worker!'

Apart from the knowledge workers, the College is establishing a presence in other emerging fields such as design and entertainment.

This breadth flows from Coman's policy of selecting 'eccentric' staff with broad backgrounds. One of his secret weapons during his time at Bradfield was that he personally selected all his staff and all of them have done much more during their careers than teach. In Germany, all academic staff in the Fachochschulen are *obliged by law* to have worked outside education. Coman's staff came from business, the stock market, television and a wide range of other callings. The pre-eminence of Bradfield in entertainment studies can be traced directly back to the employment of an ex-actor (*No. 96*) and Sydney Theatre Company education officer. Over 100 students are now signed up for the entertainment course. Coman selects high capacity oddballs as teachers, deliberately nurtures their interests and 'foibles', and waits to see what they will come up with, nourished by the Bradfield buzz. Teachers of this sort respect the 'Spanskys' of this world because they understand them and their frustrations. They have something in common with them.

Who chose Allan Coman to direct this new enterprise? He believes that the presence of a well-known entrepreneur/business-woman on the selection panel may have helped because he (Coman) *ought* to have been—and probably was—viewed suspiciously by conventional academics. Gregor Ramsay, the Director of TAFE, was also an important backer. The TAFE/DSE collaboration itself owes something to the Foundation for Education set up by the Dusseldorp family some years ago. You might say that Bradfield College had good grandparents, long before the arrival of Allan Coman. Still, Coman is important and we ought to try to understand how he came to be in the right place at the right time. He understands, as Bob Clifford does, that decisions have their special time. He says: 'The trick is, you always say *yes*—it's better to get forgiveness at the end than to ask for permission at the start! It's so easy to miss an opportunity.'

My experience of education administration in the United Kingdom leads me to think that anything so obviously successful as Bradfield must be in some kind of danger—it raises too many awkward questions about what most of the rest are up to. Coman says himself: 'The straiteners and the narrowers are trying to move in!' Bradfield compares well enough on 'effectiveness audits'—completion rates, HSCs gained and so on— but to really understand the process of a place like Bradfield, and the societal benefits that may flow from it, you need to talk at length to the students both during and after their time in the institution. Funnily enough, educational auditors hardly ever talk to students—there is always the risk that direct contact with the throughput might contaminate their data.

Allan Coman himself comes from a respectably modest background. He describes himself as a 'product of the Catholic education system', which may account for the very strong sense of institution with which Bradfield is imbued. His father was originally a clerk in Tooheys Brewery; later manager of a milk factory. Educationally, Coman was a slow starter and late reader and suffered his share of bullying. Like many inspired teachers, he was rescued by a particular (female) teacher (in Year 5), who spotted his peculiar talents and encouraged him. In Year 7, he sat for and won a scholarship, ending up at the de la Salle Brothers School in Ashfield, near Sydney.

Then he joined the Order as a trainee teaching brother and spent six years in New Zealand. It was at this time that he collected the first of a couple of Masters degrees. At twenty-five years of age he left the Order and went through a period of 'isolation'. In his late twenties he was a peripatetic teacher of science, moving from school to school and observing the practices of others. Like Robert Keep at the same age, his isolation gave him the advantage of a certain detachment. By the age of twenty-nine he was ready to put his ideas into practice; he became Principal of Kingsgrove de la Salle College, 'very determined to make the school work!' Making a school work means viewing the whole system as a working machine and understanding how it ticks. You can hear an echo of Clifford's fascination with the original hovercraft and Keep's absorption in the pattern of odds. Coman reckoned the key variables were the *clarity* of the underpinning *ideas* and the *quality* of the *people*, the whole bolted together in *teams*. It is a nice reformulation of the ternary idea—purpose, people and teams.

So, by his early thirties, Coman had 'turned Kingsgrove inside out' and was on the way to Bradfield. Five years at Kingsgrove turned into seven years at Ashfield de la Salle College for boys from Years 5 to 12. On his entry, Ashfield was a failing school with a declining roll of 550 pupils. By the time of his departure, it was a spectacularly successful school with a roll of over 1200 pupils. By that time the surrounding schools at Burwood and Lewisham, which had attracted most of the government support funding in the intervening years, had almost closed. The bureaucrats had backed the wrong horse! Ashfield was the serious dry run for Bradfield.

Ashfield really was a challenge for a new principal with ideas. Ninety-nine per cent of the pupils were of non-Australian stock: they came from Lebanese, Italian, Croatian, Greek, Chinese, etc. families, and the standards of English language expression and comprehension were generally abysmal. By this time Coman understood something about the importance of *symbolic* communication with staff, students and parents. He had read, and had been powerfully influenced by, Peters and Waterman's seminal *In Search of Excellence*. This book was not standard fare for schoolteachers in the 1980s, but Coman has always been a voracious and eclectic reader. (Over the years, Tom Peters, one of the *great* popularisers, has been an enormous influence for good. The English are sniffy about him because he is perceived as too garrulous. The point is, he *reaches* people like Allan Coman.) From Peters, and other off-line *managerial* sources, Coman had picked up something significant about the *theatre* of leadership—the need to reach people at a level *beneath* the merely intellectual. For a modest and self-effacing man, Coman has a near-genius for the transmission and presentation of *ideas*.

He foresaw three fundamental challenges for Ashfield:

- At the 'tough but fair' end of the spectrum, it would be necessary to address, quickly and ruthlessly, the language problem. Without that bedrock of capability all other aspects of education would be diminished.
- There was an urgent need to 'soften' the school's profile. This meant subverting the prevailing *macho* culture and replacing it with something less mindless and more stimulating.
- Finally, there was the inevitable need to lift the boys from their relatively stunted circumstances and to give them a glimpse of a possible better world.

The previous administration of the school had placed the first of these tasks firmly in the 'too hard' basket. The latter two would simply not have occurred to the old regime because it would not have countenanced the possibility that the riffraff in the school contained the seeds of nobility. The reason why Allan Coman is able to turn failing schools round, over and over again, is that he *knows* that every child contains the possibility of cleverness of one kind or another. Coman simply brings the skills of an impresario to the task of remaking the institution.

On the language front, they instituted a crash program of closely supervised improvement for every child in the school, working in *teams*. Within two years, the average Year 10 Ashfield child was up to the New South Wales State average. After that, they were consistently *above* the average. That gave the kids much of the confidence they had previously lacked. On the culture front, Coman went for a skill area where a core of the pupils had something ready to build on. He cajoled the most talented children into a much expanded program of drama, art and music. The first twenty to buy in were subjected by their mates to merciless teasing—until they eventually won the Schools' Rock Eisteddfod, beating a raft of well-endowed schools in State, national and international competition. Handicapped by the absence of girls in an all-boys school, they went on stage with heavily tarted up *mops* as companions! By this time, about a hundred of the kids were fighting to get into the front line of the music program and Ashfield was famous for its public performances. The school assemblies were now 'legendary' for their liveliness and inventiveness. They were, of all things, *fun*, and they celebrated the special values of the school—energy, creativity, teamwork and success.

After all this, the pupils were ready for the outdoors education program. The entire school regularly decamped to the bush just before the Easter break for a program of exploration, trekking and climbing, including, for some, a night in the open at the top of a just-climbed mountain. This was an important ritual event for inner-city, often deprived, young people. It may seem extraordinary that so much could have been achieved so relatively quickly but, as Allan Coman tells it, all you have to do is *'get the staff to re-envision the school then re-position the school in its environment!'* Well, yes, but how do you get *other* principals to do the same thing elsewhere. The answer is *by imitation*. One of Coman's greatest sources of pride is, as the great teacher he is, that half a dozen of the best and brightest of current principals of New South Wales schools were involved, as junior teachers, in the heady Ashfield experience. They saw, they learned, and they went on to conquer new fields.

After Ashfield, Coman was ready for the challenge of Bradfield—an entirely new kind of school with novel support from the two agencies TAFE and DSE. The brief account given above glosses over the difficulties and frustrations at Bradfield College—'We did stupid things at the outset!' In hindsight, Coman is remorseful about the embarrassment to which his entrepreneurial approach exposed genuine supporters up the line in the New South Wales education system. All great leaders are perfectionists and the burden of a good intellect is that you can always see what might have been. To the outsider like myself the question is, always, what do you do for an encore? How do people like Allan Coman find the next great challenge commensurate with their expanding capability?

ALLAN COMAN MOVES ON . . .

I discovered the answer to this important question in May 1996. When I first met Allan Coman, in the middle of 1995, it was clear to me that he was ready for the next challenge but almost exhausted from the relentless demands of leadership over the past three years. Achievements like Bradfield are never easily won. Working, initially, to two bosses (TAFE *and* DSE) is always nightmarish, even if the bureaucratic spirit is willing. Coman, partly in the interests of his health, left his beloved Bradfield to run a small Catholic private girls school (Stella Maris College) in Manly. The reader won't be surprised to learn that this was yet *another* school in decline. Coman arrived on 1 February 1996 at a school with a nonviable roll of just 452 pupils. Just three months later the word had got around and new enrolments were running at the rate of two or three per week. Good news travels fast amongst anxious parents. At Stella Maris, Coman is accountable to a small company board of directors, including five Sisters of the Order of the Good Samaritan—a far cry from the bureaucracy of the New South Wales State education system. Stella Maris had actually withdrawn from the formal Catholic system some years previously.

When I first heard the news of Allan Coman's departure from Bradfield, from his successor, I was startled. Surely Coman, of all people, should have been moving on to bigger and wider responsibilities? I should have known better. On arrival at Stella Maris, I learned that he had simultaneously joined the Policy Committee of the New South Wales Catholic Education Commission, the fount of his early experience in education. Thus he succeeded in combining hands-on experience of a tightly knit educational community with a stake in policy direction of the big system. Like all my leaders (look at Clifford and Keep) there is the need to *stay in touch* whilst redesigning the world. (Sculpture is the metaphor—the ideas matter but the hands must work the clay and drive the thinking.) Further-more, and unsurprisingly, there is a plan to create *another* (but privately managed) 'Bradfield' down the road, in association with the Manly Training Centre (another venture of the Stella Maris board) and Manly Council. Manly–Warringah has a substantial youth and long-term unemployment problem. Coman, it turns out, has not deserted the 'big picture' at all—he has merely found a manageable way of tackling the big, intractable problems with a minimum of bureaucratic interference and without putting himself and his family under intolerable strain

All great leaders leave behind them an arena that is different from what it was before. What do we find at Bradfield today? Firstly, the succession is secure. Coman knew that, before his departure, he would need to 'institutionalise' the changes he had wrought. Andrew FitzSimons and Phil Stabback were there from the start of the great experiment and lasted the gruelling course. They have smoothly taken the baton.

But there is much more. Bradfield's ripple effect is substantial and likely to increase. The College was one of the very first to establish an Enterprise Agreement with its staff, all of whom are better paid than the State baseline. By 1996 a third of the staff were working four-day weeks with flexible monthly work commitments (140 hours over four weeks). The physical assets were being sweated well into the evenings, again with the active cooperation of the teachers. The New South Wales Teachers Federation is not famous for flexibility, but Bradfield leadership and determination helped them to strike an innovative and farsighted staff employment deal, taking the Federation itself into a leadership role in Australia.

Furthermore, Bradfield is pioneering the *clustering* of 'subjects' into enterprise-relevant combinations. In other colleges, design, drama, information technology and entertainment industry studies are usually found in separate, carefully fenced boxes. At Bradfield they are interlinked in exactly the way that the new technology/entertain-ment/multimedia industries require. If you presume to educate large numbers of 'Spanskys', you had better make your offerings relevant to the adult world they already inhabit. You had better also attend to the entire repertoire of human intelligences. Interestingly, Allan Coman, voracious reader that he is, was unaware of Howard Gardner's work when we first met. If you examine his educational practice at each school he has directed during his career, you'll see that it is as if he *wrote* Gardner's seminal book *Frames of Mind*.

One final example of the beneficent impact of Coman and Bradfield is an apocryphal story—I hope it is true—of a meeting between Coman and the then State Education Minister (at that time a woman) and her department head. This was at the outset of the Bradfield experiment. The story has it that Coman was handed an envelope containing his instructions or rules of engagement—'marching orders'—for the task ahead. When he opened the envelope the sheet of paper inside was blank! The Minister is reputed to have said: *'Make it work!'* The rest is history. Nothing would have been achieved without farsightedness at ministerial level and sympathetic support (principally from Dr Susan Holland) along the line of authority. Women in high places have been an important influence in the New South Wales education system. At the time of writing, the head of the Education Coordination Department is another woman—Jane Diplock—with broad-band experience of banking as well as public service.

Even now, the New South Wales education bureaucracy is trying to create new kinds of student pathways through the education labyrinth. The Coffs Harbour district is the showpiece, where a Joint Board of Management has been created for the senior high school, the TAFE Institute and the local university, in order to reduce the tyranny of the subject guilds and to open up education to adult *logic*. I hope it works well—it deserves to! If there are any problems, I would ring Allan Coman in Manly. But then again, if I were the *Prime Minister* and looking for good ideas in education, I would ring Allan Coman. He is a very *senior* 'Imo'—but an 'Imo' just the same!

ALLAN COMAN AS INTELLIGENT LEADER

It will be obvious that I look on Coman as a well-nigh perfect leader. It is very nearly superfluous to list his leadership qualities, but here are just a few reminders of earlier themes which he exemplifies.

Coman *combines* the direct and indirect types of leadership. None of his achievements would have been possible without the involvement and enthusiasm of colleagues and staff. He knows therefore how to get people *attached* to a worthwhile purpose, mainly through the subtle arts of theatre and symbolism.

It appears that this motivating skill has always been *idea-driven*. It is the ternary principle made flesh; Coman may be personally persuasive but the idea is *really* persuasive. If the idea catches on (this book is meant to help), then he becomes an indirect leader too.

What is the idea? It combines:

- the *knowledge* (some might say faith) that *every* child, however disadvantaged, has the seeds of creativity and endeavour hidden away somewhere—with . . .
- the understanding of schools as *systems*, charged with *managing* inputs, value-adding conversion processes and valuable outputs

Forget the exams. If the output (resourceful young adults) *works*, then the school works.

Coman is an exceptionally modest man, yet he has a keen critical eye for the lunacies of educational systems. He has the great advantage, as role model for teachers and children, that he is another 'broad-bander' on the Gardner intelligences. I cannot vouch for the presence of the *musical* or the *bodily/kinaesthetic* intelligence, but I can vouch for the rest. It doesn't *matter* if he is tone-deaf and clumsy, and I don't want to know.

Finally, there is a transparent sense of *duty*. Like all the best leaders, Allan Coman is determined to *make a difference*. How you interpret this depends on your view of human nature. If you adopt a moral perspective, you can say that Coman is a *good* man, impelled by a higher voice to perform good works. If, on the other hand, you adopt a pragmatic or behaviourist perspective, you might say that he is a person of unusually high *capacity*, impelled by his restless intelligence constantly to stretch himself to new limits. The point is that *it doesn't matter* whether the values drive the intellect or vice versa. We should be grateful for the combination when we find it and worried about the stifling of potential in similar, but younger, people.

10

John Latham of IBM: the housetrained 'Imo'

For the corporate reader, Messrs Clifford and Keep may seem a little like Martians. It is difficult to picture either of them climbing steadily up the ranks of a bureaucracy. Unless you count his father, Bob Clifford was never anybody's employee. Robert Keep did succeed spectacularly well for a while in the Australian Army, a very substantial bureaucracy, but in the end the misfit became obvious to both sides. Allan Coman is superficially less eccentric, although not many corporate executives begin their careers as novitiate priests. That suggests a dedication to ideals of a higher order than career success or corporate profit.

My assumption is that, whilst the Cliffords, Keeps and Comans can never be fully housetrained, there are potentially more of them around than we realise and it ought not to be impossible for big organisations to contain them and use their special gifts intelligently.

Most big organisations, without meaning to, just make it very difficult for them. Clifford, Keep and Coman have a few things in common, even though they occupy completely different worlds. It is what they have in common that the big corporations most need. It is that same thing which makes it likely that only a very unusual, and smart, corporation will be able to contain them or turn them into 'intrapreneurs'—Gifford Pinchot's term for the entrepreneur within the corporation. This is a necessary prelude to the story of John Latham, the only one of my contemporary leaders to have persisted in the employ of a major bureaucracy—in this case, the IBM Corporation. Before we examine Latham, it may be instructive to re-examine what the preceding leaders have in common.

1. *Persistence*

Each of them has worried away at a particular idea or venture for year upon year. Coman was headed for the special challenges of Bradfield as soon as he took on Kingsgrove School, years before. Clifford was headed for the big ferries as soon as he started to grapple with the problems of building a small fishing boat. (It is worth recalling that all the best America's Cup skippers were dinghy racing champions before they graduated to Cup racing.) Keep was headed for the world of very complex data as soon as he started jotting things down in notebooks. One of Robert Keep's heroes is the great 16th century Danish astronomer, Tycho Brahe. It was his persistence, observing the heavens day after day, year after year, in a disciplined but openminded way, that laid the foundation for his assistant, Kepler. Kepler, a generation younger and standing on the shoulders of Brahe, devised the basic laws of planetary motion, thus paving the way for Newton. Newton acknowledged his debt to others' persistence: 'If I have seen further, it is by standing upon the shoulders of Giants!'

Probably the only people in big corporations who share the 'luxury' of persistence on this scale nowadays are a very few senior scientists in corporate labs. One exception might be Japan, where the sprightly, octogenarian inventor/founder is still to be found in or around the boardroom—still ingenious, and very wise. In the take-over-obsessed Anglo-Saxon business world, anything involving a long-term perspective has become a rarity, even for members of the board—*especially* for the members of some boards. It is only in very rare cases, like some of the 'intrapreneurs' Pinchot describes in the

3M company, that those obsessive employees who refuse to stop working on pet projects actually get away with it. For the most part, the accountants and the big shareholders want quick profit because they are always frightened of corporate predators. That fear is the enemy of individual persistence.

Of course, product life-cycles are getting shorter and shorter, but the products themselves are like plants that come and go. It is the quality of the soil that matters, nurtured and cosseted over the years. Japanese corporations have been much better than their competitors in nourishing this kind of continuity and persistence among creative people. In the West, the Keeps and the Cliffords generally have to go it alone.

2. *Complexity and keeping it simple*

This is the counterpart of persistence. Long-term projects get complicated as they develop. They suck in elaboration. Persistent people therefore have to have high intellectual capacity—the ability to juggle lots of mental balls simultaneously. Most corporate executives can ring-fence their own particular patch of turf in order to keep things reasonably simple. This is what causes departmental 'smokestacks' or 'silos' and communications blockages. Truly inventive people have to beg, borrow and steal ideas, resources and support from wherever they can get them. In the days of Internet, that means anywhere in the world. Their problem is to communicate in a *simple* way with those they need to influence. In the corporate world, that may mean their bosses. The problem for the entrepreneur is that he or she may be the only person with the grand design in mind.

I worked closely for a period with the manufacturing director of a very high-tech avionics factory. The plant had nearly three thousand employees and he knew virtually all the names. It was a subsidiary of a major corporation. The director engaged in, and seemed to enjoy, a kind of running guerrilla battle with head office. He was fiercely proud of his plant, his people, and the fact that they were rated an 'A1 Vendor' by the Boeing Corporation. He cursed and swore his way around the place, playing the rough-and-ready man of the people, watching events in every corner of the operation, and getting his hands dirty. He was a great charismatic leader who was always at pains to wear his learning, which was considerable, lightly.

I wanted to know how he held it all together. He puzzled me at first by referring to the 'vehicle'. I thought he was talking about the gleaming Jaguar in the car park, of which he was inordinately proud, and in which I had already had occasion to offer up prayers for survival. But the 'vehicle', it turned out, was a *mental construct*—a kind of rolling, aerial photograph of things as they currently are, in all their complexity, right across the factory operation and its key customers and prospects. Its special virtue was to be *simple*—'before the pointyheads [IT specialists] turn it into printouts'. The contents of the 'vehicle' differed from day to day, yet it was a continuous and stable construct.

I think all clever leaders have to have a 'vehicle' in their minds, not so much for grappling with complexity but for keeping it simple. Only the most important things stay inside the 'vehicle'. Such people don't stop working during the night—frequently their dreams influence the contents of the 'vehicle' in the morning. If they are really clever, they strive to share the vehicle with a few trusted colleagues. It helps to know how the boss's mind is working, alongside the formal planning and review routines. My avionics friend, I fear, was not good at sharing his 'vehicle'. He was, I suppose, a kind of *intrapreneur*. The problem for the company, I foresaw, would be to *replace* him eventually. He was much more like Robert Keep than most senior corporate executives. Keep's algorithm is a 'vehicle'—a way of condensing a mass of data into a simple formula. So are the 'backs of the envelopes' on which Bob Clifford works out new ferry designs, sitting on aircraft.

If corporate mentoring or coaching is to add value, it has to help quirky people like this to share the contents of their minds. Some of them regard knowledge as power and hoard it. This is a rational response to a *binary*—i.e. competitive organisational—culture. John Latham (below) had to cope with this.

3. *The oscillation between thinking and doing*
I sometimes call this 'thinkering'—a clumsy amalgam of thinking and tinkering. Clifford and Keep, in particular, are people who preserve time for thinking but they hardly ever stop playing with their mental gadgets. They are hands-on tinkerers. It seems they *need* to oscillate, on a frequent basis, between the abstract and the very concrete. Keep does not recognise the existence of illness—he has to turn up *every single day* at his computer station (during the Australian night-time) and he feels he has to *personally* dispatch his bulletins. *Then* he goes

walking and thinking. That unbending daily cycle seems to be important. It makes perfect sense for Allan Coman to go on running a smallish girls school whilst grappling with State-wide policy issues. It looks very much as though each sphere (the concrete and the abstract) is a function of the other.

Sculptors provide a good example of the same process: the idea flows into the clay—the clay assumes a character (which is never exactly what the artist meant; probably more interesting in a way)—the half-formed clay then feeds the thinking process—and so on round the loop. Significantly, Henry Mintzberg seems to have been influenced by his wife (who is a potter) in the preparation of his marvellous book *The Rise and Fall of Strategic Planning*. He says: 'Because analysis is not synthesis, strategic planning is not strategy formation!' In other words, once you withdraw yourself completely into the abstract domain, you *lose the plot*. Politicians, especially government ministers surrounded by flunkeys, are always in danger of losing contact with their *raison d'être*—the sensibilities and welfare of the people.

Theatre, our chosen metaphor so far, is similar to sculpture in this sense. The director knows what he or she intends but also knows from experience that that is not what will happen. A lot of other people will influence the outcome, in completely unpredictable ways. The task of the director is not to 'stick to plan' but to keep up with the creative juggernaut as it plunges forward, but still bearing the ideal (or the writer's intention) in mind. Bob Clifford and his colleagues are solving enormously complex design problems as they go along. All they know for sure is the general direction of the fast-ferry business, the niche they occupy within it, and that they are years ahead of the competition. All of these characters seem to have always understood that the 'practical' and the 'theoretical' must interpenetrate continuously. Mary Parker Follett (Chapter 5) made this observation about managerial leadership over sixty years ago.

Mintzberg goes on to say: '. . . strategies that are novel and compelling seem to be the products of single creative brains, those capable of synthesizing a vision. The key to this would seem to be integration rather than decomposition, based on holistic images rather than linear words.' The followers of these kinds of leaders don't know what is going to happen, any more than the leader does, but they *sense* they are in safe hands. These leaders inspire *confidence*.

4. *The ternary focus as the source of a good story*

One thing that distinguishes these three men from their corporate employee counterparts is their relative indifference to money and conventional career success. They are not primarily out to succeed or to compete with their peers. Their aim is to perfect the gadget upon which they are currently working. Joseph Schumpeter put it pretty well in 1911 in *The Theory of Economic Development*: 'There is the will to conquer, the impulse to fight, to prove oneself . . . , to succeed for the sake, not of the fruits of success, but of success itself. Finally, there is the joy of creating, of getting things done or simply exercising one's energy and ingenuity!'

Clifford, Keep and Coman range from the comfortably off to the seriously rich, but that isn't the point. This focus on the 'third corner' (the object) gives them another advantage—the ability to see their field of operation not as the whole world but as a stage on which they get to direct and act out their own play. This is probably why all three are so good at 'public relations' or *positioning*. (I discovered them because of this gift for positioning.) They are in the play but they are also simultaneously on the outside, with a good overview of how it must look to others. Each in his way (I mean this respectfully) is a high-class *ham*. This must involve an element of Gardner's *intrapersonal intelligence*. Because of this, they are much better than the manufacturing director (above) at *sharing* with others—employees, the press or anybody else—their own personal 'vehicles'. In each case, the 'vehicle' is just mental work-in-progress; the trick is to shape it for public comprehension.

In *Leading Minds* Howard Gardner lays heavy stress on the successful leader's capacity to *tell a gripping story*, and to go on telling it consistently over time: 'I argue that the story is a basic human cognitive form; the artful creation and articulation of stories constitutes a fundamental part of the leader's vocation. Stories speak to both parts of the human mind—its reason and emotion.' I prefer Gardner's way of putting it to the grandiose idea of 'articulating a vision', but nonetheless that is why some stories *work*. Let me repeat Allan Coman's apparently artless description of how you turn a failing school round: '*Get the staff to re-envision the school, then re-position the school in its environment!*' It sounds simple. But, by the time Coman got to Ashfield School, he had a terrific story to tell, based on previous success and on a *developing* idea (a 'vehicle' in his mind) about the relationship between kids, schools and learning. He must have come across as pretty persuasive (or inspiring) to the Ashfield staff, even though he could not have known *exactly* what he would do with the school.

That, in a modest way, is why this book contains stories—the accounts of the lives and achievements of a range of clever, influential people. Without the stories, the conceptual material wouldn't come alive.

JOHN LATHAM

I met John Latham for the first time around 1968. I had been appointed management development consultant to the director of IBM United Kingdom's Office Products Division, the 'downmarket' end of the Corporation since it sold typewriters, word processors and dictating equipment. There was a social gulf between the 'OP' sales division and the data processing salesmen and systems engineers, many of whom were Oxbridge graduates selling to their counterparts in the City of London and in the big corporations. I had joined IBM as a young man in Australia and, newly arrived in London, the social division was obvious enough to me. Nobody else in the system seemed to be aware of it at a conscious level, although it affected behaviour in mysterious ways.

Latham, a dozen years or so my senior, was in charge of the OEM (other equipment manufacturers) Group. Their role was to operate in the grey hinterland between the (then) dominant IBM Corporation, which didn't need to collaborate with anybody to maintain its almost monopolistic position in the market, and the other suppliers who from time to time traded with IBM or fitted their equipment (keyboards, for example) into its systems. This was good business for IBM, but it was treated almost covertly because the mighty IBM didn't officially consort with the minnows. The OEM Group was located in the aforementioned Office Products Division, because of the product overlap. This was probably a mistake because Latham and his lads were actually stalking the no-man's land where the really important market intelligence for computers was to be found—where the future was taking shape.

The obvious difference between John Latham and the three entrepreneurs above is that he joined a major corporation in early mid-life and stayed with it until a modestly early retirement. Latham was therefore technically an 'intrapreneur' not an entrepreneur, although his range of activities and interests throughout was always pretty impressive. His importance lies in the fact that, because of the almost unique positioning of his operational group within the Corporation, he foresaw what *must* happen to IBM in another ten to fifteen years or so, unless urgent corrective action was taken straightaway. Latham was therefore an Imo. His claim to seriously intelligent leadership lies in the fact that he not only foresaw the future—he foresaw how and why he would be powerless to forestall the future. He knew intuitively that, no matter how hard he tried, he would be unable to divert the bureaucracy from its collision course with one of the biggest corporate blunders in business history. He did try, however.

The story of IBM's blunder is well known, but the reader may appreciate a brief recap. Because of IBM's market dominance in computers, which amounted virtually to a worldwide monopoly, it had been able to *control* its competition by outspending them (especially in research) and holding new product developments back in order to kill off upgraded competitive equipment. All this was financed by the wide *margins* that IBM was able to charge for its product/service mix. The service, by very high quality sales, systems engineering and maintenance staff, really provided the edge. Generally, the IBM kit was nothing special but customers felt *safe* with the superconfident IBM *people*. The inherent weakness in all this was the flipside of the main strength—the belief, on the part of purchasing departments, that *'nobody ever got the sack for buying IBM!'* The competition might be offering a much better price/performance package but the *safe* option remained the reassuringly expensive IBM option. Latham saw that this was a shaky foundation for continuing market dominance because it was a *psychological* advantage rather than a realistic *technical* or *performance* advantage. *How* and *why* he was able to perceive this is the point of the story.

It would be fair to say that John Latham stood out in the IBM culture. He had come into the company not just from the Army but from the cloak-and-dagger ranks of the Special Services. Tall and craggy, with a cut-glass accent, he might have stepped out of any Hollywood-style spy/war movie of the 1940s. In fact, at the age of *seventeen*, he had been in charge of bits of northern Italy and Malta

189

in the dying days of World War II. There is a certain kind of fearless, uncontrollable youth for whom a war is a much more engaging pursuit than zooming around the country on a motorbike to the despair of his mother. Latham was one of these—precocious would be the word for it.

I have worked with many men (and fewer women) who shared the intensity of this wartime experience. They all seem to possess a detached scale of values which accepts that being alive at all is much more significant than getting a promotion or pleasing a boss. It is a pity we can't really improve on wars for teaching this sort of wisdom.

After the war, Latham stayed on in the Army. He was rejected at first by the Special Services on grounds of his 'lack of interest' (for which read: the mind wandering to more interesting matters). He became a commissioned officer in their ranks later on when he had proved his ingenuity in the field. An example of the ingenuity was his invention of a kind of spyhole for use in the big NATO war games in Germany. The north German plains are largely devoid of good cover. Latham reckoned that the cheap, civilian 'Anderson Shelters' (designed to withstand Hitler's buzzbombs) could be converted to underground observation points strong enough to withstand passing tanks. What's more, Latham was able to get them built and proven in just a few days and without permission, by enthusing his commando teams and getting his own hands dirty. It proved simple and highly effective—Latham's 'army' won the 'war'.

There are many more Latham stories of this kind, most of which cannot be revealed for security reasons. By the time John Latham entered the corporate world, as a humble typewriter salesman, he had become very experienced indeed in covert observation and in the interpretation of fragmented data. These are useful skills in the sales world too. Selling is not unlike spying—you have to simulate *particular* genuineness, while carrying out a routinised *general* task. Not for nothing do psychologists see selling as a 'promiscuous' activity. It is also no accident that corporations are obsessed by 'market intelligence'. If you can understand what is (or must be) going on by making sense of the fragments you are able to get hold of, and building up a *pattern*, then you have the drop on the competition—provided you can get the bigwigs to understand and to act quickly on what you have discovered. It was at this point that Latham, like Keep, ran into a brick wall of incomprehension.

As did all the best intrapreneurs, Latham had a mentor or 'sponsor' in IBM—significantly, a Stateside American boffin with worldwide contacts in the new technology world. Latham was appointed to sit, as the IBM representative, on the British Standards Institute, because he understood the way the technology was running. As an ex-'spy', he understood that his role on the BSI was to say nothing and to observe closely. Of course he was not the only person in IBM to see which way the wind was blowing—towards highly flexible local (personal) computing, and away from the big mainframes which still sustained IBM's market dominance. Because Latham was close to the *designers* around the world, he could see how easy and cheap it was to bolt together even the existing technology to make a new kind of product. C. K. Prahalad has observed that quite a few people in IBM had seen which way things were going. The problem wasn't the forecasting, but imagining the possibilities and capabilities.

To be fair, IBM did have special problems. Because of its market dominance, it was under constant United States Government scrutiny under the anti-trust laws. It was said that there were two Justice Department lawyers whose sole function was to watch IBM nonstop. It was also said that IBM employed *sixty-three* lawyers to watch those two. The Corporation was certainly distracted by the effort to divisionalise in order to meet the objections of the smaller competitors. What really mattered wasn't the lawsuits but what the competitors were doing with the technology. In the end IBM, by sticking to what it knew best, 'gave away the keys to the kingdom!' Intel ran away with the manufacture of chips and Microsoft (famously) ran away with the software. The IBM top dogs simply didn't *see* that in future it would be the *software*, not the machines themselves, that made the money and secured the market stranglehold.

Like many American corporations, IBM was heavily influenced by 'binary' or Darwinian notions. Product development would take place along competitive lines, with development teams fighting it out for corporate funding. It did release enormous energy, but it also encouraged turf wars. At that time the director of the United Kingdom Laboratories, at Hursley, was a brilliant designer/manager, Dr John Fairclough. One of Fairclough's teams had already lost one of these development battles over a mainframe computer design—reputedly with a *better* design—the SCAMP system. Latham used to talk to Fairclough about technical developments amongst the competitors.

They looked, for example, at the early Commodore machines, agreeing that it would be easy to replicate them cheaply—a 'typewriter with a chip inside'. Fairclough (now Sir John) had thought about all this before and knew that the competitors, generally scorned by IBM, were potentially dangerous. Later he went on to become the United Kingdom Government's Chief Scientific Officer. He was also ready for a bigger, wider and more challenging assignment by then.

Between them Latham and Fairclough tried to bend the minds of the corporate bigwigs. Latham talked to the European laboratory directors about the way the market was headed. They were sympathetic but they were locked into product development 'missions' handed down from above. They were a bit like rugby forwards—already bedded-down in a scrum and pushing hard. They felt powerless to diverge, no matter how compelling the local argument. Latham was particularly concerned about the communications side of computing—the froggish interfaces with other types of system. This was the time when limited intelligence terminals were beginning to find their way into airline check-in stations. This meant he was getting involved with process control systems, message-switching, international standards—all the spaces between systems, and a far cry from the interests of his Office Products colleagues. He foresaw the kinds of technical collaboration and interlocking between manufacturers that were bound to come. He was networked with most of his counterparts around the world—an informal cabal of inventive mavericks, taking the business forward *despite* their employing corporations.

Right from the start the OEM group, Latham's team or commando, was an oddball outfit—a motley collection of ex-garage mechanics, merchant bankers and other riffraff, carefully chosen for ingenuity by Latham himself. The parallel with Allan Coman's staff at Bradfield College is inescapable (see Chapter 9). When you entered the OEM group as a member of staff your first task, with much help and encouragement from the others, was the establishment of your personal share portfolio. Latham believed that everybody needed to be financially independent of the Corporation in order to be 'brave' enough to take bold decisions. Not surprisingly, every member of that oddball team has gone on to greater things. When I discuss people like Latham with major corporations, the tendency is to marginalise them as mavericks or eccentrics. But part of the significance of people like this is the *multiplier effect* of their leadership. John Latham was truly an innovator of great talent but he was also a fine *manager*, sensitive to the development needs of his motley crew, uncompromising in his expectations of their loyalty and effort, and expert in drawing out their own ingenuity. They certainly admired the boss; possibly *loved* him in the same gruff sort of way that commandos sometimes come to love their officers.

In the end, as history records, Latham and his like failed to redirect the juggernaut. The Corporation survived in the end by importing a tobacco baron, Louis Gerstner, to wield the surgeon's knife. The treatment was essentially financial by then and desperately necessary. The opportunity to change the Corporation by way of technological innovation had vanished by that time.

Latham's last few years with the IBM Corporation were instructive. By that stage he was engaged, on a semi-formal basis, with a wide range of leading-edge projects, working with sponsors from all over the worldwide IBM Corporation. But his employment was still officially with the original Office Products management bureaucracy in the United Kingdom. They had never really understood Latham. His final months bore an uncanny resemblance to the exit of Michael Phillips from the Bank of California (see below). Once Phillips lost the protection of his boss, Bob Person, his corporate enemies nailed him. First he lost his sponsor, then he lost his job. He said: 'Bob Person understood and could explain what I was trying to do in terms other bankers could comprehend.'

Michael Phillips and the widows

Gifford Pinchot, the inventor of the 'intrapreneur' (internal entrepreneur) concept, tells the story of Michael Phillips, then Director of Market Research for the Bank of California. Phillips was an 'Imo', encouraged and protected by Bob Person, one of the bank's top team. Phillips subjected all the bank's personal investment products to an exhaustive market analysis and discovered that one particular customer group not only produced a disproportionate profit for the bank but did so for minimal marketing or account management effort. This group was the widows—some of them very wealthy indeed; all of them bereft or grieving; most of them unused to managing money. Phillips concluded that not only were the Bank of California's widows getting a raw deal—all the widows in America were. Phillips set his sights on that wider market. His idea was to offer them an easy-to-understand personal account in the form of a special Certificate of Deposit, which would help them to take responsibility for their own affairs and, more important, to earn substantially more from their investments.

Like all the leaders celebrated in these pages, Michael Phillips began by immersing himself in the data. Gifford Pinchot continues the story:

> He was motivated by a personal ideal: to provide a better savings vehicle for older people. As the head of marketing research, he had assembled groups of older bank customers with substantial savings and asked them to discuss their investment needs. Many of them said they had heard of Certificates of Deposit, but they knew very little about CDs except that they were a desirable form of investment but suitable only for investors more sophisticated than themselves.
>
> Beginning with the typical tasks of his job, Michael had to determine why these customers were putting their money in 4% savings accounts instead of 5.25% CDs. He discovered from his market research groups that customers were puzzled by the term 'certificate', since in most cases the actual certificate or bankbook-type of record had been replaced by a ledger entry held somewhere in the bowels of the bank. Furthermore, the fact that CDs were only sold in large denominations such as $10 000 intimidated many potential customers, including many who had savings accounts far larger than that.
>
> But Michael did not stop with discovering these facts, as his job description warranted. He went much further in his research. There was, he found out, no legal or operational reason why Certificates of Deposit could not be offered in small denominations; rather, the intimidating Certificates were based on a longstanding tradition in commercial banking that Michael abhorred—that dealing with individual customers was unprofitable and somehow beneath the dignity of a proper banker. Michael, on the other hand, saw consumer Certificates of Deposit as an opportunity to better serve customers and attract substantial deposits by offering them a higher return. His idea was simple: to create and advertise a Certificate of Deposit in small denominations ($500).

At this point he came into collision with the bank's senior management cadre. They patiently explained that the primary task of a business is to widen, not to narrow, the profit margin. If the widows were complaisant and ignorant, that represented a marketing opportunity—the task was to extract *more* from them. This is the binary model in pure form: if I gain, you lose! Phillips argued that the bank's focus was too narrow and too short-term (Imos always argue like this), and that it was locked into the existing customer base. Phillips had his eye on the Widows of America—no less. The task, as he saw it, was to create an entirely new product which broke all the rules by bringing very substantial benefit to an exploited group.

The story has a sort of happy ending. In the end Phillips won the argument, the new product was created and marketed, and the Bank of California went on to manage a chunk of the investment income of widows right across the United States. This *ternary* (wide-view, long-term) vision transformed the fortunes of the bank in just a few years (by transforming the fortunes of widows). By really looking after the customers the bank looked after its own interests, as a by-product. But defeat at the hand of the upstart Phillips rankled with some of the binary heavyweights. Three months after Bob Person (Phillips' sponsor and protector) left the company, they sacked Michael Phillips.

In order to survive in IBM, Latham also needed such a sponsor. In fact Gifford Pinchot argues that the corporate survival of the 'Imo' depends on an array of talents, probably located in different people:

- The inventor: the person who really understands the new product or service but not how to make a business of it.
- The 'intrapreneur': the person who focuses on the business realities but who may, in enthusiasm, neglect the realities of organisational politics.
- The sponsor: the person who gives tactical advice to the intrapreneur and removes organisational barriers.
- The protector: the very high-level sponsor who approves and protects but who rarely meets the intrapreneur.

Latham's problem, as a quintessential Englishman of higher social status than his immediate bosses, was that he needed protection from another culture, IBM being in essence as American as blueberry pie. When he ran out of protection, he was sunk.

With the decline of IBM's fortunes, the United Kingdom Office Products management needed to 'lose' seven managers. As they didn't really understand what Latham was up to, they didn't really value his eccentric gifts. Latham went on a skiing holiday and broke a leg. In recuperation he received a message that on his return he was to report to one of the branch offices as a common or garden salesman: the role in which he had entered the Corporation twenty years before. He was then fifty-five years of age. He never went back; all that remained was to brief his lawyers.

Most of the corporations I deal with would prefer to believe that this kind of thing could not happen today, at least in *their* corporations. In Chapter 1, I drew attention to firms like Hewlett-Packard, Herman Miller and ABB, where neglect of cleverness is less likely. But the problem remains with the broad-band capability, or lack of it, up the managerial line. Even if you institute policies and programs designed to root out creativity and protect the creative, you must still be limited by executives who cannot grasp what they are being told by junior 'Imos'. In the end, the core task for intelligent leaders is to ensure that the higher you go in the hierarchy the smarter the people—right across the Gardner repertoire of intelligences. How this is achieved is addressed in Chapter 14.

11

Boys, girls, role models and parenting

The alert reader will have noticed that the heroes celebrated thus far (with the exception of Imo and Mary Parker Follett) have all been men. That is partly a function of my narrow exposure to intelligent leadership in Australia in the last few years. In the course of re-searching this book, I have now started to penetrate a much wider society of interesting leaders, especially in science and technology, politics, and also amongst women. Any new edition should be enriched by a wider and deeper *dramatis personae*. At any rate, it is vitally important to expose the subtle differences between the *char-acteristic* leadership styles of women and men. The overlap is huge, but the differences are still important. Howard Gardner, whose theory of multiple intelligences underpins much of my argument about the nature of intelligence, suggests that there are few sex differences amongst the 'intelligences' except for the spatial intelligence and, notably, the interpersonal intelligence. This is captured nicely by the title of a conference session late in 1996: *Why Men Never Listen and Women Can't Read Maps!*

The suggestion that sex-based behavioural differences are inbuilt has to be considered in the context of special environmental factors.

Lyn Carlsmith, a research student at Harvard in the 1960s, came up with one of those hunches that precede really interesting research. Thinking in much the same inductive way as Robert Keep, she got a *feeling* about the cohort of young men passing through the university at that time. She thought there was something odd, and unusually nice, about them; but why? She then carried out an exceedingly elegant piece of research which required no research protocols, or interviews, or surveys, or complicated analysis.

Her main achievement was to grasp that World War II represented a kind of research goldmine. These young men had spent their infancy in the first years of the war. Some of them had had a 'normal' upbringing in the sense that their fathers (for one reason or another) did not go away to war. Others had lost their fathers for the duration, and some of them permanently. This was an abnormal kind of upbringing.

Carlsmith's research approach was simplicity itself: she went back to the records of the Scholastic Aptitude Test that all the students had completed in order to get into Harvard in the first place. She extracted their verbal and mathematical scores (in those days, the pattern almost invariably was that men excelled in the mathematical and women in the verbal). She divided the students, all of whom were male, into two groups: those whose fathers had been away for at least two years during the subjects' infancy and had then permanently returned; and those, from matched social backgrounds, whose fathers had remained at home.

The outcome was striking, and pretty much as Carlsmith expected. In the 'father-present' group, eighteen out of twenty students had the typical male bias towards the mathematical part of the SAT but only seven out of twenty in the 'father-absent' group did so (see Figure 15). These young men were (so far as their test profiles suggested) very like the bold, confident, slightly androgynous young women you find in the top American women's colleges—the kind of young women who tend to have been regarded throughout their lives as omnicompetent by their fathers and/or to have grown up in tomboyish friendship and rivalry with a raft of brothers. They are intelligent young women with the same cocky self-assurance as young men and they tend to do very well in their careers.

What this suggests is that, without too much social engineering, it ought to be possible to produce young men with much of the

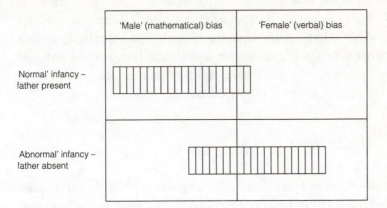

Figure 15   Lyn Carlsmith's Harvard Class of '64: Scholastic Aptitude Test Scores

> Lyn Carlsmith's wonderfully simple and elegant study of Harvard undergraduates suggests that if infant boys are brought up without male role models (either the parental or the peer-group kind), but with very positive female role models, some thirteen out of every twenty of them will end up thinking very like the best and most resourceful women.

subtlety, sensitivity and guile of 'typical' young women and, at the same time, to produce young women with the same assertiveness and risk-taking capabilities as 'typical' young men. Such young men and women are already very similar to each other and generally work and get on well together. The genetic differences remain in the behaviour patterns, but they don't get in the way of effectiveness. Viewed in this light, the single-sex school may be a mixed blessing. Of course, mixed schools need to keep an eye out for the special needs of both girls and boys. *Elements* of quarantine will always be required but, overall, the output today of the very best mixed schools is impressively ahead of that part of its parental generation educated in purdah. They will be *much better* managers and many more of them will be women who really know how to relate to the best kinds of men.

By the way, the Carlsmith generation was my cohort and her findings ring true for me and, I think, for most of my male and female contemporaries. It was and is an unusual generation, containing sensitive men like Clive James (whose father was killed on *the way home* from the war) and tough and resourceful women like Germaine Greer. It is a great pity that nobody, so far as I am aware, has conducted a similar study of the young women of that generation. If you read Greer's poignant book, *Daddy, We Hardly Knew You*, you get an intimation of what it must have been like to be brought up during a war by an omnicompetent mother and to see that mother reduced to relative impotence by the return of a less than perfect man. It was mostly that generation that produced the great feminist tracts.

THE TROUBLE WITH BOYS

In the next section I touch on the trouble with girls (or female executives)—the natural reaction against dominance by male gangs. Sometimes female dogmatism may seem to be the only defence against collective male strength. If it is true that boys brought up solely by women have a wider repertoire of 'intelligences' than the average, does this tell us anything useful? What about all those little boys officially in the 'father-present' state who hardly ever see their fathers? Since I came upon the work of Howard Gardner, I have discovered that one of the best ways of getting through to the real concerns of chief executives and other very senior male managers is to take them through the theory of 'multiple intelligences'. A good many of them are gripped because they themselves have had to overcome poor academic performance in order to demonstrate their prowess in making things happen. Others are gripped because they are worried sick about the behaviour and capabilities of their own children—especially their sons (whom *they* hardly ever see).

There is not much doubt that *criminality* in society is directly associated with the Y-chromosome. Most of the inhabitants of jails are men. About 90 per cent of indictable offences are the responsibility of men. Around sixty young men are incarcerated for every one young woman. Are we dealing with genetics here, or with social conditioning? What are the implications of all this for developing effective (i.e. useful) leadership? In their fascinating book *Demonic Males* Wrangham and Peterson point out that, whilst many animals routinely kill, in the interests of survival, only humans and chimps (our nearest cousins) actively *seek* the *death* of prey, apparently for its own sake. If so, it must have been usefully adaptive in the past. They describe how apes will gang up on individuals with positional power in order, not merely to depose them, but to tear them limb from limb in a form of extended torture. Once the new order is installed and, in due course, another realignment of power, another episode of torture will ensue. It is horribly reminiscent of boardroom power struggles—just bloodier. Out on the street, amongst the gangs of young men, you get the blood too! We should bear in mind that it is only about 130 000 years ago that we achieved 'full' humanity as *Homo sapiens sapiens,* a mere moment in evolutionary time.

If we consider the social conditioning of the typical young modern male, it amounts to a predicament. Very few men are closely associated with the boy. He may catch glimpses of men at work, doing whatever it is that men do, and his father (if any) may swoop down and throw him excitingly in the air, but that is usually a fleeting thrill. His sister, on the other hand, is much more likely to get to observe adult women at useful work, at first hand and continuously. For her, the future is not so far away. By the age of around three, little girls know that they will probably grow up to be (inter alia) mothers and homemakers, and they know roughly what that entails. To a 'liberated' female adult, homemaking may seem limiting but, to a three-year-old, it must be reassuringly comprehensible. By three, girls are behaving like women; practising being *grown up.* The outstanding entrepreneurs in this book, men and women, mostly got to watch a parent *making something happen* at first hand. The experience gives a good sense of process—how the world can be improved or transformed by concentrated human effort.

If boys try out copying their mothers, they will be told that boys don't do that. If they cry and ask to go home, that isn't on either. Angela Phillips (in *The Trouble with Boys*) comments:

> Perhaps the reason why so many boys run around and shout a lot is because they don't know what else to do. They don't have a complex role to inhabit, or a joint understanding of an imaginary world in which to play together. The only thing they know about what it is to be male is that it isn't like being a girl. They start to define their whole sense of themselves, not in a positive sense as 'like' someone but in a negative sense, as unlike the people who surround them.

Phillips points out that boys therefore confront a vacuum; they *have* to find out, somehow, what it is to be male (as opposed to non-female). In the absence of satisfactory adult role models, they pick it up from male peers, mainly in groups:

By the time they are seven, the coercive process of masculinisation is well under way. Boys mercilessly tease those who do not conform to the group idea of masculinity. Those who don't fit will be edged out in order to create a clearer idea of what it is to be a proper boy.

Pretty soon, in the early teens, the prospect of violence looms. If you don't fit in, you have to find a way of avoiding trouble. A substantial majority of the great comedians (Clive James was no exception) are clever and sensitive people who grew up surrounded by toughness and who coped by taking on the role of class clown. The most dangerous kids are those who have been excluded by peer pressure and who are desperate for reinclusion in the group. They will do just about anything, however criminal and violent, to earn approval. Once 'toughness' and the art of male-bonding is learned, those at the top of the tree can go on to bully other people in the business world. Those at the bottom, like Spansky and his chums, will very likely swell the ranks of the jailbirds.

Of course there is more to this than social conditioning and the absence of male role models. We have only to look at the completely natural patterns of young male behaviour amongst our primate cousins. Lionel Tiger pointed out a long time ago (in *Men in Groups*) that the all-male hunting band far preceded the evolution of our big brains a couple of million years ago. The hunting band had the capacity to act *as* a brain, even if its individual members were still relatively primitive. The hostile takeover clearly offers more than financial excitement and satisfaction to human predators. All the evidence suggests that hostile takeovers usually benefit the few at the expense of the many. The evidence suggests that *both* firms involved frequently underperform afterwards. The business community as a whole, and hence the nation, may be weakened as a result. But the predators' leaders never had higher-order aims in mind, just short-term aggrandisement, like hunters slavering for red meat. If business leaders were less primitive (better brought up?) maybe business as a whole might flourish. The best leaders for today need their primitive instincts, because it can get nasty at times, but they also need a longer and wider view of the future. Starting off as a boy may not be the ideal preparation for that.

In the meantime, the new consensus is that successful *nations* have business communities in which *trust* coexists with competitiveness.

With trust, you can set about building and sustaining long-term businesses with valuable purposes and outputs. If the price of success is the hostile takeover, why bother with building anything—become a raider! When I first adopted the terms 'binary' and 'ternary', an American colleague, conscious of the primitive psychology of the takeover, commented: 'You might as well talk about *raiding* and *building*.' It comes to much the same thing. Raiding is binary, because all that really matters is winning. Building is ternary, because the relationships are much less important than the objective or ideal.

'THE TROUBLE WITH WOMEN IS THEY DON'T GIVE PUTTS!'

I am indebted to Robert Joss (Chief Executive, Westpac) for this quote from one of his senior managers. The statement could mean a number of things, from 'women are inflexible' to 'women have high standards'. The point is that it was a man, and a senior one, who said it.

For the reader unfamiliar with golf, an explanation is in order. There is a convention in friendly golf of 'giving' a short (say half-metre) putt on the green, the last half-metre the ball has to travel in order to fall in the hole. These short putts can be 'knee-tremblers'— they should be easy but if much hangs on them (like a substantial wager) the distance can seem much greater. When you are given a putt, you simply pick up your ball and treat it as if it had been holed-out. In an informal way, you are now in debt to your opponent. Your opponent is entitled to expect you to give him an equally tricky putt later on. The emphasis is on *him*—this is generally a male-bonding kind of ritual.

When Robert Joss passed on this excellent quote (in the course of an interview for Amanda Sinclair's major study, published as *Trials at the Top*, about women's difficulty with the 'glass ceiling') my immediate reaction was: 'They don't give putts in the US Open either!' In other words, if you are engaged in a serious, international competition for big stakes (like the modern business world), there is absolutely no room for sloppiness. It may well be that the female executive's uncompromising approach irks her male colleagues, but it might be just the ticket for the serious business of satisfying foreign customer requirements. My guess is that when senior businesswomen methodically cross the *t*'s and dot the *i*'s, they remind men of their own mothers, or bossy sisters, or strict school teachers or (worse) their wives.

The best thing about the putt-giving statement is that it underlines the reality that *both* sexes have characteristic strengths and weaknesses. That is not to argue that no men share the feminine weaknesses or that no women share the masculine weaknesses; simply that each sex has its special and distinctive pattern of behaviour. Whether that behaviour represents a strength or a weakness depends entirely on the *context*. I believe that the male reaction: 'women don't give putts!' tells us something important about both the strengths *and* weaknesses of women in big and responsible jobs. If women are serious about breaking through the 'glass ceiling' it will be useful to *learn* from this.

Let us go back those 130 000 years—to the point of pre-history where we have become recognisably *homo sapiens sapiens*—upright posture, big brain and all. The men are bigger and stronger than the women and there is a clear role specialisation which has proved valuable for adaptive natural selection. Those with the capacity to flick the wrist will be launching lethal projectiles at animal prey. No woman can do to a 160 gram cricket ball what a professional male cricketer can—send it seventy metres on an almost flat trajectory at bullet-like speed. Genetically-speaking, the trick is located in the mechanism of wrist, elbow and shoulder. Women can throw, but they can't throw like *that*.

Because hunting is necessarily a group effort, especially if you are slower or weaker than some of your prey, then the task has to be performed according to the implicit understandings within groups of stalking men. In the heat of the hunt, there is no time for elaboration. Anybody puzzled by the atavistic glee of corporate raiders mounting an ambush on other unsuspecting businessmen, need look no further than the hunting band. That is the genetic endowment of the human male. Any sympathy for the prey would be counter-productive. The activity hardly requires thought—mainly high adrenalin levels and a very deep-seated capacity to work together on a limited, dangerous task. You could predict, however, that the hunting males would acquire highly developed *spatial* skills; the capacity to 'see' the terrain as if from above.

Meanwhile, back in the cave, there is a lot of elaboration. There is actually a form of *society* which involves a certain amount of diversity. After all, there are the relatively elderly and the young, and the possibility for communicating in a different and more complicated way. As language develops, the talking is bound to be about the system and its survival requirements. The presence of a relatively settled society or community means the development of *empathy* between people. This doesn't mean that the hunters will lack empathy, simply that their relationships are likely to be of a different, and less sentimental kind. The physical requirement for specialisation by sex (reinforced by genetic coding over hundreds of thousands of years) means that men and women are characteristically good at different things. The skill overlap is substantial but the differences remain.

The shift to organised farming, our species' first chance to share labour between the sexes, occurred a mere 300 generations ago—a fleabite in evolutionary terms and far too short a time for men to adapt to the new circumstance. The modern bureaucracy is the product of the last couple of hundred years. We haven't got the hang of it yet. We may be in the process of disinventing it.

There is a point to this speculative tour around our pre-history. It is that the evolutionary process is unimaginably gradual. Our ideas may be modern but our instinctive behaviours, as men and women, are programmed and very slow to change. Our problem is that, as a species, we have got control of too many of the environmental forces which used to control us. We are changing our circumstances more quickly than we can evolve. The characteristic behaviours of the stronger sex used to be functional for species survival, supported by the women. It now looks very much as though the characteristic behaviours of men might be our undoing. Once it becomes possible to apply technology to the social control of big populations, then Saddam Hussein's big brain becomes a liability. Because his father treated him like a dog, his behaviour is no more 'advanced' than that of his prehistoric ancestors.

The most important problems which beset us now are *relationship* problems. It doesn't really matter all that much whether or not the Hubble space telescope sends back terrific pictures of deep space, if our own world falls apart in the meantime. Most of the men celebrated in these pages are fiddlers and tinkerers. They happen also to be charming and persuasive, but their special strength lies in the ability to fool around with materials (aluminium, currency movements, student throughput systems, computer peripheral devices, etc.) in such a way as to produce wonderful outcomes. As Chapter 2 suggests, they have a *spatial* way of overviewing complex phenomena. It is no great surprise that the seminal work of Mary Parker Follett died the death, because the core of her understanding lay in human relationships. The powerful men surrounding her clearly had difficulty in grasping her meaning fully. In the sixty years since her death, a succession of famous male thinkers and writers has been slowly struggling to catch up with her. My own 'ternary' notion is merely a warmed-up (masculine/spatial) variant on her 'law of the situation'.

This is a well-known psychological experiment which demonstrated the truth of all this charmingly. The setup was an ante-room, scattered with various toys and devices. Young children of both sexes were asked to wait in this room for the experiment to begin. They didn't know it, but the experiment had begun already. The boys fell on the toys and proceeded to manipulate or disassemble them, demonstrating fierce concentration. Communication was limited to the odd monosyllabic grunt, always to another boy and always about the device in hand. The girls completely ignored the toys, and the boys, and created an instant society. Within five minutes of arrival, all the girls knew an astonishing amount about all the other girls. The speed and richness of the exchanges was stunning.

Now of course there may be women as captivated by tinkering as these boys, and men as sociable as these girls, but it isn't the norm. The leaders celebrated in these pages seem to me to be people with a very wide repertoire of behaviours and skills. Clifford, Keep, Coman and Latham all come across as pretty butch, but with their 'feminine' skills intact. Mary Parker Follett, Noel Waite and Liz O'Shaughnessy (the stories of these latter two are still to come) are entirely feminine but their useful 'masculine' skills have helped them to exercise leadership. All of these people appear to spread right across the Gardner 'multiple intelligences'. If we could determine what caused that, we might be able to replicate the process in families and schools.

I said above that the characteristic behaviours of men and women are neither good nor bad; it depends entirely on the situation. I hinted also that women might have something to learn from the 'women don't give putts' anecdote. There is a clue here, I believe, as to the avoidable mistakes that female executives make. I am thinking now

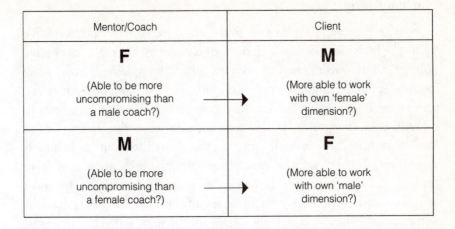

Mentor/Coach	Client
F (Able to be more uncompromising than a male coach?) ➡	**M** (More able to work with own 'female' dimension?)
M (Able to be more uncompromising than a female coach?) ➡	**F** (More able to work with own 'male' dimension?)

Figure 16   Executive mentoring: male/female synergy

As the fashion for one-to-one executive mentoring and coaching develops, it turns out that some of the most effective mentors to very senior men are resourceful women *of a certain age*. And vice versa. It may be that, within the security of the mentoring relationship, the yin and the yang come together harmoniously.

of women who want to succeed in conventional, large organisations. I am not preaching to the increasing number of outstanding women who are turning their backs on such organisations because they are bored by the childishness of their male colleagues' behaviour. *Trials at the Top*, which both male and female big company executives should read, charts this development admirably.

However, the big corporations are going to have to find some way of retaining the most talented women (the ones most likely to lose patience with the executive 'boys'). Otherwise the monoculture at the top will lose creativity, along with its diversity. Altering the group behaviour of the boys is the obvious place to start, but isolated female executives probably also need a modicum of mentoring. Noel Waite has specialised in providing this service for female executives over many years, but there is also an argument for the kind of mentoring provided by an older wiser *man*. Sometimes the male mentor can adopt a more uncompromising stance than another female. The same thing works in reverse; a remarkable number of the most trusted and successful mentors of male European chief executives are women. It works for the same reason—the female mentor can be more uncompromising (tougher, if you like) than another man would dare.

The fatal flaw

Now, with trepidation, we come to the characteristic female executive 'failing'. It is less serious than the characteristic male executive failings about which senior women often complain. These male failings generally include crude competitiveness, rampant careerism, unmanaged aggression and a loss of identity in the rugby-scrum mentality of the group. If the typical male executive failing is the loss of identity and integrity, the typical female executive failure is *dogmatism*. I have seen a number of promising female executive careers self-destruct on this particular rock. It is one of the most common and important presenting symptoms in role consultations with senior women. It is the main blind-spot amongst powerful women and it automatically causes a failure to learn. It follows, if you *know* you are right, there cannot be anything to learn.

This is entirely understandable, if not entirely excusable. If you are a lone, or nearly lone woman surrounded by slapdash men, it will be necessary to cross the *t*'s and dot the *i*'s. If the men are locked in 'groupthink', the woman may be excluded and disempowered. As she cannot sup at the well of male group power, she must derive her strength from somewhere else. It is as if she is forced to say: 'All right, if I can't be strong with the group (and I can't) I'm going to be *right*!' I would guess that the executive quoted by Robert Joss of Westpac might have been reacting against this form of dogmatism. Women who have been forced into this position throughout their lives can find it very difficult to start 'giving putts' at work, after so much struggle. That is why the off-line mentoring approach is more likely to be helpful. In that setting, it is possible to consider the possibility of being wrong and it is possible to 'unpack' situations which have cropped up at work and which have put the woman under pressure.

In Britain, Margaret Thatcher is regarded by many people as the archetype of the bossyboots woman who never acknowledges, because she never *registers*, that she may be wrong. John Major, her successor, got into trouble in her eyes because he (in her words) 'lacks an unswerving belief that you have to be right!' As a matter of fact, John Major *is* wrong rather much of the time, in the view of most Brits, but at least he appears to be aware that such things are possible. Thatcher was in the habit of tapping her forehead and saying: 'I have a filing system here—I always remember things correctly!' Female

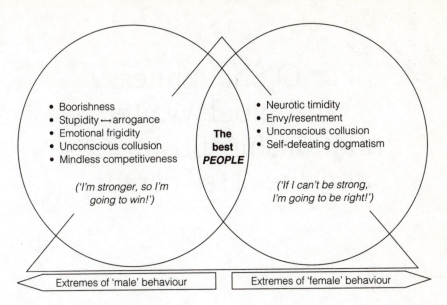

- Boorishness
- Stupidity — arrogance
- Emotional frigidity
- Unconscious collusion
- Mindless competitiveness

('I'm stronger, so I'm going to win!')

The best PEOPLE

- Neurotic timidity
- Envy/resentment
- Unconscious collusion
- Self-defeating dogmatism

('If I can't be strong, I'm going to be right!')

Extremes of 'male' behaviour

Extremes of 'female' behaviour

Figure 17   The best people

The worst (most boorish and untrustworthy) men and the worst (most neurotic and dogmatic) women have a kind of *modus vivendi*. It is called the war of the sexes and everybody understands the rules. The *best* of both sexes are very similar to one another, as the illustration shows, and don't need to fight at all. They ought to marry each other more frequently than they seem to.

executives in Britain tend to disown Margaret Thatcher, on the ground that she is really a man (because of her competitiveness and aggression). In truth, she was the quintessential dogmatic woman. Her failure *ever* to give a putt weakened Britain's position in the world, especially in Europe.

Obviously the giving, or not, of putts is a behavioural variable, partly independent of the presence, or not, of intellectual firepower. There are a few dogmatic bright people and there are many dogmatic stupid people. There are more of the latter, for obvious reasons. I remarked earlier on that arrogance and stupidity are different sides of the same coin because the one causes the other, and vice versa. The need is for female leaders who combine the best of male and female—tough cookies with hearts of gold, and never prey to self-destructive dogmatism. As we move forward to Waite and O'Shaughnessy, Figure 17 sums up the overlap between the sexes.

12

Liz O'Shaughnessy and Noel Waite: relationship businesses and the 21st century

This chapter is built around two further mini-biographies. Both of the subjects are contemporary Australian women. Their achievements are separately interesting but it is the connections between them that concern us most. Their businesses create value through *relationships* and, characteristically, one helped to launch the entrepreneurial career of the other. Helping is the very essence of human relationships. Their stories provide the perfect opportunity to introduce two interlinked themes.

1. *Tomorrow's Company*
The relationship company is *healthy,* in the sense that its network of relationships within and without the organisation create a climate of *trust.* This, in turn, acts as a kind of antibody against environmental turbulence. The 'Tomorrow's Company' initiative, described here, works on the proposition that business analysts always get it wrong because they use too narrow a scoresheet for assessing organisational health. They usually let down the farsighted shareholder by dealing only with relatively short-term financial elements, leaving out the elements that women tend to understand intuitively, and which *bring about* durable, long-term success.

2. Art and the entrepreneur

One of the characteristics of newly-founded organisations is that they are still *attached* to their original purposes—they have not yet become merely self-serving devices for looking after the well-being and careers of their members or shareholders. They have this in common with artistic enterprise which, at its best, is always concerned with the *object*, never with peripheral aims like money or success. In one sense these two female entrepreneurs are *artists* and the intriguing thing about them is their respective *methods*. This offers a chance to reflect on the way that outstanding artists, sportspeople and business leaders develop their unique *methods* of operation, and how this is the real source of the respect and admiration they attract as 'leaders'.

In Chapter 1, Imo the little monkey symbolised the difficulty that ingenious women have in making their presence felt in a patriarchy. In Mary Parker Follett, we have a near-perfect example of an (American) intellectual leader who achieved prominence for a time but who dropped from sight for want of a cohort of other reinforcing and supporting women. In order to illustrate the above themes, I wanted to highlight ingenious female 'Imos' who had confronted the usual difficulties and surmounted them through intelligent and timely mutual support. There are a great many outstanding Australian women from whom I could have chosen—in business, education, the sciences and the arts. My own great-great-grandmother, Georgiana McCrae, one of the first women in Melbourne (she arrived, accompanied by her four infant sons, in February 1841) and certainly amongst the most capable, is an excellent example of great talent underused. Brenda Niall's brilliant biography of Georgiana is required reading for anybody interested in Gardner's theory of multiple intelligences. Georgiana combined the gifts of an artist and musician with the fluency of a linguist, with the skills of a society networker/hostess, with the practicality of a navvy.

I leave the reader to pursue Georgiana. The two women I have chosen are linked by the fact that the older provided transformational mentoring for the younger at a crucial time. The separate achievements of each of them are remarkable but it is relevant that the contact was a generous, *helping* contact. When Liz O'Shaughnessy needed to break away from a (financially successful) career that was destroying her personal morale, Noel Waite was on hand to provide the kind of acute observation and advice that she has supplied to hundreds of Australian women. Liz O'Shaughnessy's business (Puddings On The Ritz) really dates from that transformational moment. It is a new business, so its inclusion here represents a calculated risk—the same risk Tom Peters ran when he created *In Search of Excellence* around real business cases. Some of his companies, my old *alma mater* IBM amongst them, slid into decline soon afterwards. By including these two women in the text I can make a double point about the distinctive kinds of businesses that women generally run, and about the ways that women can provide support and advice to each other.

Just as Bob Clifford's defining moment was the destruction of a bridge, you could say that Liz O'Shaughnessy's moment was the reinvention of the Goolgowi campfire pudding, which first saw the light of day in the 1830s. It is a succulent confection of breadcrumbs, vinefruit and bananas. Making it just right for airline and other bulk catering meals is the tricky part. By the end of 1996 something approaching a *million* Goolgowi puddings had been consumed on (mainly) Qantas and Ansett flights. Every single pudding was essentially *handmade* with tender loving care. At the time of writing, United Airlines, Air Vietnam and Air Caledonie have joined the select Goolgowi club. The Goolgowi has now been joined by a range of other puddings, all made to the same exacting standards and using similar high-quality, natural ingredients. Hospitals, hamper companies and gourmet restaurateurs are now in the Puddings On The Ritz loop, plus the Diabetes Foundation of Australia. The hospitals, such as the Royal Melbourne and the Royal Womens, get a special pricing deal because Liz O'Shaughnessy believes that really good food is spiritually nurturative for the convalescent.

The big stores—Coles-Myer/Grace Brothers, Daimaru and David Jones—have now joined the club and the corporate gift market, based on personalised packaging, is expanding exponentially. The export market beckons, based on the logic that Australia has a huge advantage in the quality and range of its natural foodstuffs. Puddings On The Ritz simply adds value by deriving classy niche products from the very best natural ingredients and packaging them with stylish, theatrical flair. All this has been achieved by a workforce of talented and dedicated youngsters ('CES kids') selected by Liz O'Shaughnessy from the ranks of the disadvantaged or unemployed. Why? Because she knows what it means to have a tough time of it as a kid and she likes to help. The Puddings On The Ritz philosophy is to 'employ long-term jobless young people and those from disadvantaged circumstances, and to provide support, encouragement, friendship and training in every aspect of our business in a nurturing work environment'. The company is 'committed to the youth of Australia'.

Waite Consulting, Noel Waite's organisation, is obviously a 'relationship business'. Its core business is in executive search, advertised recruitment, vocational and career counselling, outplacement and training. Even here, a major part of this highly successful business arose out of informal and unpaid counselling. As Noel Waite puts it: 'Women gravitated to me for career advice . . . I had no intention ever of getting involved in "women's affairs".' In those early days, around 1980, the only money charge was for the psychologist for vocational appraisals. The relationships preceded the business. It is the ternary principle made flesh: the valued object causes the money-making—virtually as a by-product of that object. The business is financially more valuable because its underpinning values are human values. It is valuable because it is valued. By contrast, Puddings On The Ritz ought by rights to be a straightforward manufacturing and service business. After all, the output is steamed puddings, not advice or support. Yet, probably because it is run by a woman, the company *feels* like a relationship business. It is hard to say whether the human satisfactions or the puddings are the by-products. At risk of corniness, maybe a pudding made with love always tastes lovely.

TOMORROW'S COMPANY

Before we look in detail at the biographies of these two women, it will be useful to examine the *context* of their enterprises. All over the world there is a mounting critique of the kinds of organisations in both the public and private sectors (but especially the latter) that have served to dehumanise workers whilst, so far as possible, exploiting consumers. The feminist part of the critique avers that such organisations are natural outgrowths of masculine competitiveness, selfishness and aggression. What matters to the male power blocs at the top, according to the critique, is *success*, however achieved. Intelligent collaboration with other organisations, in order to better serve customers, is less exciting than the well-timed and stealthy corporate *ambush*. What the organisation actually *does* for a living, and how it may despoil its environment, is of no real concern, provided that the short-term economic indices hold up. If there is a choice between *keeping the team together* in order to serve new markets, or driving out cost (via attrition) to flatter the bottom line, the latter option nearly always wins.

Charles Hampden-Turner makes the important point that all this is short-sighted from the *national* perspective, even though it makes a kind of sense for the most powerful individuals in the *firm* in the short term. He points out that the smart countries are getting out of the pernicious trades. The Japanese are majoring in pollution prevention and control, because the world *has* to change its polluting ways. The Americans and the British, driven by the 'masculine' leaning to technology and short-term gain, have been slower to grasp this logic. British industry is disproportionately represented in slow-growing or declining sectors like drink, tobacco and armaments and underrepresented in fast-growing export sectors like information technology. As we come to terms with *needs* (as opposed to *wants*), the future will inevitably belong to the *useful*. You could argue, I suppose, that eating *nothing but* Goolgowi campfire pudding (or Boambee date and walnut pudding, or classic chocolate and macadamia pudding, or pear and ginger, or orange and zucchini, or chestnut and tokay, etc.) would mean an unbalanced diet, but we are not talking about serious side-effects here.

Before the move to puddings, Liz O'Shaughnessy was a senior executive and part-owner in the custom carpet manufacturing business. She was alienated not from the basic business but from the way it was run. Women often can't stomach the sort of practices that men embrace or turn a blind eye to. In the future that will be a plus, not a minus. If the purpose and outputs of a business are pernicious or merely frivolous, the presence of women in senior management may well be counterproductive. If they can't put aside their conscience, they will simply slow things up. But once you get into the virtuous businesses, where the rights of all the stakeholders are meticulously preserved, then the women start to look more attractive.

One of the most valuable initiatives in Europe in the last three years has been the 'Tomorrow's Company' project, based on the Royal Society of Arts. This project has been driven by a group of about thirty of the most forward-looking blue-chip firms, including IBM,

Guinness, Rothschilds, Coopers & Lybrand, Cadbury Schweppes and Natwest Bank Group. All of the firms were worried about their international competitiveness. They were worried also that they might have been measuring the *wrong variables* in their attempt to compete, or to catch up.

Their research makes interesting reading for anybody concerned about the waste of female talent in large corporations.

The four principal obstacles to effective competition were:

1. *The adversarial approach*

Coopers & Lybrand's 1994 Middle Market Survey indicated that 73 per cent of companies still believe they are doing the intelligent thing by screwing their suppliers to the floor. The idea of *managing* a relationship business (an idea first trawled by Mary Parker Follett back in the 1920s) has penetrated into the rhetoric of top management but not into the the practices of buyers. In the carpet business, Liz O'Shaughnessy was in charge of production and buying all the yarn. It is a very good place to learn about the continuities of *trust* upon which long-term success has to be built. The Puddings On The Ritz policy statement says: 'Our aim is to provide first-rate products, backed by superior service and expertise, and to create solid relationships with all customers, large and small. Each customer is important to us. Our commitment to excellence is reflected in our dedication to creating and maintaining personal relationships with our clients by means of active communication.' But in her final years in the carpet business she was under constant pressure to scrimp on the degree of yarn going into the product. She was deeply offended by the sloppiness but she also understood that, in the long run, it was inefficient and costly when they came up short on jobs. One of Bob Clifford's founding experiences was managing the buying process for the very first (fishing) boat. The Coopers study makes it pretty clear that the binary approach (I win, you lose) is alive and kicking, and the ternary (let's build a relationship that works for both of us long term—let's get it *right*!) is still pretty precarious, despite all the rhetoric.

2. *Complacency and ignorance of world standards*

The IBM/London Business School study showed that, whilst 2.3 per cent of the companies studied met the criteria for world-class operating standards, 73 per cent of those companies *believed* that they were world-class. We are back again to the giving of putts in male monocultures. When it comes to the standards required in the global marketplace, there is no room at all for sloppiness. It is where women's most irritating pernicketiness becomes a potential corporate strength, handled properly. Barings Bank, funnily enough, was always ternary at the top—a family company, wedded to good works and public spirit. The rot was in the sloppy, overoptimistic, shortsighted, greedy men in the middle, giving putts all over the place. After the collapse the new corporate director of human resources, Frank-Jan de Leeuw (a methodical Dutchman from the new owners), issued all 5000 employees with their *very first job descriptions*! And after the tragic sinking of the ferry *Herald of Free Enterprise*, with the loss of more than 100 lives, the independent Sheen Report on P&O European Ferries said: 'From top to bottom the body corporate was infected with the disease of sloppiness.' The inquest returned a verdict of unlawful killing but the judge declined to prosecute the directors for corporate manslaughter. More putts?

3. *Over-reliance on financial measures*

The Tomorrow's Company team observed tartly that of the eleven companies that topped *Management Today's* profitability league table between 1979 and 1989 four subsequently collapsed and another two fell to hostile takeovers. Their conclusion was that companies that rely solely on financial measures of success are exposing all the stakeholders to unwarranted risk. As yet, very few shareholders are putting the squeeze on the institutional investors and pension fund trustees to evaluate the whole 'frog'—not just the disembodied financial bits of the corporate 'bicycle'. In the end they will have to devise a 'balanced business scorecard' which will reflect *all* the variables that go to make up a healthy organisation. That will include, of course, the core values and purposes, the long-term reputation, and the hedging against the sort of risks that Barings and P&O fell prey to. We are talking about the 'relationship company'—a concept that Liz O'Shaughnessy and Noel Waite never needed to be taught. Of course, this kind of shortsightedness on the part of institutional investors is both stupid and a gross failure of *leadership*.

4. *Misunderstanding of directors' duties*

This is partly a question of the interpretation of company law. The issue is whether you regard directors as responsible solely to the *existing* register of shareholders, or whether they ought to be held accountable to *any* shareholders at any time in the future. If, as director, you acquiesce in going for the short-term buck, you are probably shortchanging tomorrow's investors and employees. You are almost certainly helping to weaken the long-term viability of the corporation as a national asset. Bob Garratt's wonderful new book *The Fish Rots from the Head* is required reading on the role and function of the company board and, in particular, the key role of the tough, nosy and independent non-executive director.

I have included the Tomorrow's Company material here because it connects directly with the findings of a report on the operation of 'glass ceilings' in Australian companies, *Trials at the Top*. Section 2.3 of that publication, on 'The Australian Executive Culture', reads like a paraphrase of the obstacles noted above:

- *I've lived and worked in the United States in several cities . . . This* [Australia] *is by far the most 'clubby', closed senior executive environment that I've seen. I guess all seems very comfy and very cosy . . .*
- *They were fed up with the sloppiness, the lack of a sense of opportunity, the lack of fairness, that maybe some sort of old boy values will get you ahead . . .*
- *It really is a club. It's a boys' club and they act like it's a boys' club so that manifests itself in the shady jokes, the whisperings, the jokes off to the side . . .*

Finally, on the matter of the adversarial culture of the big corporation (the reason why bright women want out), Amanda Sinclair writes:

The language and metaphor . . . are of physical combat. Being in meetings is described as 'taking body blows'. A new appointee to a Board is, with relish, expected to 'give the Board a bit of stick'. Potential entrants need to demonstrate their eligibility by 'pounding at the door . . . clawing at the door to get the visibility . . .' The environment is described as a 'rat race', populated by 'some men of limited ambition, some big rats'. An 'adversarial culture', the executive environment is widely portrayed as combative, where pain is publicly inflicted. In its best example, this was cast as 'well-directed aggression'; something close to thuggery and bully-boy tactics, at its worst.

PUDDINGS ON THE RITZ: LIZ O'SHAUGHNESSY'S RELATIONSHIP COMPANY

Happily, the Australian Institute of Management has already picked up on the Tomorrow's Company work. Under the leadership of Brian Hirsch, the AIM is taking a different and more independent tack—keeping the big firms at arm's length. Big Australian firms have come a long way in recent years but the *Trials at the Top* report suggests that most of them are still uncongenial for very clever women like Liz O'Shaughnessy—and for plenty of men as well. In fact, it is exactly this kind of male mindlessness that led, indirectly, to the creation of Liz O'Shaughnessy's business. She had started out at fifteen years of age as an insurance clerk with the T&G in Melbourne. That was in 1966. In those days the men were paid more for the same work and the women weren't even allowed to smoke at their desks. You may wonder whether the smoking at fifteen was a sign of rebelliousness—it was. O'Shaughnessy fought for, and won, the right for the women to smoke wherever they wished. It didn't do much for her popularity with the bosses. She moved on to a stuffy, Lloyds-associated insurer where it was even worse—deferential and grossly inefficient: 'I got sick and tired of doing the work of a broker, and covering for him whilst he was at lunch or the pub!'

The O'Shaughnessy career proceeded along these lines for the next few years, always shouldering an enormous burden of demanding work; never getting the full credit or reward for it. By the time she was twenty-one, and just married, she was working in PVC piping with a company that eventually became part of James Hardie Industries. It was, she confesses, 'an incredible learning experience—I was the GDB [general dogsbody]. I performed the task of office manager, receptionist/telephonist/secretary, accountant, purchasing officer, salesperson, order clerk, pay officer, packer and loader. But, more importantly, I was a dedicated and loyal assistant to my boss—I shared his vision!'

Furthermore, she and her boss had created the business from scratch; she had seen at first hand how a new business with a new kind of product grows and develops. I believe this is a crucial factor in the development of entrepreneurs. Bob Clifford had a similar experience (in the printing trade) at about the same age. Allan Coman created a realistic simulation of the same experience in his real-life projects at Bradfield College. When his students actually *go* to market it stops being a simulation, of course.

Predictably, Liz O'Shaughnessy became *too* useful to promote. She was performing an enormously complex task but she was never afforded a proper title. Furthermore, she was clearly dangerous—a 'power behind the throne'. Her condition for helping to set up a new operation (as an outcome of the James Hardie takeover) was to move to a consultancy contract. When her boss went overseas for a few weeks his replacement, jealous of Liz's power, 'relieved' her of her consultancy duties. She finally saw red. A friend mentioned that Noel Waite, head of a career development consultancy, had helped hundreds of men and women to convert bad experiences like this to good. Within a few weeks O'Shaughnessy was on her way to the carpet trade, courtesy of a transforming meeting with Noel Waite.

It will be obvious from all this that Liz O'Shaughnessy is 'bright'. Yet the narrative records her going out to work at fifteen years of age. There has to be a story, and there is. One defining moment was the sudden death of her mother (aged forty-two) when Liz was about to turn twelve. This precipitated a long separation from her father, who remarried shortly afterwards and 'chose' his new wife over his children. But even by then there were signs of an iron will. Her mother was desperate for her to go to MLC (Methodist Ladies College) as she had done herself. Liz won the scholarship but refused to go to MLC, preferring the downmarket high school in Heidelberg where her friends and brother were. She was grossly understretched there, but happy, and excelled in everything, including an astonishing array of sports. Even in primary school she had been a boisterous and disruptive class clown. The headmaster, ahead of his time, understood that her problem was boredom and secretly rewarded her with jelly beans (having officially admonished her on behalf of the teachers). He can take some of the credit for buoying up her morale at a time when her family placed all its gratitude with God.

Home life had always been an odd mixture. She was brought up in a stiflingly religious extended family of Methodist ministers and laypersons. Both her parents were trustees of local churches and her mother was the organist. Her father was originally a carpenter/builder from the Victorian country and her mother an English emigrant from the coalmining county of Durham. Her childhood memories are of spending all Sunday at church, of camp pie sandwiches for the 'alcos', of spraying Airwick over the back pews of the mission, of mattresses laid out for sleeping in the back of the station wagon on long-distance missionary work. Anyone who has read Jeanette Winterson's novel *Oranges Are Not the Only Fruit* will recognise the atmosphere. Liz O'Shaughnessy's mother had high expectations of her daughter and was an excellent soundingboard, but it was not a warm or nurturing relationship. Her mother's death virtually destroyed her faith in deities but not in the goodness of human nature.

Forced by her father to leave her beloved high school in order to decamp to another school which she hated from the start, she rebelled again. She had already won a Commonwealth Scholarship to support her studies for the Leaving/Matriculation years. Instead, desperately unhappy and unloved at home, she quit school halfway through her Leaving year, got a job, and also left home. Some of her experiences in the next year or so were of being 'exposed to moral danger', as the courts used to put it. Many of her similarly rootless friends and associates succumbed to 'drugs, booze, nightclubs, sex'. She was lucky to be more or less adopted by a loving couple in South Melbourne, both recovered alcoholics. For the first time in years, she felt safe and loved. Even in the dark days she felt 'totally conscious that some higher power was protecting and guiding me. I had absolute awareness that I was meant for better things and that what I was experiencing was just preparing me.' You can take those words to have a religious significance or—if the uses of *theatre* are central to the book you happen to be writing—you can take them as powerful evidence of the protection and inspiration that flow from imaginative *fantasy*. The main thing is that now Liz O'Shaughnessy is in a position to provide challenging employment for kids like herself thirty years ago—talented but probably unemployed or understretched or otherwise at risk.

Perhaps the best way to describe this caring process is to spell out what happened when Puddings On The Ritz went, overnight, from making 4000 puddings every four weeks for Qantas to making 3000 puddings *per day* for Ansett. Prior to that the business had been run as a weekend venture, parallel to the carpet business, until O'Shaughnessy walked out of that job. Like Bob Clifford, Liz O'Shaughnessy has a good feel for showbiz. Clifford says: 'My boats sell my boats!' Liz knows her puddings sell her puddings. Her very first order for 2000 puddings came, on the spot, as a result of setting up a display on the occasion of David Jones's establishing its Melbourne Food Hall. The display involved a theatrical combination of calico trimmings, parchment, silver platters and great dollops of King Island cream. On that occasion she had to pull out of the proffered contract because her company wasn't ready to produce in bulk. Shortly after, she invested in a brace of ex-hospital steamers. The Ansett order sprang from the Melbourne International Food Fair in September 1994, where 'Puddings' had laid on another jazzy, olde worlde display, in partnership with an antiques dealer. They won the best stand award.

This time they had just three weeks warning: 'The [name withheld to protect a household-name food] product has failed—you're on!' Liz took on the job with no equipment, no staff, no money. In three weeks she had to find and buy the right equipment for the contract, including the fundamentals like commercial dishwasher, vacuum sealing machine, electronic scales and, crucially, the banana processor for 750 kilos of bananas per week. She also had to work out appropriate packaging to preserve freshness, design and contract out the packaging work, source all the raw materials and, above all, find, hire and train the staff. She went straight to the Commonwealth Employment Service for three long-term unemployed young people.

In the end, the interviews were conducted *four days* before the first puddings had to be dispatched.

They did it. The first delivery of seventy-five cartons (7500 puddings) went out on time on 21 October 1994, the second seventy-five cartons three days later. The kids were working about twelve hours every day and Liz and her production supervisor (an ex-school-teacher) around twenty hours per day. Production went on twenty-four hours per day, including several minor contracts for different puddings in the runup to Christmas. There was a campbed in the office for those 'babysitting' the puddings. For those young people, this was best form of caring—an assumption that they could and would perform to a high standard, that they would care about the quality of the output, that they would work together responsibly and in harmony. (Naturally, this was Allan Coman's assumption about the youngsters who passed through Bradfield.) Of course, the big boss was there too, working harder than anybody. The entire Ansett contract was completed to specification, without a hitch.

Liz O'Shaughnessy says, and she means it: 'I really wanted to give these young people a chance. I felt that if someone were to believe in them, support them, not punish them, but encourage them to learn from their mistakes, that it would bring out the best in them. In a sense, the business is more about the social aspects than *about* making puddings. Puddings just happen to be the vehicle for the project!'

The debt of these young people is, indirectly, to Noel Waite. She was the person who originally hauled Liz O'Shaughnessy out of a dead-end situation into a new conception of enterprise. It is an example of one relationship business (a career development consultancy) instigating another. When any human being is empowered like this, the ripple effect is always palpable—the power multiplies itself. That is why schoolteaching is a noble profession.

ROBERT CLIFFORD AND LIZ O'SHAUGHNESSY—THE PARALLELS

It may seem far-fetched to connect the manufacture of big fast ferries with the making of puddings. But look more closely and you can see that the only important difference between these two (sex aside) is the old male/female split of tinkering and socialising. For Clifford, it is really the technical challenge that matters most, though he is an inspired 'man-manager'. For O'Shaughnessy, it is the people and the relationships that matter, though she is an inspired cook. The point is that similar conditions need to be in place in order to produce people like this who make things happen. The same is true for my other leaders but the parallels are more striking with these two:

- *The broad repertoire of 'intelligences'*
We should not be fooled by Clifford's dismal academic performance at school. When he had something important to read about, he got reading. Anyway, he could always do the mathematics, he just didn't know *how* he did it. Both were outstanding sportspersons (bodily-kinaesthetic and spatial intelligences) as well.

- *Observing the entrepreneur*
Clifford and O'Shaughnessy both got to watch an entrepreneur build a business (in printing and plumbing respectively) when they were young enough not to be too frightened of risk. This is a bit like toddlers skiing fearlessly fast—they never really learn fear properly. Allan Coman recreates these conditions at Bradfield College. It doesn't matter what the business is; it is the process of *formation* that matters. If you have lived through it once, it isn't frightening any more.

- *The content role model*
This seems to be a different kind of role model—the adult who engrosses you in a *particular* field or medium. Robert Clifford's father was originally a butcher, but when the family turned to fishing, father and son worked closely together in what was already established as the boy's medium—*water*. Liz O'Shaughnessy's maiden Aunt Adelaide (whom she adored) was an Army cook and 'keeper of the foods secrets'. Liz got to watch an expert making things happen, transforming materials into delicious finished products, displaying effortless *mastery*. It left a mark.

- *The ham*
Both of these creatives are essentially hams—using whatever razzamatazz it takes to promote their causes. I am not sure where theatricality falls amongst the Gardner 'intelligences' but I suggested, in writing about Robert Keep, that it must have something to do with 'spatial' and the 'intrapersonal' intelligences. Both of them are engrossed in their businessses (as actors) yet they both know when

and how to take up a position on the outside in order to present the business in the best possible light (as impresarios).

• *A plug for the ANZ Bank*

Perhaps this is a frivolous connection. I have already recounted how Tony Travers (manager of the Sandy Bay branch of ANZ in Tasmania) bankrolled Clifford's entry into the ferry business when all other bankers fought shy. When Liz O'Shaughnessy got the enormous (verbal) Ansett contract, nobody in banking and venture capital wanted to know, despite her track record, because she had not run her own business before. In the end, Andrew Wise of the St Kilda Road ANZ came through. I hope the ANZ and the other banks still have local managers authorised to exercise judgement in this way.

• *Moving on personally*

Significantly, very intelligent entrepreneurs usually have to leave somebody behind if they are to maintain momentum. Robert Clifford and Liz O'Shaughnessy parted with both a spouse and a business partner at the same key point in the course of their odysseys. Liam Hudson suggests that this is almost inevitable and that evidence suggests a strong correlation between the most revolutionary scientists, in terms of their breakthroughs, and the frequency of divorce. He says: 'An ability to breach the walls of convention in the intellectual sphere is associated . . . with the propensity to breach them in the personal sphere as well.' For the true entrepreneur, the enterprise is the first love. It takes a special kind of spouse to cope with this.

• *Moving on corporately*

At the time of writing, both Incat and Puddings On The Ritz are at growth thresholds. One is a medium-sized firm of less than a thousand people and the other is a small firm of less than ten. Nonetheless, the problem is the same—how to become a different *kind* of company and how, in particular, the leader can let go some of the direct control of everything. Of all the services available to SMEs (small to medium enterprises) there is usually insufficient attention paid to the nature of these threshold points of growth. At these points, the leader needs a particular kind of mentor. There are very few around who understand what kind of support is required; which brings us back to Noel Waite. I return to this important issue of mentoring in Chapter 14.

WAITE CONSULTING: NOEL WAITE'S RELATIONSHIP COMPANY

Liz O'Shaughnessy's story is typical of the hundreds, perhaps thousands, of people who have been influenced in a similar way by Noel Waite, AO. Waite Consulting is the ultimate relationship business. How the company evolved is worthy of study. The turning point of Noel Waite's career was a tragedy—the death of her husband, John Waite, and her own facial disfigurement—in a car crash in the United Kingdom. At that time she had four children back in Australia, aged from twelve to four. She spent months in hospital having her face brilliantly reconstructed by a team of surgeons who had worked under the great New Zealand plastic surgeon Archibald McIndoe. After those months she caught the ship home (flying was out because of her damaged sinuses), first buying a couple of wigs and a special makeup kit. On her arrival home all the kids recognised their mother: the surgeons had done a superb job. So good was the reconstruction that I had to be told about it after my first meeting with her, but that was much later.

The business, originally a personnel and vocational consultancy, nearly disintegrated without its founder, John Waite. Attempts were made to replace him but no one could quite pick up the reins. It became obvious that only Noel could do it, so she did; but the business fluctuated for six years because, as a single parent, she was *determined* that her children should come first. Then she married her present husband, Bruce Gandy, and seriously turned her mind back to the business. She kept her first married name, however, an unusual decision in those days. It made sense—the Waite name was a valuable asset. In the early, nerve-racking days, it was also reassuring to hide behind her androgynous given name, Noel. Like all the leaders celebrated here, she always understood that the *product* and all it stands for must be *centre stage*. The rest, as they say, is history. Waite Consulting steadily enhanced its reputation as a national (and increasingly international) leader in career development. The firm is now established in every Australian State and represented in four Asian countries. Canada, South Africa and possibly the United Kingdom are next.

In 1989–90, in the depths of the business downturn, Noel Waite took the bold step of shifting to central Melbourne and setting up the Waite Career Development Centre alongside the core search and management services practice. She became the first female president of the Australian Institute of Management in 1990 (and was reappointed in 1993). Also in 1993, in the Queen's Birthday Honours List, she was appointed Officer of the Order of Australia (AO) for 'service to business and management, particularly through the development of women in management'. Waite Consulting is doing something practical about the 'glass ceiling'. Its 'Top Steps' and 'Ultimate Step' programs are probably Australia's best hope of enriching the capacity of top management by bringing in well-prepared women of the very highest calibre. If you look at Noel Waite merely as a successful businesswoman, then you could adopt the binary (competitive) view of her success—after all, she has prevailed over most of the competition, winning the race to new market niches. If you look at her as an *intelligent leader,* then the view is ternary, because the *effect* of her success is to strengthen the cadres at the top of Australian management in the medium and long term. Waite Consulting gains too, of course, but that is a by-product.

Where did this remarkable woman come from and what were the shaping forces? At this stage the reader might expect me to refer back to Howard Gardner and the seven intelligences. Very well, then: Noel Waite is another broad-bander. Like Liz O'Shaughnessy, she was always 'bright' at school and loved it. As I noted earlier, she has perfect pitch and played piano from the age of three, and sang well enough to consider it as a career. Apart from schoolwork, her other passions were art and acting. This accounts for at least the verbal, musical, spatial and bodily/kinaesthetic 'intelligences'. Mostly, the family's aspirations for Noel centred on the music. In the end she became a very successful commercial artist, until fate took a hand. Like Liz O'Shaughnessy, she was visited by family tragedy at around twelve to thirteen years of age. Her mother nearly died from meningitis and lost her eyesight and her hearing for a substantial period (a tragedy for such a music lover). Noel took over management of the household—cooking, shopping and washing in the copper.

Noel Waite, 8 years

Like the other entrepreneurs, Noel Waite had an early exposure to mastery of a craft. Her father was a master tailor and her volatile and temperamental grandmother (with whom she lived through most of her Melbourne schooldays) was a gifted dress designer. The more you look at successful entrepreneurs, the more important the early exposure to dedicated craft working seems to be. During the war her father moved from Deniliquin to a £4/10/- per week Public Service job in Melbourne and made suits at night, sending two of his children to grammar school. Noel helped her father sometimes and also made all the dresses for her mother, her sister and herself. After school, the move to Swinburne Art School and a four-year Commercial Art course was a natural progression. The year 1946 was an interesting time to be going to art school. There was an atmosphere of expectancy and a motley collection of 'rehab' students from the armed forces. It must have been an eye-opener for a young lady from a 'school for little ladies'. Nobody got a formal qualification, which seems a pity because it was a distinguished cohort, containing soon-to-be internationally distinguished artists like Norma Redpath, Ray Crooke and Kath Ballart. Noel Waite had to go to Victoria/Deakin in 1980 for a *fifth* year in order to get a diploma.

In 1950, at the age of twenty-one, Noel joined an exclusive accessory house as a window dresser but quickly moved on to illustrating all the advertisements. Myers poached her shortly afterwards; she worked there full-time for the next six years, infuriating her six-years-older civil engineer brother-in-law by earning much more money than he did. By this time she was married to John Waite, previously head chorister at her church. As he set up the Waite business, she persuaded Myers (ahead of their time) to retain her on a fee basis to carry on her art/fashion work from home, whilst she brought up the children. The late Wally O'Donohue, the advertising manager and a notable Myers 'Imo' with a good eye for talent, fixed it. There is an echo of Liz O'Shaughnessy in Noel's reflections on those next nine years: 'Business was not for me; as an artist I worked for love! Money came in as a result of a job well done and it honestly never occurred to me that I would be running my own little advertising art business in my own studio with a nucleus of regular clients—very lucrative, I might add!'

Once again, we see the ternary approach paying off—look after your vocation, and the valued product or output, and in the long run life will look after you. The accident destroyed all that, so far as art is concerned, although Noel did her best to keep the art business running in parallel with the consultancy. In the end, her 'art' moved onto a bigger and more complex 'product'. If we take the Jaques levels of capability seriously, it might be that somebody as intelligent as Noel Waite *needs* at a certain point to move on to the next level of challenge. Technically, Noel 'ought' to be considering retirement now. In practice, she is probably just about ready, and gearing up, to make her *real* contribution to her country. Waite Consulting–Executive Search and Selection is already in the safe hands of her son, Peter Waite. Really, the point about many female entrepreneurs, like Waite and O'Shaughnessy, is that they are impelled to do something *useful*. They make money all right, but it is not always the primary driver that it is with so many male entrepreneurs.

ART AND THE ENTREPRENEUR—THE IMPORTANCE OF *METHOD*

Noel Waite and Liz O'Shaughnessy are near-perfect illustrations of Howard Gardner's central thesis that the 'multiple intelligences' interact and reinforce each other in powerful ways. Noel Waite used to be embarrassed about being just 'an artist in business'. No longer. Now she believes more than ever that intelligent business leadership is always about visualisation and conceptualisation *as well as* detail. This is not just a matter of having a good overview of the scene but of *shaping* something completely new out of the available fragments. The true entrepreneur, in other words, has a cluster of intelligences very similar to that of the artist.

All outstanding people seem to have a more or less conscious *method*, whether they work in business or the arts. To take the business world first, in Chapter 10 I described an outstanding technical executive with what he conceived of as a *'vehicle'* in his head—a kind of rolling, constantly fluctuating map of the territory. He found the 'vehicle' difficult to describe to others but he knew it was his secret weapon. Robert Keep's algorithm is sufficiently robust that he has no need to be clever, on a day-to-day basis, about currency movements—once his clients understand what the algorithm *does*, all he has to do is log the daily changes in the markets and pass on the details for the clients to act upon. He deals with his clients *via* the algorithm. An intelligent strategic plan serves the same purpose, provided it is infinitely flexible, serving as an organising *principle* for day-to-day action.

This is only speculation, but it is easy to see how a young child with a craftsperson parent (or similar role model) would learn *early* in life how *method* gives rise to *mastery*. The craftsperson probably can't explain in words how it is done but *watching* it all happen is bound to be instructive. Liz O'Shaughnessy's Aunt Adelaide made wonderful-tasting food. *How* she achieved this was initially mysterious for the watching child. That same trick now benefits thousands of airline passengers otherwise doomed to bland and unimaginative in-flight eating. The trick is to *reframe* airline food as some other kind of meal—more classy, stylish and relaxed—as if you were *not* crammed into an aluminium tube five miles up in the sky. Having the vision is crucial, but it comes to nothing without the practical *method*.

Something very similar occurs in the arts, as young practitioners are apprenticed in formal and informal ways to great masters. You can teach the arts, up to a point. At that point, each tyro artist has to begin to fashion his or her special and idiosyncratic *method*. Nearly all the great actors have a *routine* or *ritual*, sometimes childishly simple, to which they resort under pressure or as a gateway to deeper levels of work. Sir Alec Guinness can't get the character until he has got the character's *walk*. The great mezzo-soprano Dame Janet Baker never talks about her *voice*: she always refers to 'the instrument'—a God-given object of which she has stewardship. This kind of ternary thinking is characteristic of great artists. The words don't matter— *vehicle, method, algorithm, routine, instrument*—the idea is the same; the outcome is achieved *through* some valued object or principle which has been devised by the individual concerned, generally as an outcome of years of endeavour. It is always a personal thing; not the gift of a teacher, or guru, or flashy consultant.

Over the years I have been more or less obsessed by the self-portraits painted by Rembrandt throughout his long life. Never a great beauty, he got less and less pretty as the years passed but he always painted himself with a cool, almost brutal detachment. The last paintings in the series reveal a wonderful humanity and nobility, yet the effect is achieved with progressively *less* brushwork; he achieved more and more impact with less and less *obvious* effort—true economy. The self-portrait, it seems, was his personal 'vehicle'. The wonder of it is that the whole development of his method can be traced through these marvellous paintings. The same is true of the great actors—the achievement of more with less, as time passes.

There is a curious parallel between the worlds of art and sport— both fields that call on the bodily/kinaesthetic intelligence. Because these worlds rarely mix, it is not commonly known that Julian Bream, possibly the world's leading lutenist and one of the greatest guitarists, shares a technical or *craft* experience with Nick Faldo, one of the greatest golfers of all time. Both of them were faced with the need to *break* their basic *methods* in mid-life in order to sustain their success. Bream was largely self-taught. His method had made him an internationally known virtuoso but, as time passed, it became evident that it would limit his continuous development and probably doom him to muscular difficulties and possible arthritic complications. There was no alternative but to go back to square one and relearn his method, like a child or tyro. It took him years, but his art demanded it of him. The method will make it possible for him to continue his life's work for almost as long as life persists.

Faldo faced the same problem. He was already a leading golfer, but he was determined to be the best in the world. That meant the creation of a method which was so simple and so fundamentally sound that it would never crack under pressure. The aim was a *swing*—the basic tool of the professional golfer—that would deliver good results even when it was operating suboptimally. The solution was the same as for Bream—to go back to school in order to rebuild the method from scratch. It took some years, under the eye of one of golf's great technical gurus, during which time Faldo made virtually no money at all from the game. But he was patient and he emerged with a method that will see him through to the end. His great rival, Greg Norman, now also in his forties, still has a 'young man's swing'—endlessly exciting to watch but always fragile under pressure. (As we go to press, Norman too is finally seeking advice from David Leadbetter, the great guru of the swing.)

By the way, Faldo has done another clever thing. He has dispensed with the series of male caddies (club carriers and advisers) and formed a long-term professional association with the wonderfully equable Fanny Sunesson, previously one of better female golfers in Sweden. When the going gets tough, as it always does in professional golf, Fanny is there to exude calm professionalism and to bark polite Scandinavian instructions at spectators and officials. Meanwhile, the almost invariably male caddies of other golfers share in any *binary* panic going. The calm and ultra-professional female caddy is part of the Faldo *method* and *mystique*, along with the rebuilt swing. It is a potent combination. The only technical difficulty is that American caddies are obliged by the big golf clubs to wear *trousers*. Fanny has invented the *skort*—a sort of comfortable and practical pair of baggy shorts or culottes with a kilt-like front—a typically inventive way of pleasing everybody.

Artists and sportspeople offer a good example of the *ternary* principle in practical use. If you have a personal method that has been shaped over the years by your own struggle, you have a *binary* advantage over any competition.

Take the example of the great hurdler David Hemery. It was Hemery who sliced a whole *second* off the world 400 metre hurdles record in the Mexico Olympics. Very few athletes have destroyed a world record so comprehensively, and few ever will again. Few people know how this was achieved.

Four years previously, at the close of the Tokyo Olympic Games, Hemery and his coach sat down and calculated what speed would be required to *certainly* win the Mexico hurdles, takng into account the general improvement in performance standards and coaching methods. They concluded that 48.4 seconds should do it—nearly a full second (or about *eight metres*) faster than the existing world record. From that point on, their joint endeavours were focused on sustaining that particular (48.4) pace for the full 400 metres of hurdling. The *pace* became the *method*. At first, this was only achievable for about 200 metres or so but, as time passed, they continuously extended the range at the same, almost metronomic, pace. By Mexico, they were almost there, but not quite. The hope was that, under pressure of competition, Hemery could find the extra few metres at that same gruelling speed.

As it turned out, by the time of the Olympic final most of the best American opposition was already in awe of Hemery, who wasn't talking to anybody much (so focused was he on the *method*) but who everybody knew was going incredibly fast over the hurdles. The other athletes probably realised by then that Hemery was not engaged in a *binary* contest with *them*, but in a personal odyssey with the gods of athleticism. He and his coach had *defined* the race four years previously; all that was required on the day was the execution. When the time came, Hemery was a bit worried about one other competitor and *consciously* went out at what felt like about 48.3 seconds pace. After the race, which Hemery won by a *mile*, he could not believe that he had actually sustained a 48 seconds flat pace, even in the thin air of Mexico City. By cutting adrift from ordinary competition with ordinary athletes, they had *reframed* the race. The nice thing about athletics, as golf, is that there is not much room for referees or judges—the outcome is *obvious* to all. Now, David Hemery teaches the mysterious secrets of *method* to others, and notably to senior business people.

It doesn't much matter whether the field is sport, art, craft or business: the player with a *method* usually has the edge. That competitive edge comes, oddly enough, from eschewing direct competition with all the other *people*. The truly creative entrepreneur is engaged in a higher-order contest for perfection against the '*elements*'. The point about people like Noel Waite, whose story prompted these musings, is that they built their method laboriously and patiently over the years, just as craftspeople must. All of the heroes celebrated in this book, from Bob Clifford to Bill Hudson, did the same thing. This is probably the main reason why they became *admirable* people—they manifestly built something of value and the process of building improved them. That is one reason why sporting heroes *become* heroes—people can *see* how the natural talent has been developed and sharpened by effort and dedication. It is impossible to follow a leader you don't *admire*. Leadership is like love—it dies when admiration cannot be sustained.

This means that it is much easier for the SME (small to medium enterprise) leader to appear admirable in the eyes of his or her people. They can *see* at first hand the match between the person and the corporate object and values. In the big firm, those values need to be very clear, very admirable and very consistently reinforced in order to compensate for the isolation of the leader. In companies where such strong values exist (Hewlett-Packard and ICI, for example) there have generally been outstanding broad-banders in charge over a long period—the kind of people who really do value their people, who really do care about fashioning valuable outputs, and who also have the theatrical knack of embodying those values in their behaviour and in their symbolic communication. Where the narrow-banders get the upper hand (those who can only see the money and the short-term gain), life gets increasingly difficult for young 'Imos' in the engine room. They need *intelligent* inspiration.

If you believe, as I now do, that the outstanding people I have described are merely *normal*—apart from being lucky enough to have had an upbringing that allowed natural development of *all* the intelligences (through guidance, encouragement and role-modelling)—then the *clever* country would be the one to remove all the obstacles to such natural development, or at least to seek ways to ameliorate the effects of stupidity in parenting and schooling. You have to believe, to start with, that all the talent is there in the first place. Allan Coman can always turn schools round because he knows this is the case. I am sorry to say that most of the business schools with which I am familiar have a narrow view of the talents that leaders need. All this talk of relationships and art merely puzzles the more *macho* management academic. But then, business schools are generally uncongenial places for the best women.

COACHING, MENTORING, COUNSELLING
AND SO ON . . .

In Chapter 14 there is a full description of certain *methods* for helping people to come to terms with their own best ways of working and achieving. These go under such titles as *Executive Role Consultation, Career Path Appreciation* and so on. In essence, they are no more than elaborations of the process that goes on between a master and an apprentice. In order to achieve the remarkable results that Noel Waite has had with her clients over the years, more is required than the application of mechanical formulae. When Waite took Liz O'Shaughnessy in hand, her first task was to determine what kind of resource this person represented. She was charged with *moulding* the material to hand, not with manufacturing a particular or routinised sort of manager. The good golf pro does the same thing—observes the trainee's *natural swing* before beginning to shape and control it. You go against the grain at your peril, and your pupil's.

This may sound simple, but it seems to be the hardest thing of all for managers, parents and teachers of all kinds to understand and practise. All those callings demand *leadership*. The easier part of leadership is the creation and sustaining of the *vision*. The artist or sculptor usually knows in advance what is intended. Most parents know exactly what kind of offspring they want to have. The harder part is the moulding and shaping required, because this is always perplexing and frustrating and there is no certainty at all that it will work out 'right' in the end. I suspect that the great coaches and mentors are those who understand in their bones about *craft* and *method*. Of course, that goes for the great leaders too. Noel Waite has had an extraordinary long-term impact on the quality of Australian management, mainly, I think, because she understood these things from a very young age. Not only was she 'bright', she saw at first hand how each of the suits her father lovingly crafted turned gradually from an undifferentiated jigsaw of bits and pieces into a beautiful, practical three-dimensional object.

13

Weaving the threads

I warned the reader at the outset that this book deals with a quirky selection of leaders—from monkeys to major business entrepreneurs. I don't pretend that they cover the entire territory, either as to leadership capacity or as to intelligence. They are in the book because they are *interesting* cases and because they are, to my eyes at least, *admirable*. What I want to do in this brief summarising section of the book (before we pass on to the 'helpful hints') is to weave together as many of the threads from the earlier chapters as possible. This *ought* to be when the different yards (no pun intended) begin to make up a recognisable pattern in the cloth. This means that this section, as you would expect, contains a great many cross-references. I also want to say a little about the kinds of intelligent and *well-known* leaders for whom there is no space in the book. I touch on just four eminent Australians—a businesswoman, a jurist/diplomat, an economist/banker and a scientist.

THE *ADMIRABLE* LEADER

One problem with too many modern 'leaders', especially in politics and business, is that they are difficult for decent people to *admire*. There is a view amongst many young people that top dogs are tainted *by definition*—if you have succeeded in grabbing or inheriting power, there

235

must be something dubious about you. I noted above that leadership has something in common with love—once admiration is lost, so is everything else. You can't love, or follow, a person you no longer admire. The continuous enrichment of mediocre 'fat cats' at the top of big organisations, and the simultaneous impoverishment of those at the bottom, or at the margins of systems, simply means that top people, unless they are obviously very, very good, are collectively relinquishing their claim to admiration. Once it becomes clear that they are in pursuit only of *binary* goals such as wealth or power, rather than useful *ternary* end products, then they can forget the admiration of decent, sane people (including their own children, if any) and the claim to 'leadership'. As Sumantra Ghoshal points out, Western business leadership has become 'extraordinarily timid', downsizing to restore profit rather than transforming: ' . . . it doesn't really take a great deal of managerial imagination or guts . . . and the thing is we have made a macho-ness out of the timidity'. The characters in this book have all done pretty well and those still with us are pretty happy too, but their claim to fame lies in their outputs and innovations—in their *contributions*.

As I said at the beginning of this book, I have access (directly or indirectly) to the heroes described here and this means I can tell their stories in slightly more depth than most treatises of leadership are able to attempt. Tom Peters and Charles Handy are the masters of these kinds of parables in the business world. For my money, John Pilger's wonderful book *Heroes* is the model for transmitting important messages via stories about admirable people. (He is another admirable Australian 'leader'—a hero, if you like—who has stuck to his ethical guns through thirty distinguished years in the journalistic swamp.) More important, the heroes described here share a number of characteristics and talents. These characteristics underpin the book's argument about the nature of intelligent leadership. Once we are clear about the elements, we can begin to think clearly about getting ourselves more intelligent leadership in every walk of life, but especially in the nation's schools.

THE INTELLECT/DAMAGE SYNERGY—THE SMART AND SANE LEADER

Although there are always many variables involved when leadership is influential, this book sets out to reduce the variables to the most important two: the capacity to think clearly and the relative *absence* of psychological damage (see Figure 14, earlier). *Smart* and *sane* should be the watchwords. The difficulty with this simple formulation is that both aspects require a deal of 'unpacking'. What do I mean by 'intelligent', and what sort of 'damage' always undermines leadership?

On the intelligence front, the reason I have enlisted Howard Gardner and the theory of 'multiple intelligences' is that there is little agreement, even amongst psychologists, about the nature of practical or operational intelligence. The highly 'educated' tend to be dismissive of those from the university of life. The relatively uneducated often assume that the educated are 'all theory'. People who think in a holistic way (seeing systems as densely interconnected 'frogs') have difficulty with serial or compartment thinkers (who have to work their way methodologically around the 'bicycle')—and vice versa.

Connections and patterns

We began our trawl of clever leaders with Imo, the inventive monkey on the island of Koshima. Her special ability was to *connect* one phenomenon (a creek) with a process (the removal of sand from sweet potatoes). Her discovery could not have arisen by chance—she *had* to conceptualise the possibility before carrying out the first crucial physical experiment. What she did looks simply enough *after* the event. It looks like an amalgam of Gardner's *logical* and *spatial* intelligences. Bob Clifford did much the same thing when he *connected* commercial ferry operation with catamaran design. The first of these necessarily involved an understanding of the psychology of marketing and hence of the *interpersonal* intelligence. The second required *spatial* awareness, learned through *bodily/kinaesthetic* experience.

In a similar way to Imo and Clifford, Robert Keep was able to visualise battlefield situations in advance by making patterns out of previously inchoate material. He 'knew' the Viet Cong attack was imminent because he could 'see' in his mind's eye the meaning of a pattern. Later on, his eminence in the world of finance flowed from seeing the psychological *connection* between horse racing odds and the operation of currency markets. Mary Parker Follett was one of the first people to see clearly how the operational aspects of organisations are *connected* to human nature. Her view was therefore holistic, as opposed to the mostly mechanical models popular at the time. She was really the precursor of the 'socio-technical systems' idea.

These are all 'intelligent' people but the aspect of intelligence that distinguishes them is this ability to *connect* in order to make *patterns*. All of them are more or less gifted in all the Gardner 'intelligences' but this is their notable strength. I have had the privilege of talking at length with most of these heroes and it is clear to me that making patterns has motivated them and largely *caused* their creative breakthroughs. The obvious link is with my account in Chapter 2 of the seven- and eight-year-olds engaged in highly sophisticated systems thinking. I argue that this kind of pattern-recognition and pattern-making is a natural gift which we often neglect in parenting and schooling. Only when education is alive to this capability do you get the extraordinary results (in terms of creative, practical outcomes) achieved by Allan Coman at Bradfield College. As a form of work, pattern-making is simultaneously very disciplined but also essentially playful.

Seeing or envisioning are usually regarded as creative or artistic skills, and why not? My guess is that what these gifted people do (when they envision something) is to employ an enormous amount of the neural circuitry, just as the most complex software eats up capacity on a computer. The outcome may be simple and elegant but the processing usually involves lengthy, complicated and more or less continuous processing. This probably explains the pre-eminence of the chess grandmasters—it is hard to discern what exactly distinguishes them from other front-rank players, apart from the fact that they generally *win*! When the grandmaster beats the biggest computer in the world, the trick goes beyond the *logical/mathematical* skills—there is evidently some kind of complex *spatial* pattern-making going on, with a time dimension built in. The best players are usually obsessional, thinking about chess more or less nonstop, but some of them are notably uncrazy. Bob Clifford is as sane as they come, but he hardly ever stops thinking about his beloved boats.

All the great artistic endeavours are accompanied by this sort of night and day perseverance. A well-known example is Wagner's 'discovery' of the great E flat major Rheingold theme (after a nightmarish half-sleep on an uncomfortable couch in La Spezia): '[When] I awoke from my half-sleep in terror . . . I at once recognised [that] the orchestral prelude . . . which for a long time I must have carried about with me, yet had never been able to fix definitely, had at last come to being within me!' It is by no means frivolous to compare with this Paul McCartney's 'discovery' of the 'Yesterday' melody. He woke up with the tune in his head, wrote it down, and spent the next few weeks asking everybody in the business where he had heard it before. The *shape* of the song looked so obvious to him that it was inconceivable that he had *invented*, rather than *rediscovered* it. 'Yesterday' was *sui generis*—completely unlike all the other Lennon and McCartney songs but, crucially, it emerged out of their most concentrated period of joint creative productivity, but from just the one overheated brain.

The obvious link with Howard Gardner in these two cases lies in the simultaneous mobilisation of the *musical* and *spatial* intelligences (because composers usually 'see' the shapeliness of their output—see Mozart's reflections on this subject in Chapter 2). But, at another level, both of these composers reveal an insight about *intrapersonal* self-awareness. They are fully engaged in their creative work, but simultaneously *aware* of themselves as instruments or conduits for the output. Throughout the book I have referred to the theatrical metaphor and to the crucial ability of effective leaders to occupy the stage whilst holding in mind the shape of the whole play. If you adopt Gardner's logic, there is no essential difference between the business entrepreneur and the creative artist—both need perseverance and a vision. The point is that this demands brainpower, not just 'flair'.

In the concluding part of the book I outline a few methods for enhancing the mobilisation of broad-band mental activity. The *Career Path Appreciation* method actually sets out to test, amongst other skills, the capacity of an individual to reframe visual patterns, on the assumption that this ability underpins some aspects of managerial effectiveness. In order to do this, subjects are obliged to hold a greater *quantity* of information in mind for a sustained period of intensive work, and to sift and order it under time pressure. The *Executive Role Consultation* method helps individuals to a more self-aware state in their working and life environments, on the assumption that this will amplify their *impact* on events generally. A number of organisations, notably Body Shop, now involve their staff in big, theatrical collaborations, on the assumption that this is good not only for 'creativity' and teamwork but excellent also for developing thinking capacity. It forces people to think at two levels simultaneously, it forces them to hang on to a visualisation whilst coping with running emergencies, and it absolutely demands the fusion of rational discipline with emotional messiness. Art, as we know, mirrors life.

The point is that intelligence counts when it comes to effective and admirable leadership, but you have to define intelligence in a broad, *interconnected* way. It all comes down to brainpower in the end but business schools generally neglect any outcomes that seem to be passionate, or heartfelt, or unsupported by the 'facts' and by 'logic'. Howard Gardner agrees, of course, on the importance of logical/ mathematical intelligence; but it is *not enough*. Daniel Goleman, the author of *Emotional Intelligence*, is right to stress the importance of social deftness in leadership but a sense of space, shapeliness and *interconnection* also seems to be important. In fact, *all* Gardner's intelligences matter when we set out to bring up or educate children, or to develop managers.

Readers of this book are free to make connections which have not occurred to the author. This happens all the time, as I know from readers' letters past. One such is the connection between bogus statistics (described in Chapter 3) and the phenomenon of *under*management in the downsized organisation (described in Chapter 14). Today's most spectacular blunders and cockups often involve this combination. The extraordinary cases of Nick Leeson (who *broke* Barings Bank) and Peter Young (who cost Morgan Grenfell half a billion pounds—and rising—by doing more or less the same thing as Leeson a year later) demonstrate how greedy, low-capacity bosses will always trust statistics that please them, especially when they hardly ever see the rogue subordinates they are supposed to be supervising. In order for Morgan Grenfell to learn from the Barings fiasco, it was necessary for *somebody* to make the essential connection between so-called 'performance measures' and the absence of proper supervision up and down the anorexic organisational hierarchy. Nobody made the connection. The intelligent, systemic question to ask is: do the designers of 'performance management' systems and the *separate* groups who carry out downsizing understand the *connection* with subsequent cockups? Does anybody in senior management factor in the huge cost of big cockups when they think about how to *manage* the system in future? If such things only happen every

240

few years (even if they can destroy institutions and lives) it probably won't happen on your watch and, in the meantime, look at all the lovely money.

Psychological damage

My argument, as the reader will by now be aware, is that such intellectual deficiencies or bad habits are bound to *interact* with latent psychopathology. If a manager brings too much of his psychic damage to work, that will always cloud his thinking and lead eventually to mental muddle. Even slightly crazy people have to get reality to fit the mad internal map. On the other hand, if a manger lacks the agility of thought to keep up with events, he or she will come under increasing pressure and, sooner or later, behave badly. In Chapter 6, I set out the probable causes, early in life, of the kinds of psycho-pathology that cause bullying, deceitfulness or cowardice in the workplace. Most of the organisations in which I work are very slow to discipline—or to help—the many managers who cause workplace fear and irrationality. There is so much of it about that it hardly seems worthy of comment, even assuming you are aware of it.

All bullies and totally selfish people are damaged, rather than 'bad'. Very dangerous people, like Slobodan Milosevic, the Serbian tyrant (just clinging to power at the time of writing), are usually *very* damaged. Hitler, Stalin, Saddam Hussein and most of the great tyrants of history were themselves tyrannised in childhood. Milosevic's back-ground is about par for the course. When he was seven, his favourite uncle blew his brains out. His father, a Serb Orthodox priest, followed suit when young Slobo was twenty-one. Twelve years later, his mother hanged herself from a light fitting in the Milosevic living room. Like his fellow Balkan dictator Nicolae Ceaucescu, he married a fiercely ambitious and ruthless woman—the redoubtable Mira. Together, they were more dangerous than apart, feeding each other's fantasies and ambitions in the grip of a *folie à deux*. Her father got him his first crucial political appointment. Egged on by Mira, he ambushed his principal mentor, Ivan Stambolic, the man who had helped him most in his meteoric rise through the Communist Party ranks. Stambolic, one of the more principled of the old party *apparatchiks*, was appalled at the way Milosevic was prepared to stir up all the old Balkan ethnic

241

demons in order to get *binary* power for himself. Therefore, Stambolic had to go.

The point to bear in mind about damaged souls like Milosevic is that they can be extremely skilful in their political machinations. Part of their psychopathology is an almost superhuman understanding of the uses of fear and suspicion in human relations. Higher-order *ternary* logic always catches up with them in the end, but by that time the entire system (region) is likely to have been poisoned—old wounds reopened, new atrocities committed, and a whole generation infected with hate—all to serve the ambition of a crazy couple. Political tyrants provide the best possible illustration of the way in which intelligence and psychopathology relate to one another. They are essentially independent variables, but when they interact—in the form of the clever madman—watch out!

I cite the case of Milosevic to highlight the issues. I don't suggest that the petty tyrants in organisations are as 'wicked' as this, but they *are* pale imitations of the same phenomenon. When ordinary, decent people are hurt in organisational life, it is often at the hands of a relatively damaged individual who has aggrandised himself (or herself) in the pursuit of personal ambition. The *binary* ambition has supplanted the ordinary human interest in doing something useful. Of course, none of us can claim to have escaped all psychological damage. The outstanding Australians described in this book are not exactly perfect but, I contend, they are notably uncrippled by psychopathological baggage. If they have a failing, it lies in a kind of obsessiveness. In this respect they resemble the great artists rather than the greediest businessmen. This means that they are, so to speak, *married* to their creative endeavour. In most cases, this seems to create some difficulties for life partners. With a couple of notable exceptions, my heroes have had stormy or discontinuous relationships with partners. As the psychologist Liam Hudson points out (see Chapter 9), major discontinuities in creative work often spill over into social life.

The difficulty for the creativity-driven person may lie in finding a suitable (that is, *similar*) partner. When it comes to obsessives, it takes one to live with one. Figure 17 suggests that the 'best' (most creative and productive) people don't always get hitched to one another. Sometimes, highly binary women ambush gormless but potentially ternary men—what might be described as the Macbeth

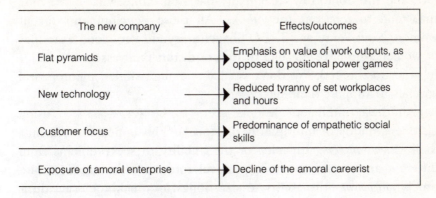

The new company		Effects/outcomes
Flat pyramids	→	Emphasis on value of work outputs, as opposed to positional power games
New technology	→	Reduced tyranny of set workplaces and hours
Customer focus	→	Predominance of empathetic social skills
Exposure of amoral enterprise	→	Decline of the amoral careerist

Figure 18   The 'glass ceiling' good news

syndrome. This was apparently the case with Mesdames Milosevic and Ceaucescu—strong but crazy women using weak and malleable men as a front for their own ambition. Something not dissimilar occurs in the senior ranks of the big corporations, although this has not been much studied. Over the years, I have worked with numerous very senior men, many of them deeply frustrated and unhappy, who were driven, in the main, by the expectations and desires of their wives and/or demanding offspring. Until we get many more women in top jobs, we won't know whether the reverse is likely to occur. I have seen overstretched male executives, grey with exhaustion at the end of the long working day, restored overnight to fighting-fitness by a backstage *impresario*.

The 'Tomorrow's Company' initiative (discussed in the previous chapter) suggests that in future there may be a shortage of the kinds of admirable people I have described in these pages. In a relationship organisation, where trust and reputation are the building blocks of success, there is not much room for the old-style machine politicians. As most of them were men (possibly propped up by ambitious partners) life is arguably going to get better for women. The emerging fields of networked home-working, media, theatre, health and public relations are all, if not dominated by women, at least female-friendly. As Figure 18 depicts, in the longer run things are moving towards women's advantage—flat organisational structures extrude unnecessary timeservers, new technology loosens up the working day, customer focus helps those with natural empathetic skills who really *care*, and the Tomorrow's Company focus on ethics will, in the long run, tend to root out the crooks. All these developments favour women. Noel Waite and Liz O'Shaughnessy are very good examples of women who have not had to trim or distort their essential natures in order to succeed. We don't yet have enough skilled mentors and coaches to support their successors.

All these intelligent leaders seem to be *broad-banders* (using Gardner's notion of multiple intelligences). This appears to enhance their *systems thinking* capacity, or their ability to see problems from different angles and to envisage novel futures. This translates into timely *judgement*—the ability to size things up quickly and act decisively. This is how we are defining *leadership* in tomorrow's company. As a matter of fact, it is not much different from the array of characteristics usually associated with famous 'leaders' like Winston Churchill, even though such leaders have generally been viewed mostly in the light of *character* rather than intelligence. Churchill, of course, was a first-rate journalist and writer. Like the leaders in the book, he was also something of an obsessional, but his psychopathology never completely disabled him. Arguably, it was exactly what his life's task demanded. He was pretty badly parented, by today's standards, but he did have a wonderful, kindly, caring nanny. Without her, possibly none of his *talent* would have been realised, because the damage might have swamped the intellect. Nanny Everest, you could argue, exercised a remarkably important leadership act in the context of 20th century history.

WHO'S NOT IN THE BOOK?

This roundup of the book's characters, and their connection with leadership and intelligence, points up the *absence* of many outstanding Australians from these pages. As I discussed the emerging book with colleagues the constant refrain was: 'Why didn't you put in Janet Holmes à Court, or Ninian Stephen, or James Wolfensohn, or Allan Synder, or . . . ?' The short answer is that I wanted to pick out just a few people, not all of them grandees, who exemplified the core intelligences and aspects of leadership that are the book's subject. I also wanted people with whom I could spend quite a lot of time, in the endeavour to get behind the public entrepreneur to the intellectual and ethical reality beneath. This means I needed their *permission* so to explore. I also wanted to expose the less famous (like Liz O'Shaughnessy and Robert Keep), the underappreciated (like Bill Hudson) and the neglected or forgotten (like Mary Parker Follett) on the grounds that we should all worry about the prominence of flashy but shallow charismatics when so many *substantial* leaders are unknown. Once I step beyond the core characters, it is invidious to leave out *anybody* of merit, and just as invidious to deal with only the four 'absentees' noted above.

But I want to give a sense of the kinds of *establishment* figures who are the spiritual brothers and sisters of the book's heroes. You don't *have* to be obscure in order to be virtuous. These four are all *extraordinary* Australians (maybe we can include them in a subsequent edition of this book, after it has been improved by first-tranche readers). Janet Holmes à Court, for example, is another woman (such as Noel Waite) who came to prominence through a tragedy—the untimely death of her husband Robert. She was already a very significant upholder of *communitarian* values in Australia and a lifelong *non*-conservative. To start with, that made her *unusual* amongst business leaders, most of whom lean, without much forethought, to the political *right*. What has happened since to Heytesbury Holdings (the grazing to theatre empire pieced together by Robert) is that it has become a more *stable* organisation, partly as a result of overdue business reshaping but partly also as the result of female levelheadedness.

All of the collapsed business empires of the 1980s, put together by male financial engineers, were essentially *virtual* corporations. Of course, there were tangible assets but the ascribed value depended mainly on the *opinions* and *expectations* of the traders and dealers that Robert Keep so expertly scrutinises. Knowledgeable women tend to be as sceptical about financial-engineers' figures as they are about flashy men. They generally need to understand the *substance* of the business. The main problem for female inheritors of business empires is usually a *control* problem—how to ensure that all the men surrounding you really share your value set. If they don't they are bound occasionally to perpetrate cockups with the best will in the world—by simply trying to do their *binary* best (see the reference to *The Adversarial Approach* in Chapter 12). This is not meant to be an *apologia* for the Heytesbury group of companies, just an observation that the stable organisation is not necessarily the stodgy organisation and that women, by and large, value stability.

Systems thinking tells you quickly enough that if women need to spend at least twice as long in the lavatory as men (and if theatre audiences split roughly fifty-fifty), then in order to operate efficiently your theatres are going to need toilet capacity in the ratio 2:1. It's only a small thing but, all over London, the female clientele of the Stoll Moss theatre chain owe an unconscious debt of gratitude to the sort of leader who *connects* systems thinking with ordinary human needs (the *substance*) whilst driving 'strategy'. Most of these theatres have been around for a long time; it took till the 1990s for this aspect of *throughput process* to be addressed intelligently.

It ought to be reassuring to Australians that that kind of level-headedness is to be found, for example, on the Reserve Bank Board. The story goes that, when Janet Holmes à Court joined the Reserve Bank, she was the only external director game enough to say 'what does that mean?' when the experts tried to baffle the non-executives with science, even though most of the others were baffled too. That is one of the most difficult, useful and underrated leadership acts of all. In Chapter 10, I refer to the practice of 'thinkering' or amalgamating high thought with hands-on tinkering. This is the combination of subtle thinking, ethical value and no-nonsense straightforwardness that outstanding women can bring to high office. It is tragic that it so often requires a tragedy to make it happen. It is no surprise, therefore, that Janet Holmes à Court is the prime mover behind the Australian Children's Television Foundation (ACTF) and that Gardner's ideas about 'thinkering' provide the basis for the ACTF's early childhood program.

Most of the beleaguered inhabitants of Ireland, both north and south, are unaware of the crucial role of Sir Ninian Stephen in drawing the warring factions together to talk as intelligently as possible to each other. Wisely, the British Government recognised that the midwife for the 'peace process' had to be somebody of enormous wisdom, patience and detachment. That doesn't mean that Sir Ninian lacks passion for the task at hand, merely that, as an Australian, he can combine a lawyer's clarity of mind with a cultural affinity that is just about right—not too close (an English person wouldn't do), nor too distant. Above all, he reinforces the point that wisdom goes on accreting in the minds of those who remain ablebodied. A much younger mediator than Sir Ninian is difficult to imagine. It is surprising, in a way, that more distinguished Australians are not called upon to act the referee in world affairs. The Irish work, of course, calls for the very *opposite* of flamboyant leadership. Theatrically, the need is for the subtlest and most sensitive *direction* of the negotiation system—the lightest touch, backed up by the big brain.

Observers of the World Bank say that that institution is undergoing a revolution, and not before time. The more thoughtful economists have argued for years that the bank had become part of the problem, rather than part of the solution to the world's economic and political stability problems. Previously, crude economic intervention, based on oversimple 'bicycle' assumptions, were applied to immensely complex socio-economic 'frogs', especially in those underprivileged parts of the world that were most difficult for Americans to understand. James Wolfensohn, the newish chief, has effectively asked two questions: *What exactly is the World Bank for? What, in reality, have been the long-term effects of previous World Bank interventions in other people's economies?* This particular Australian is merely applying high-level systems thinking to an urgent world problem. In order to effect change, he needs most of the repertoire of the Gardner intelligences, from social deftness (*interpersonal*) through self-deprecating unpompous humour (*intrapersonal*) to the big brain (*logical/mathematical* and *spatial*). There is no obvious application for his *musical* virtuosity (he plays the cello) but Gardner would argue that it probably helps the big 'frog' (Wolfensohn's brain) to work well. No reader of this book will be surprised to learn that he was previously a world-class fencer (the *bodily/kinaesthetic* intelligence).

There is a curious parallel to Wolfensohn's top teamwork at the World Bank in the Nick Faldo/Fanny Sunesson story in Chapter 12. Wolfensohn has brought in the redoubtable Rachel Lomax as his deputy. She was previously one of the most senior Treasury mandarins in the British Civil Service, famous for being about the only person who could handle Margaret Thatcher. There is a famous account of the return of Lord Carrington and Sir Ian Gilmour from Brussels, after a notably successful renegotiation of Britain's contribution to EEC funding. On their return they presented the outcome, with some pride, to the Prime Minister. She, for reasons nobody could fathom, found fault with everything, complaining, amongst other things, about the impact of the renegotiated settlement on foreign aid. As it had absolutely nothing whatsoever to do with foreign aid, this was perplexing to Carrington, Gilmour and all the aides present. As Gilmour put it, it was a bit like being a soccer goalie in some arcane version of the game where the object was to kick the ball into the crowd—the best you could manage would be the odd despairing lunge as the ball sailed out.

But, Gilmour noted, Rachel Lomax had the Prime Minister's measure. Whenever Thatcher was plain *wrong*, Lomax would calmly but firmly point out: '*I believe, Prime Minister, if you refer to section X, subsection Y, on page Z, you will see that . . . !*' The PM, sensing she was outgunned, went quietly. In the end, Gilmour concluded that there was no logic in Thatcher's disagreements; it was simply more important for her emotionally to have the *binary fight* with Brussels than to achieve an intelligent, realistic, *ternary* outcome. That realisation filled him with dread. Anyway, James Wolfensohn, our Australian hero, has done what smart leaders do—post really smart lieutenants at key strategic points. It is a nice touch that the key lieutenant should be a woman.

The fourth 'absentee' is Professor Allan Snyder, head of optical research at the Australian National University in Canberra and recent winner of the Australia Prize for science. I would dearly like to have explained his work (so far as I could understand it) and its origination in these pages. Given time and space, I would have recruited Robyn Williams—a *unique* science broadcaster/populariser in all the world— to assist with this task. Snyder, like Williams, is Australian by adoption, a nice compliment from one of the world's leading photonics researchers and the impresario behind a number of leading-edge Cooperative Research Centres. Here is another broad-bander, drawn from primarily *musical* stock in New York but steeped also in high finance and psychology. One of his obsessions, *parallel* with his groundbreaking hard science, is the nature of perception and the workings of the human mind. (In this respect, he resembles Howard Gardner, whose main contribution to this book arose from the *connection* between hard science and the practical problems of education—see Chapter 9.) Snyder, like Robert Keep (a friend), has persevered for years with scientific ideas and experiments which, if ultimately successful, will completely transform the relevant field, worldwide. Bob Clifford would agree with both of them that Australia, partly *because* of its physical isolation, is a fertile source of scientific innovation and creativity, provided the worldwide connections are in place. It helps to be distinctive, but networked.

With the possible exception of Janet Holmes à Court, all of these notables are probably better known outside Australia than at home. That is perhaps as it should be but, if inspiring role models are needed by young Australians (and they are), what is the best way to expose these kinds of people and achievements, in schools, for example? How many Australians really understand what the jurist/diplomat, the economist/banker and (perhaps most important) the scientist represent, and what their likely impact on the world well into the next century will be? We can anticipate that the eyes of the *sporting* world will turn to Australia and New Zealand at the millennium, as the Olympics and the America's Cup come south in the same year. It would be a crying shame if this merely reinforced the world's view of a region entirely peopled by amiable athletes. Intelligence, in the practical and broad-band form I have described in these pages, has always been an Australasian speciality. The trick is to celebrate the fact and to ensure that it is nurtured and reinforced over the very long term.

It would be no bad thing, by the way, to institute a major Down Under celebration of the *mind* (especially the active, applied, problem-solving mind) to coincide with all this *physical* activity. As we enter the new millennium, why not bring the world to the South Pacific to look afresh at the big issues? If the great economic shift is, as the pundits say, to the Asia–Pacific region, maybe Australasia can play a leading role in integrating and mobilising practical—and *multiple*—intelligence in the region. Mounting something like that would require the support of clever politicians with a long-term perspective and, dare I say it, a view of *the big picture*.

PART III

Nurturing intelligent leadership

In this final part of the book I outline a number of useful hints and ideas for anybody interested in helping the kinds of mavericks celebrated in these pages, or in supporting maverickdom in big organisations. On the whole, the former task (helping the entrepreneur to *grow* his or her enterprise) falls to government—in the Australian setting, to State government. On the whole, the latter task (loosening up the buried cleverness of all the 'Imos' in big systems) falls to management educators, consultants and researchers. These were matters confronted by David Karpin's Federal Government Task Force on Management and Leadership Skills in Australia, which produced its valuable final report, *Enterprising Nation*, in 1995. I had the honour of helping the overseas touring arm of the Task Force as it examined the thinking and practices of foreign corporations and education systems.

Be warned: the 'helpful hints' set out below in Chapter 14 are not *tools*, not step-by-step procedures, to be taken away and used in work systems by readers. I have included them in the book as a source of optimism. There *are* practical and user-friendly ways of intervening in systems but they require mastery, and hence understanding. I include therefore some suggestions for further reading around the main themes of the book. And I am always happy to talk to anybody about *how* to attach good ideas to messy realities.

Much of what I want to say concerns the *sizes of systems* and of their subsystems. That is why Gregory Bateson's 'polyploid horse' serves as the text for Chapter 1. To shift the organic metaphor, Australia is just a big frog. Any attempt to get it to function as a highly efficient frog must depend on our capacity to understand how all the parts relate to the whole. No consultant, however Machiavellian, can *make* it into a bicycle (see Chapter 3). We have to understand it *as a complex system* in order to help it to grow and develop *naturally*. In the United States and the United Kingdom, there are too many examples of dogmatic force-feeding or starvation of systems in evidence. As I remarked earlier, if you have more of your citizens in jail or on remand than you have in college (as in the United States) then the big system *cannot* be functioning well.

Viewed from the outside, the relationship of an organisation like Bob Clifford's Incat to Tasmania, and to Australia, and to the specialised world of fast ferry transportation, is downright fascinating. But so is the relationship of a *system* like Tasmania itself to its environment. From the outside, it is difficult to comprehend that a system of just three industrial clusters, with a population about the same as a big metropolitan *county* in Britain, should be a fully fledged *State* with all the trimmings (including a bloke in a silly hat to open Parliament). Yet there is the reality of Bass Strait to reinforce the psychology of separateness. Potentially, Tasmania, given a few more Bob Cliffords, could teach the mainland about creating and sustaining *coherent systems*—systems that *feel* right and function smoothly. Half a million people is a terrific starting point, provided you can bring them all together into a realistic sense of community.

The tragedy of Port Arthur makes it clear that the presence of sound political institutions (the structure of the bike, if you like) is no guarantee of social coherence. As with any disaster, there was a prescient 'Imo' sounding a warning. In 1991 Barrie Unsworth, then Premier of New South Wales, prophesied: *'It will take a massacre in Tasmania before we get proper gun control in this country!'* He had tried harder than any politician to *anticipate* impending danger by responding intelligently to the Hoddle Street, Queen Street and Strathfield massacres. No one could argue that there wasn't a *pattern* building up. After Port Arthur, he tended to blame himself: 'The events at

Port Arthur made me very sad and depressed, with the sense I failed in 1987 to effectively start the process which would remove the weapons of war from our society and achieve a real reduction in guns. Therefore, I felt I had contributed to the tragic circumstances' (*Herald Sun*, 6 May 1996).

Barrie Unsworth is the last person in Australia who should blame himself for the failure of the country to come to its senses. But his anguish shows the burden of the intelligent leader when the system cannot respond to intelligence. Such people are always uncompromising with themselves. They are able to comprehend the complexities of the big system (the frog, the country as a whole) but sometimes they lack the political clout, or the time needed, to act upon that understanding. They are often surrounded by intellectual pygmies with narrow-span, short-term perspectives. Those pygmies rarely share the sense of anguish or guilt because they were helpless to begin with. Understanding is a terrible burden because, in the relatively undamaged personality, it imposes *duty*. This is the stuff of tragedy.

If we take Tasmania as a case study, we can see that understanding the nature of the beast, and beginning to bring it to blooming health, must be a long-term process, very carefully undertaken. Michael Porter's important book *The Competitive Advantage of Nations* has much to say about the natural economic *clusters* that sometimes grow, like algae, around networks of entrepreneurs. Those clusters are in the nature of mini-frogs. One of the best known, described by Porter, is the cluster of ceramic tile manufacturers in the north of Italy. Beginning with a few natural (geological) advantages, the tilemakers combined fierce commercial competition with intelligent technical collaboration, supported by a network of publicly funded training establishments and research and development centres. Porter argues that that trick lay not in the dominance of free enterprise OR state control, nor in the dominance of competitiveness OVER collaboration, but in a subtle admixture of all the elements—binary AND ternary. If you really understand the *natural* properties of the system, there is no place for political dogma.

Tasmania could be the ultimate example of a big socio-technical system repairing itself. But it will require very intelligent and persistent leadership. The economic fixes, though difficult, will be the relatively easy bit. The *integration* of natural economic activity with long-term social healing will be the complicated, and therefore hard, part. The 'collective unconscious', an idea first mooted by Jung, will dog the rational process of economic rebuilding. Without integration of the rational task aspect and the underlying demons, the project of rebuilding may fail completely—or make things worse. The helpful hints given below will make more sense if the sense of *system* (or frog) is held in mind. To make it easier I reproduce a shortened version of Bateson's 'polyploid horse' as a reminder of what happens when a system is constructed according to the logic of a completely different kind of system:

> . . . a horse precisely twice the size of an ordinary Clydesdale. It was twice as long, twice as high, and twice as thick. By the time the horse was shown to the public it was not doing any standing. In a word, it was too heavy. It weighed eight times as much as a normal Clydesdale.
>
> For a public showing, Dr Posif always insisted on turning off the hoses that were continuously necessary to keep the beast at normal mammalian temperature. After all, its skin and dermal fat were twice as thick as normal, and its surface area was only four times that of a normal horse, so it didn't cool properly.
>
> Every morning, the horse had to be raised to its feet with the aid of a small crane and hung in a sort of box on wheels, in which it was suspended on springs, adjusted to take half its weight off its legs. Dr Posif used to claim that the animal was outstandingly intelligent because it had eight times as much brain (by weight) as any other horse, but it had very little free time for thinking, what with one thing and another— always panting, partly to keep cool and partly to oxygenate its eight-times body. Its windpipe, after all, had only four times the normal area of cross section.
>
> And then there was eating. Somehow it had to eat, every day, eight times the amount that would satisfy a normal horse and had to push all that food down an oesophagus only four times the calibre of the normal. The blood vessels, too, were reduced in relative size, and this made circulation more difficult and put extra strain on the heart.

My recommendation to senior executives is usually to read this passage once, just to get the physics and the biology clearly in mind, then to read it carefully again, with the big corporation in mind. The fable demonstrates what inevitably happens when two or more variables, whose curves are discrepant, interact. This is what produces the interaction between change and tolerance. As a species we have been pretty good, over a few million years, at coping with bands, gangs and smallish societies. The modern corporation is a very new and unfamiliar system, connected by entirely novel electronic linkages. It is hardly surprising that primitive behaviour sometimes bubbles up from the depths.

I illustrated the change/tolerance phenomenon earlier by describing how a frog will absorb gradual change (removal of bits, for example) for a surprisingly long time, until *suddenly* the threshold of tolerance is passed and the entire system collapses. The 'polyploid horse' illustrates how big, cumbersome corporations usually get out of kilter with their component parts (living, breathing, thinking, feeling, hurting, inventive human beings). The fable doesn't help us to decide what to *do* about it. 'Downsizing' clearly exposes the system to the same problem in reverse—the changing of any variable always exposes a critical value of another variable.

THE ORIGINS OF INTELLIGENT LEADERS

The reader is entitled to take the view that the people I have described in this book are really oddballs or mavericks. They are mostly people who don't fit very well into conventional social or employment systems. They are also people who present as exceptionally 'bright'. The purpose of this book is to suggest that people like this are the only 'normal' ones among us. It is the big employment bureaucracy that is odd, historically speaking. If we were all better at parenting, educating, supporting, encouraging and stimulating, then *everybody* would be as bright and focused as these heroes. They are people who escaped most of the damage attendant on normal upbringing. I accepted in Chapter 6 that 'intellectual firepower' may be the most intractable of the successful leader's qualities. That is halfway to admitting that intelligence may be partly heritable.

On the other hand, I have had the opportunity to observe, close to, the work of obstetrics pathfinders like Dr Frederic Leboyer. His babies always emerge into a peaceful, unhurried world without stress, panic or noise, save for J. S. Bach, softly. Such babies are not upended by the rugger-bugger type of gynaecologist and slapped on the bottom in order to elicit evidence of lungpower. They are allowed to crawl at their own pace around mummy, exploring this new environment. They appear completely focused, as though checking out a place overheard and imagined, now available for inspection. They do not cry; they are just *interested*. The point of this is that Leboyer claims that his babies always end up clever, because they have curiosity and calmness soldered in. This is quite impossible to prove because the kinds of parents who opt for a Leboyer birth are already, by definition, highly selected. Still, it makes you think. I often watch other people's babies on public transport. There is an extraordinary difference between the blank, enclosed and disgruntled visages of some babies and the probing and inquisitive scanning of others. It matches the behaviour of the mothers. The recent discovery of the correlation between sucking dummies in infancy and subsequent low IQ fits neatly with this prejudice.

SOCIO-TECHNICAL SYSTEMS THEORY

At any rate, the idea to hold in mind is that almost *anybody* can operate in a similar way to the heroes in this book. If that is to happen inside large organisations, we have to pay some attention to the structure and processes of such organisations, bearing in mind that *human nature* changes very slowly—more slowly than we can observe in a 70-year span. We are dealing here with the theory of 'socio-technical systems', a phrase coined in the 1950s by some of the Tavistock Institute pioneers. The classic study took place in British coal mines. An efficient new technology had appeared on the scene—the so-called 'long wall' method of coal-getting. You could prove easily, on paper, that the new technology would produce much more coal per hour because it was technically much more 'efficient'.

It didn't work out like that. It turned out that if you permitted the technology to dominate the process, the inevitable effect was to destroy the social 'glue' that held together the work system. One effect of the new technology was to break up the *logic* of the work sequence, leaving the miners to carry out only a fragment of the task, rather than seeing the whole cycle through. This removed *meaning* from their work. Furthermore, the new technology broke up the work *groups* that underpinned trust and respect across the whole system. Those groups, like the subassemblies of frogs, were part of the total system. If you messed them around, the whole system suffered. In a closely knit mining community, the families and the local community were part of that big system too. The damage to the big 'frog' was widespread and insidious. From the management standpoint, production rates following introduction of the new technology actually suffered.

The 'solution', famously, was to *satisfice*. If you designed a system around the technology alone, you ran the risk of distorting or destroying the social glue. If you designed a system around the social needs, you simply wasted the benefits of new methods and exposed yourself to smarter competition. The trick was to *integrate* technical and social requirements into a sub-maximal but workable alternative, drawing upon the knowhow of all the 'Imos' in the system. It was an early example of what we might now call 'team working' or 'multiskilling' or 'empowerment'. The new multiskilled groups accepted responsibility for each activity in the extraction cycle, from initial shot-firing of the coal and its removal to conveyor belts, through the moving forward of roof supports as the face advanced, to the final packing of the worked face and the management of a controlled roof-fall. When something works well, because it *makes sense*, it motivates and stimulates. The outfall is more interest and creativity. The people who work the system always understand it better than their bosses but, even now, as we approach the millennium, their wisdom is rarely tapped. Their 'resistance to change' varies inversely with intelligent involvement in decision-making.

The interesting thing about the socio-technical systems work of the 1950s in the British Coal Board is that it predates 'business process re-engineering' (BPR) by nearly fifty years. The basic idea was the same—isolate the fundamental throughput processes and encourage those people with the operational responsibility to improve the processes for themselves, using statistical data. The basics flowed directly from the 'operations research' approaches which coped with the logistics of the Normandy landings in 1944. I have long argued that BPR is merely operations research rebadged. It is what intelligent people do *naturally*. There is, however, a big difference in the starting points of the 1980s re-engineers and the socio-technical pioneers:

- BPR was a godsend (a sort of intellectual figleaf) for the 1980s asset-strippers driven by stock market demand for short-term profit in the United States and the United Kingdom. The simplest way to improve the bottom line fast is to strip out cost. The quickest way to achieve that is to 'downsize', or 'rightsize' as it soon came to be known. The moment to get into 'outplacement counselling' was the early 1980s. The human asset-strippers *sensed* that they were taking the easy, short-term route, so the outplacement package eased a few consciences. Most of them believed that they had no alternative—that BPR was holy writ. Read Professor Enid Mumford's book *Systems Design: Ethical Tools for Ethical Change* for the evidence that the longer term effects of this sort of restructuring have usually been deleterious. She says 'United States companies that have drastically reduced the size of their labour forces have proved to be less financially successful than those in the same industry that did not do so.' By 1996 the arch-apostles of BPR, James Champy, Michael Hammer and Tom Davenport, had all recanted. Davenport has gone as far as calling BPR, when it is distorted and misused just for downsizing, the 'last gasp of Taylorism'.

- By contrast, the Tavistock Institute pioneers set out to improve the health and well-being of the whole 'frog'. That meant the *long-term* viability of the total system—its technical capability *and* its resourcefulness and ingenuity. Originally, the enormous improvements in productivity that flowed from socio-technical systems design surprised the Tavistock and Coal Board initiators. They had not yet fully grasped the link between 'soul-destroying' work and system productivity.

CHANGE AND THE CHANGE-MERCHANT

A comment on *change* and so-called *resistance to change* is in order here. It is true that we live in a world of constant change, and we have to be able to adapt as quickly as our environment changes. That really is the iron law of natural selection. *But*, and it is a big but, we also have to deal these days with an army of 'change-merchants' who feed off instability and chaos. Some of these merchants are academics but most are management consultants. Their *unconscious* project is to destabilise systems, because destabilisation is the source of their power and wealth. Note the use of the word 'unconscious'. A *few* of the change-merchants appear to be tightly controlled Machiavellians, deliberately and consciously sowing the seeds of anxiety, much as secret agents do in wartime. But the great majority are persuasive because they really are attuned to chaos and deeply believe in the need for incessant change. In my experience, top management is frequently taken in by such people; the rank and file (the 'Imos') *never*.

A change-merchant, in the sense in which I am using the term, may be defined as *'an individual with a pathological need to create external chaos commensurate with his or her internal state'*.

In offering this definition, I am not denying the existence of chaos or the need for systems to change and adapt. All I am doing is pointing out the presence of dangerous destabilising forces in the 'machine'. A good mechanic *senses* when a machine or system is close to the edge. Bob Clifford knew, just before the event, that part of one of his catamarans was about to bang him on the head. I am suggesting that the change industry is sometimes part of the problem rather than part of the solution. On the whole, the 'Imos' in the system know this but they can't get through to their bosses. They can generally see through consultants. Because they understand the basic processes, they can see the inbuilt stabilities and continuities. They can usually see the possibility for cheap and simple *evolution*, as opposed to heavyhanded revolution. Some of the change-merchants I have encountered appear to be *threatened* by stability and continuity because it is so much out of kilter with their own psychological condition. The effect of the all-singing, all-dancing 'change program' is frequently to belittle the scope and value of the changes that operatives and front-line staff are coping with day in and day out.

Some of the executives and consultants I have encountered, especially in the last ten years of BPR and 'change programs', seem to me to be somewhat damaged characters with a pathological need to get their immediate environment into the same chaotic condition as their own insides. It is as if they require that equilibrium in order to cling to sanity. If the environment contains too much stability, this is threatening for them. Such people *export* their fearful inner states— they are usually perceived as bullies. Generally, they are *binary* in character—fearing submission and getting their retaliation in first. It helps, sitting in a meeting dominated by one of these characters, to remember that *inside* they are very frightened and confused people. This doesn't alter the fact that they do much damage and export *noise* into a work system that always needs clearheadedness. How do they get promoted to these positions? We come to that shortly.

14

Helpful hints on organisational leadership

My 'helpful hints', are all based on certain fundamental assumptions about the operation of systems, both big and small. If the reader is unconvinced about the assumptions, the hints won't look so helpful. We are dealing here with what is commonly described as 'systems thinking'. There are three basic assumptions:

1. *The group is the building block*
I don't like using a static, construction metaphor to describe a fluid process but the point is that there are some aspects of systems that really are as stable as a stone building. Our prehistory has soldered in our dependence on groups and our helplessness without them. Any big organisation that works well must have a stable foundation of coherent groups 'at the coalface' where the crucial customer/client–facing work is done. The way to build a resilient organisation is *from the ground up*.

2. *People need purpose and to be at work*
Whenever you see a human being 'on song' you can be sure that that person is bent on achieving something that makes sense (to him or her). Human beings are at their best when they work (individually

and collectively) to solve problems that matter to them and to their kin. That is what we did well, as a species, in order to 'rise above' the other apes. There is a limit, therefore, in the extent to which you can persuade people (e.g. employees) that 'Micky Mouse' purposes are real. 'Motivation' is a word much misused, mainly by Americans. It is a *noun* that describes an inner human state. When it is misused as a *verb* (I am going *to motivate you!*) intelligent people (subordinates, 'Imos') can see through it easily. The verb *to motivate* is binary because it depends on personal persuasiveness. The noun *motivation* is ternary because it depends on identification with a 'good enough' *purpose*.

3. *Organisations have a depth structure (a hierarchy)*
This is a fancy way of saying that if you find yourself accountable to a relative airhead, it won't work. Whatever the 'delayerers' or leaderless workgroupers say, the only way that big purposive task systems can operate well is when some people are held *accountable* for the work outputs of others. That means *hierarchy*. The person *in charge* has to be superior in capability as well as authority because, by definition, his or her work is more *complex*.

Taking these three simple assumptions or propositions together, you can set about creating an organisation which is focused, which *feels* right to people, and which has the capacity to learn continuously because all the 'Imos' are in play. I begin with the trailblazing work of Christian Schumacher.

HELPFUL HINT NO. 1: SCHUMACHER'S SEVEN PRINCIPLES

As it happens, Christian Schumacher is the son of the late E. F. Schumacher, author of the seminal book *Small is Beautiful*. Not surprisingly, the seven principles are entirely consistent with the message of that extraordinary and prophetic book. Christian Schumacher calls his approach simply 'work structuring', on the assumption that the most important thing an organisation does is to 'export' useful products (not necessarily overseas). The way you structure the organisation must be governed by the way you structure the *work*. The work-structuring approach is similar to 'business process re-engineering' (BPR), in that it examines the way in which 'imports' are converted (via value-adding) into 'exports'. The big difference is that the human dimension (or socio-technical dimension; see above) is built in from the start. In his latest book on BPR, even James Champy has acknowledged that 're-engineering is in trouble'—because 'management culture' gets in the way of intelligence. The big difference these days is the power of computing technology, which is tending to dissolve traditional organisational boundaries. This is just another reason why women, who are much better networkers than men, will soon take over the world.

The work-structuring principles are as follows:

1. *Work should be organised around* BASIC TRANSFORMATIONS *in order to form 'whole tasks'.*
As throughputs flow through work systems they undergo various transformations, some of them minor (like storage or transportation) and others *basic*, like the chemical transformation of materials in manufacturing. Any work system can be analysed so as to clarify these fundamental transformations. They are the nucleus of the perceived 'whole task'. Intelligent people know about this intuitively. If the structure of work flows fits the intuition of the people, it will obviously 'feel right'.

2. *The basic organisational unit should be the* PRIMARY WORK GROUP.
This principle simply builds on the evidence above, that people work best in groups and that if the group formation makes sense (because it is built around a basic transformation) the whole is always greater than the sum of the parts. In practice, work groups ought to range from about four to twenty people. The very small organisation has the advantage that the entire system feeds off this intellectual and emotional nourishment.

3. *Each work group should include a* DESIGNATED LEADER.
Schumacher takes the view that the so-called 'leaderless work group' is a nonsense. The leader is part of the group but he or she has also to accept responsibility for high-level coordination, for efficient operation and improvement, and for the personal development of the group's members. For this, he or she requires the capability to work at a higher level of complexity and accountability. The 'leaderless work group' will always stay within its comfort zone. The more

successful a group is the more it requires a single, designated leader to fight its corner and to drag it, if need be, *out* of its comfort zone.

4. *Each work group and its leader should, so far as possible,* PLAN AND ORGANISE *the group's work.*
If this responsibility is detached, there will be a loss of *meaning* (see above) and collective satisfaction. With this responsibility, groups are more committed and learn faster.

5. *Each work group should have the responsibility of* EVALUATING *its own performance against agreed standards of excellence.*
This means that all work groups get to complete the 'plan–do–review' cycle, ensuring coherence (a good *collective* understanding of the group's connection with and contribution to the wider system). Group members always have to remember that they exist to *add value*. If the conditions are right, the self-evaluation of groups will always be more uncompromising than external evaluation will. (See Figure 19 for a depiction of this and the next two principles.)

6. *Jobs within groups should be structured so that each individual can plan, do and evaluate at least one significant* TRANSFORMATION *in the work process.*
Using a technique known as 'transformation analysis', *core jobs* are identified. A core job is the cluster of activities around at least one value-adding activity. A core job may require the full-time effort of two or three people, depending on the workload. To it is added the responsibility for planning, doing and evaluating those secondary activities that tie more closely to it than to other core jobs. These secondary activities are described as 'enhancements'. A core job plus its enhancements comprises a 'whole job'. This is the basis for real *empowerment*—through this process, individuals get real ownership and responsibility for something they really can control.

7. *Personal and structural conditions that encourage* TEAMWORKING AND PARTICIPATION *throughout the whole organisation should be established.*
The essence here is to ensure that every group and every individual gets connected to the overall primary task. (Sir William Hudson's dictate that *all* staff should be exposed to the Snowy Mountains Scheme's progress flowcharts on a weekly basis is a good example.) The main structural conditions for organisation-wide teamworking

265

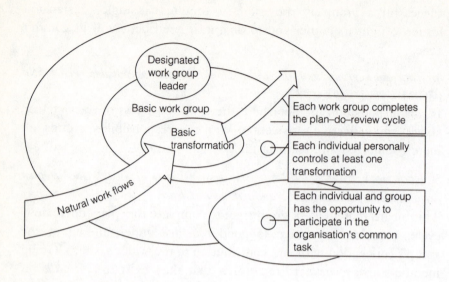

Figure 19 Work-structuring principles

include flexible working arrangements, common conditions of employment, regular work group meetings and a reward system compatible with teamworking.

Work Structuring Ltd has been installing processes like these all over the world for many years with consistent success, notably in manufacturing and service organisations, health services, government departments and agencies, finance houses and banks. Unlike some of the crasser BPR merchants, Work Structuring Ltd works in a admirably low-key way, striving always to *enhance* client capability. It will be obvious to the reader that the general approach meets my three assumptions head on: the need for work groups as organisational building blocks, the need for meaning in work, and the need for enhanced capability in higher-order jobs. It will also be clear that the work-structuring approach, because it involves real participation and empowerment, makes it much more likely that the 'Imos' will be listened to and understood. After all, they are the clever ones when it comes to really understanding transformational processes. There is a chance, therefore, that they may stay *inside* the organisation and become one of Pinchot's *intrapreneurs*. The alternative for them is to leave, taking the cleverness away, or to stay and create mischief.

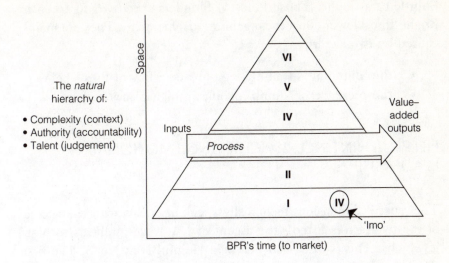

Figure 20   The space–time continuum

> This diagram demonstrates that the natural *spatial* hierarchy of an organisation (the way that complexity, authority and talent have to increase the higher you go) is just as important as 'time to market'. The fashion for 'business process re-engineering' (BPR), which simplifies processes to save time, has (important though time is) obscured the significance of the 'spatial' dimension. If leadership flaws exist in this dimension the risk is that a lowly (Level I) employee with high (Level IV) intelligence can't get a hearing. Space and time both matter.

The space–time continuum

The work-structuring principles share with business process re-engineering a concern with *time*. The whole point about the simplification of work processes is to shrink *time to market* at least as quickly as the competition does. It is no exaggeration to say that compressing time has been the dominant focus of business improvement over the past ten years, and quite rightly so. This has led to a partial neglect of the *space* dimension. I glorify this linkage as the *space–time continuum* (see Figure 20). It is a grandiose way of saying that all systems have to exist in space and time, and the neglect of either dimension is dangerous. The proof of this, despite all the BPR initiatives and the speeding up of processes, is the apparent proliferation of large-scale cockups and blunders—from the Barings Bank fiasco to the Challenger Space

267

Shuttle catastrophe. These kinds of blunders are *always* foreseen by bright 'Imos' lower down the organisational hierarchy. They are mainly caused by two factors:

- the 'dumbing' of all-male groups (see Bay of Pigs—below)
- the presence of 'dumb' people in high places

HELPFUL HINT NO. 2: ACHIEVING EMOTIONAL LEADERSHIP

The 'space' dimension, technically speaking, deals with the second of the two factors listed—the ascent of low-grade intellects to high-level jobs. This is discussed below in Helpful Hint No. 3. The first, the 'dumbing' of senior decision-makers, is a common outcome of the preponderance of male monocultures at the top of big organisations. Any group is a potentially powerful medium—for good or ill. The commando group in wartime is capable of quite extraordinary achievements, buoyed up by adrenalin and absolute mutual trust. The scientific team, driven by curiosity, can achieve leaps of logic that defy subsequent analysis. These are commonly all-male groups. John Latham's 'OEM' group in the IBM Corporation (Chapter 10) brought a remarkable, SAS-like esprit de corps to the selling of humble typewriters and word processors. But because any group has its primal origins in the unspoken understandings of the hunting band, it can degenerate into a primitive and mindless state. Youths in street gangs are usually astonished to discover that they have murdered somebody else. They didn't *mean* it—they simply lost their identity (and therefore their adult responsibility) in the mass.

One thing is certain: when tricky or dangerous situations are encountered, the leadership has to 'carry' the group, whether it is a commando or, in the case of General Bernard Montgomery on 13 August 1942, the entire staff of Eighth Army Headquarters. Montgomery's first address to the assembled top brass, on the very day of his arrival to take command, has gone down in legend. He faced a highly skeptical audience that evening. He was their fourth new commander in a year and their record was of almost continuous reverses and failures. In hindsight, his address was almost a parody of the British stiff upper lip style of exhortation:

I want first to introduce myself to you. You do not know me; I do not know you. But we have to work together; therefore we must understand each other and we must have confidence in each other. I have only been here a few hours. But from what I have seen and heard since I arrived I am prepared to say, here and now, that I have confidence in you. We will then work together as a team; and together we will gain the confidence of this great army and go forward to final victory in Africa. I believe that one of the first duties of a commander is to create what I call 'atmosphere'; and in that atmosphere, his staff, subordinate commanders and troops will live and work and fight. *I do not like the general atmosphere I find here.* It is an atmosphere of doubt, of looking back to select the next place to which to withdraw, of loss of confidence in our ability to defeat Rommel, of desperate defence measures by reserves in preparing positions in Cairo and the Delta. *All that must cease!*

There was much more in the same vein. We know this because one of the audience, presciently, took down the whole speech in shorthand. The contents do not bear close analysis. The point is that this was one of the great galvanic pre-engagement addresses, reminiscent of Agincourt, because it connected with the collective unconscious of all those present. Montgomery 'found' the emotional pulse of those present. This was two months before Alamein and it played a crucial and necessary part in shifting perceptions quickly amongst the top seventy officers. On this occasion, Montgomery attuned himself emotionally to his audience just as Hitler did in addressing a mass rally. The purpose was different but it was the same underlying phenomenon. The notable variable is *consciousness* on the part of the speaker—is the skill mobilised consciously (that is, under control) or does it, as it were, take over the speaker? Joachim Fest describes the mutual attunement of Hitler and his audiences:

For a few moments he would linger before the platform, mechanically shaking hands, mute, absent-minded, eyes flickering restively, but ready like a medium to be imbued and carried aloft by the strength that was already there, latent, in the shouting of the masses. The first words were dropped mutely, gropingly, into the breathless silence; they were often preceded by a pause that seemed to become utterly unbearable, while the speaker collected himself. The beginning was monotonous, trivial, usually lingering on the legend of his rise: 'When in 1918 as a nameless soldier at the front I . . .' This formal beginning prolonged the suspense once more, into the very speech itself. But it also allowed him to sense

269

the mood and to adjust to it. A catcall might abruptly inspire him to take a fighting tone until the first eagerly awaited applause surged up. For that was what gave him contact, what intoxicated him, and 'after about fifteen minutes', a contemporary observer commented, 'there takes place what can only be described in the primitive old figure of speech: The spirit enters into him'. With wild, explosive movements, driving his metallically transformed voice mercilessly to its highest pitch, he would hurl out the words. Quite often, in the furore of his conjuring, he would cover his grimacing face with his clenched fists and close his eyes, surrendering to the spasms of his transposed sexuality.

We have come a fair way from the clipped homilies of Montgomery but, as they say, different folks require different strokes. An analysis of Churchill's great radio broadcasts reveals that he touched the hearts of the British people through poetry, not by quotation but by expressing himself with the elegance and grace of poetic language. If your audience can't see you, the language itself carries a greater weight. This confers advantages and disadvantages. Poetry easily evokes the 'motherland'—the beloved object to be defended against barbaric hordes. World War II was a *ternary* war for the British—no matter how fierce the fighting, the *good object* always provided the justification. As aggressors, the Germans' war was all *binary*—conquest was the aim, fuelled by paranoid fantasy; the classic 'fight/flight' position. But, effective as it is for celebrating the good object, poetic language can so easily go over the top. Apparently a great many down-to-earth Britons assumed, without offence, that Churchill must have been drunk during some of these broadcasts: *'Advance Britannia!—Long live the King!'* It didn't matter. Robert Menzies, no mean orator himself and always prone to the OTT speech, put it well in referring to Churchill: *'His real tyrant is the glittering phrase—so attractive to his mind, but awkward facts have to give way!'*

The point is that these three quite different orators—clipped and critical, insane and transported, sentimental and poetic—found a pathway to the collective emotional state of their audience. The ability to do that, even in the humblest circumstances, is the best trick in the aspiring leader's armoury. How is it done?

Bion's 'basic assumptions'

The great psychoanalyst Wilfred Bion (also a senior Army officer and main inventor of the War Officer Selection Board group selection

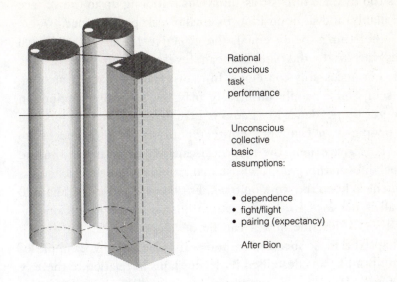

Rational
conscious
task
performance

Unconscious
collective
basic
assumptions:

- dependence
- fight/flight
- pairing (expectancy)

After Bion

Figure 21 **'Basic assumptions' in group life**

method) made use of his wartime experiences with groups to unpick the primitive and unconscious 'basic assumptions' that take hold of groups. He argued that these basic assumptions were 'instantaneous, instinctive and inevitable'. Whatever rational work the group was engaged in, there was always a parallel, emotional group life, just beneath the surface (see Figure 21). He dubbed the principal basic assumptions Dependence, Fight/Flight and Pairing. His observation was that *leadership* of the group always hinged on the unconscious belief that it could depend on somebody or something, or that it had to flee from or attack some enemy or threat, or that it would be delivered from doubt by the union of two of its members, usually the 'leader' and somebody else. Effective leadership therefore entailed *mobilising* the primitive basic assumptions in the interests of the *task*. The basic assumptions are always present so you can't ignore them. If the leader needs emotional commitment to a course of action (as well as intellectual understanding) then he or she must either align the task work with the prevailing assumption, or tweak the assumption. If all this sounds excessively psychological, think back to the last time a business meeting turned really nasty. Amanda Sinclair's descriptions (Chapter 12) of ritual public humiliations captures the essence of basic assumptions bubbling up to the surface uncontrollably, and in opposition to a calm task performance.

All other things being equal, the effective leader is the person with easy access to this subterranean level of group process. The access is not necessarily conscious. In many years of leader watching, I have seen some people intuitively play the basic assumptions in order to get things done. My guess is that these 'natural leaders' are always people with Gardner's entire repertoire of 'intelligences' to call on. This gives them the theatrical capacity to participate in the emotional life of the group, whilst maintaining enough intellectual detachment to keep the work on track. For those who lack this natural ability, all is not lost. In the discussion on Executive Role Consultation (below) I describe how it can be developed.

Perhaps the most spectacular, and well-documented, example of male 'groupthink' was described by Irving Janis in relation to the Bay of Pigs fiasco. Here was a situation where a highly intelligent group of men around President Kennedy, every single one of them (as it turned out later) with deep misgivings about the enterprise, blindly pressed forward to one of the most predictable and preventable blunders of all time. No one could speak out; everybody else *seemed* to be comfortable with the decision. Probably, the group seesawed between basic assumption Fight (against the threatening Cubans), basic assumption Flight (in relation to the fantasised Russian threat) and basic assumption Dependence (on the credibility of the generals, or on the charisma of the President). All we can be certain of is that rational task performance went out the window. This sort of thing is not so uncommon; we have all failed to speak out at meetings out of fear or confusion. The leader (male or female) who is comfortable with emotional process has an enormous advantage here.

The emotional life of business schools

This leads to an awkward question about business schools and MBA-type programs. If it is true that effective leadership depends partly on the ability to tune into emotional states, how do traditional programs tap into, or enhance, this ability. I refer the reader to my book *The Dynamics of Management Education*. This describes an attempt to understand how the psychological underpinnings of business school programs can get in the way of useful learning outcomes. I carried out an in-depth study of a long (twelve-week) executive program at the London Business School—an institution sufficiently confident to open up its underlying processes to scrutiny.

It quickly became evident that the input–conversion–output process was the opposite of that which obtains in a hospital—another type of 'people-processing' institution. As a general rule, the hospital obliges you to bring in your guts (for processing) but to hang up your brains at the entrance, like cowboys' firearms at the saloon door. Most patients are treated as if they had no brains at all. In the business school the deal is: bring in your brains but hang up your guts at the front entrance. The idea that management is *also* about emotional life is hardly recognised at all or, worse still, is treated as a technique for manipulating behaviour.

The institutional processing of *people* (in business schools, hospitals, etc.) is always tricky because the customers are made relatively helpless and anxious by the risks entailed and by the processing itself. The suppliers (professors, surgeons, etc.) can unconsciously ease their own anxieties by *partialising* the customers—that is, by trying to deal only with the part that concerns them, and not with the *whole person*. This is the human throughput equivalent of the bicycle-repair shop. Hospitals, for example, have ways of making you feel neurotic if you take too keen an interest in your own case. Business schools are sometimes made very nervous by the outbreak of actual *behaviour* amongst their students, particularly if it involves passion, skepticism or anger. They are much more comfortable with 'behavioural studies'.

I don't need to remind the reader that none of the outstanding people described in this book owe their success to formal business education. They are all 'broad-banders' *attached* to useful, concrete outcomes and all of them convey their passion. They never unlearned their natural, *multiple* intelligences and, had they ever gone to business school, they might well have been made ill by the experience. I have tried to imagine Sir William Hudson as a 35-year-old member of a long executive-development program—and have failed. It follows that if I have a criticism of the Karpin inquiry it lies in the task force's touching faith in formal, academic subject-based business school programs.

HELPFUL HINT NO. 3: JAQUES' CONTRIBUTIONS

Sometimes when the 'Imos' fail to break through with their good ideas it is a function of conscious jealousy and deliberate political sabotage. John Latham suffered from this, at the hands of people with no shame at all. More frequently, the plight of the 'Imo' is the result of dumb incomprehension in high places, especially when broad-band 'Imos' come up against narrow-band seniors (those with power, position and very advanced technical skills in one field or another). In Chapter 6, on the qualities of successful leaders, I drew a distinction between knowledge, skill, motivation and personality quirks as disqualifiers for high rank. I suggested that the most common cause of blunders was the shortage of 'intellectual firepower' in top jobs. This means, simply, the capacity to cope with complexity.

In Figure 22 I present once again Elliott Jaques' famous 'strata' of work complexity. Those who have worked with this theory, including major Australian organisations like CRA, Westpac Bank and the Electricity Trust of South Australia, know that it accords closely with reality. Jaques (another of the Tavistock luminaries) is asserting that there *can* be no more than around seven levels of hierarchy, no matter how big the organisation. A substantial non-international organisation of up to, say, a thousand employees ought to have no more than five hierarchical levels from CEO to operative. This means that many big organisations have been top-heavy in the past. If there are more levels than this, some of them must be 'pseudo-levels' and the pseudo–role incumbents will be effectively bypassed by other people, especially subordinates. The smart subordinate can always identify the 'real boss'.

The spate of 'delayering' we have seen in recent years is therefore justified, *provided* that it has been carried out according to a consistent theory of organisation—provided that it is the 'pseudo-levels' that disappear, and not real flesh-and-blood connections which help to sustain the whole organisational 'frog'. Jaques doubts that this is always what has happened. Much of the downsizing has been driven merely by cost-hunting. This has led to the *illogical* excision of functions and roles. We are back to the concept of the frog again. If you propose to remove anything from the body corporate, you need to know in advance the likely impact on the totality. That means understanding how the bits connect and how they are ordered.

VII	Global corporate prescience	Sustaining long-term viability; defining values, moulding contexts	(25–50)
VI	(Group) corporate citizenship	Reading international contexts to support/alert level V strategic business units	(15–20)
V	Strategic intent	Overview of organisational purpose in context	($\rightarrow$ 10)
IV	Strategic development	Inventing/modelling new futures; positioning the organisation	($\rightarrow$ 5)
III	Good practice	Constructing connecting and fine-tuning systems	($\rightarrow$ 2/3)
II	Service	Supporting/serving level 1 and customers/clients	($\rightarrow$ 1)
I	Quality	Hands-on skill	

Figure 22   Levels of work authority, complexity and talent

The point about the strata is that they are linked in a stepwise fashion. The 'good boss' (all other things being equal) is the one who can 'context' your work. This means that he or she has the capacity to encompass a system bigger, wider and higher up than yours. If the boss lacks that capacity, decisions will be slowed up and subordinates will be frustrated—or maddened. There are few things more infuriating than being obliged to report to somebody who cannot cope with the demands of the boss's role. This is mainly what the 'Imos' moan about in the pub after work. Jaques' theory asserts that you can easily render an organisation *anorexic* by taking out too many layers, thus leaving a vacuum in the chain of authority. This happened to a number of organisations around the world in the financial services business. Very significant Level II, III and IV lending decisions were being taken without the coordination and supervision of Level V, which had been taken out to save cost. The global Level VI work was usually still in place but unconnected. The result was very expensive, as a raft of ill-conceived lending initiatives (taken by people not *quite* up to the job) came home to roost. The diagram shows how the relationships between bosses and subordinates (the line of accountability) are the atoms that make up a successful, energetic organisation. A lot of the current management literature is anti-hierarchy. Anybody who has ever felt powerless or crushed by bad parents, teachers or bosses is likely to harbour an

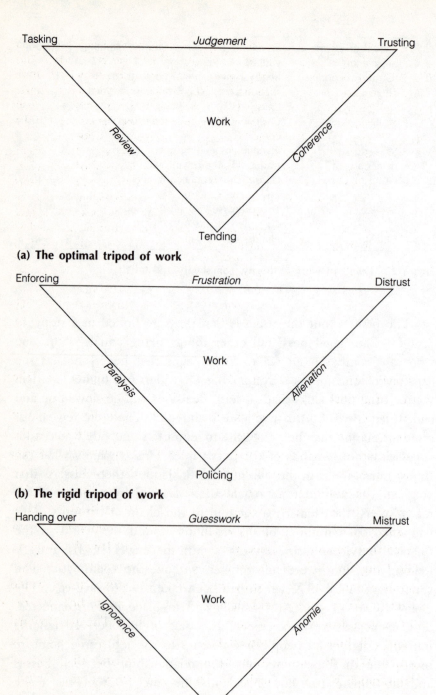

(a) The optimal tripod of work

(b) The rigid tripod of work

(c) The diffuse tripod of work

Figure 23 These three diagrams show how it *feels* when the hierarchical strata of organisations shift from the optimum and get out of kilter. This can be caused either by poor organisational design or by inadequacy in bosses—or both. In the OPTIMAL state, the boss TASKS a subordinate clearly (not specifying what will be done but specifying *outputs* required from that subsystem, along with time frames). He or she then TRUSTS the subordinate to get on with it (this doesn't work if the subordinate has been *wished on* the boss without the latter's consent). But trusting is not enough—subordinates also need bosses to be minimally *watchful*. TENDING means that the good boss appears at your shoulder just at the moment you were beginning to wish he or she would. Effective and sensitive tending loops back to intelligent retasking, and so it goes on. *Balanced* tasking, trusting and tending form the kind of bossing that people pray for. It is partly a function of the layers in the structure. If there are too many layers and/or the boss lacks confidence (capacity), the system goes RIGID. If the company has overdone the 'delayering', it goes DIFFUSE. This handing over of responsibility is often dressed up as 'empowerment'. Really it is a form of casting subordinates adrift.

irrational hatred of hierarchy, as if human pecking orders were the source of all disharmony.

It is a bold theory, which irritates some people, because it asserts that the levels are immutable—it makes no difference if the organisation in question is a manufacturing firm, a solicitors' practice, a government or a diocese. If you have ascended to Level IV capacity, you will be able to take on strategic development work of that complexity in any field for which your knowledge, skills and motivation suit you. If I deal with my architect, or my accountant, I do not receive the product or service *directly* from a Level I worker, as I do when I buy an object made by factory workers and sold to me by a shop assistant. I will deal with the professional *direct*, and I would expect to notice quite quickly if he or she seems not to be up to the job (i.e. unable to hack the complexity required). The professional person will however be served by Level I/II/III staff within the practice. Why do the levels of human capacity match the levels of organisational work complexity so neatly? The answer, according to Jaques, is that organisations are merely and necessarily reflections of human nature and human ability as it develops over *time*. The one is a natural function of the other.

Talent vs age

Before I actually put forward Helpful Hint No. 3—be patient!—there is one more important angle to the theory of work system stratification. The levels of work complexity are stable. The capacities of people clearly are *not*. While it is true that all people can be developed quickly to some extent with intensive instruction and support, it is also true that some people develop *precociously* when it comes to intellectual firepower. Even as I write, one of my clients (this is in the United Kingdom) is ascending *fast* from Level IV to Level V capability. He is very young; much too young in the eyes of his employers for any sort of conventional promotion through the system. He has also put a few backs up because he habitually pokes his nose into all sorts of organisational crannies (always important ones; that is why they attract him). He is able to do this because his formal obligations (at Level III) are met in about a third of the working week. He represents therefore a 'problem', both for his immediate superiors (who can't keep up with him and who think he is 'arrogant'—he is not!) and for the human resources director. People like this are very difficult to deploy in their twenties. They come into their own in their thirties and they *usually* turn out not to have been arrogant at all—merely impatient.

Figure 24 shows the differential rate of the increase in capacity to exercise judgement in complex or ambiguous situations. This is the normal pattern, *all other things being equal*—but of course life does not always run so smoothly. Thousands of managers from the former Soviet Union are now being exposed for the first time to modern management development and ideas. Most of their growth curves have been distorted by overmanagement and understimulation in the past. Those of lower capacity merely resume the flat trajectory (see Figure 24). Those of high capacity jump, almost overnight (given the chance to stretch themselves), to the high trajectory they would probably have pursued had they worked in the West. Clearly, some people ascend more quickly than others. These are the people who (none of the other disqualifiers being present) need to be 'fasttracked' to the most senior echelons of organisations. The array of growth curves looks pretty forbidding and deterministic to most people. It should be said that it pertains to quite a narrow area of capability. There is no suggestion that the work of high-flyers in this sense is more *important* than the work of anybody else. We all have our special contribution to make.

Figure 24 also reveals that the accumulation of *wisdom* does not cease at the 'normal' age of retirement. The kinds of people celebrated in these pages go on getting smarter, and encompassing *more*, as they age, provided that their physical/mental equipment holds out. If any country is serious about mining its talent, this raises an interesting question. I am conscious of this because my own father produced *five* new books after he passed the age of ninety. He was lucky that writing is one of those trades unconstrained by physical barriers; you can do it from anywhere. But there are substantial numbers of smart fifty-plus year-olds being 'spilled' from large organisations these days, with no obvious sluice for their energy and ingenuity. This is where the *not-for-profit* sector comes in. In the United States there are now more than 1.4 million not-for-profit organisations with total combined assets of over $500 billion. This sector already contributes more than 6 per cent of GNP, and growing, and is responsible for 10.5 per cent of total national employment.

Any intelligently led (i.e. farsighted) government these days would be making a direct investment in expanded job creation in the not-for-profit sector, as an alternative to welfare for the increasing numbers of people who find themselves locked out of the stream-lined, downsized, high-tech global marketplace. The British thinktank 'Demos' puts it succinctly:

Powerful vested interests are likely to resist the idea of providing a social wage in return for community service. Yet, the alternative of leaving the problem of long-term unemployment unattended could lead to widespread social unrest, increased violence, and further disintegration of society!

It is an attractive idea that high-capacity executives can be spilled into the not-for-profit sector, in order to stay useful, when they get to be fifty or so—but what about the relative youngsters back in the corporations? It is probably no coincidence that we are seeing an explosion of concern about 'stress' in the workplace, especially amongst senior executives. Some executive boards are nowadays dogged by the ill-health of their members. They are working much too hard because they are at full intellectual stretch—just coping with the complexity, if they are lucky. The thing to remember is that these groups of (mostly) men are usually a good ten years *younger* on average than their equivalents ten to fifteen years ago. An examination of

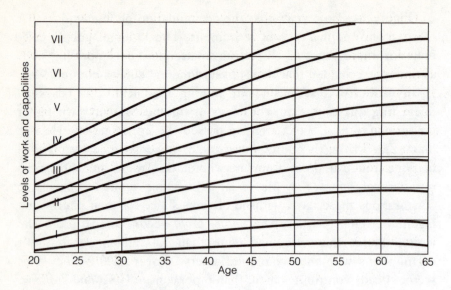

Figure 24   Array of growth curves

This chart refers to the development, over time, of the mental aspect of managing—the capacity to process complexity under situations of uncertainty or ambiguity. Obviously there are other important factors. Given a good following wind (unusual), the development of this capacity in individuals is remarkably steady and predictable. It can be seen that some people are relatively precocious in this respect. Smart primary school teachers can spot exceptionally bright young-sters easily. Big organisations need to get these people to the top (if they can keep them) relatively quickly—provided that none of the main *disqualifiers* is present. But just as valuable, in a different way, are those people in technical organisations who ascend *slowly* to Level II supervisory work, carrying with them a huge wealth of knowhow, nous, gut-feel, insight and so on. Such people are 'natural leaders' (at a key, supervisory, level in the system) for those people who do the real work—at the front line. These days, many older and wiser supervisors are stripped out to save money, or to create 'leaderless work groups'. This is usually a false economy because they represent the last line of defence against the big technical blunders which are always very expensive.

Figure 24 reveals that some of these struggling executives might have been able to cope, as their capacities expanded, a few years later—particularly their capacity for 'judgement'. Unfortunately, they jumped at the chance to fill the shoes of some wise old bird now (happily or not) *under*stretched in the voluntary sector or on the golf course.

Once you accept the notion that the nucleus at the core of any effective organisation is *sound judgement*, then it follows that the way to design organisations is to ensure that there is both space for judgement and active encouragement and stimulation of individual decision-making. The organisation will work well if every individual within it is at full stretch and is given exactly the right amount of elbow room for exercising *discretion* that he or she can cope with (see Figure 25). That means there must be a boss capable of gauging how much discretion is appropriate for the job and for the person.

Career Path Appreciation

Career Path Appreciation (CPA) is the essence of Helpful Hint No. 3. It is a method, originally designed by Gillian Stamp, based on Jaques' theories about levels of work complexity, for assessing/predicting individual capacity for the exercise of discretion and judgement in situations of complexity and ambiguity. If you accept that it is the *intelligence* of the leader that is most important of all, then you need a way of judging judgement. If you are very lucky, you may have available one of those gifted people who *know about* these things, and who *never* make mistakes in the assessment of capacity and character. If not, you need a method.

In one of the CPA procedures, a fiendishly difficult symbol card exercise, the individual is faced with an obscure *logic* in the form of an array of symbols of different shapes and colours. The task is to try out, in a step-by-step sequence, the different possibilities for determining the pattern or logic of the symbol cards, explaining each successive strategy to the assessor. This part of the CPA is essentially an exercise in continuous *reframing* (see Executive Role Consultation, below).

Stamp has conducted twenty-year studies of correlations between these assessments and the subsequent career trajectories of the individuals concerned. The results are impressive. People who are outstandingly good at this sort of reframing are always outstanding at the *intellectual* side of managing—sorting and crunching the data and making serendipitous *connections*.

I have spent some time leading up to the CPA method (there are numerous others of the same kind) because I want to stress, by so doing, the point that business failures are caused—mainly—by

A
SYSTEMATIC set of
RELATIONSHIPS between
INDIVIDUALS (and groups) which allows just the right amount of
space for the exercise of
DISCRETION in making
JUDGEMENTS

Figure 25   Sound organisation structure

failures of *judgement*. The hot issue in 'leadership studies' ought not to be personality, or charisma, or even 'vision'—it ought to be *brain-power*, or the ability to handle complexity under fire. This is so obvious to me, as a student of worldwide cockups and blunders, that I have difficulty in seeing how anybody could see things differently.

Remember that methods like CPA deal mainly with the *cognitive* aspect of leadership. All the other potential disqualifiers (knowledge, skills, motivation and quirks) still have to *judged* by intelligent people with good, proven, judgement. You use CPA if you want to be sure that an individual can handle complexity, and to check on the pre-cocity—how quickly that ability will increase over the years. The human resources director needs this kind of information for medium-term succession planning and for *protecting* the best 'Imos' from envious attacks by their peers. One Australian mining company chairman put it like this: '*I have to identify and protect the radical!*'

The space–time continuum revisited

In the preceding section, I have offered a seal of approval to two methods of intervening in organisations, both of them based on the broad 'socio-technical systems' idea. The first is the 'work structuring' method devised by Christian Schumacher and the second is the 'career path appreciation' method, which grew out of Elliott Jaques' 'stratified systems theory'. I suggested that the former superficially resembles 'BPR' (business process re-engineering) because it is concerned principally with *time*—getting work done in a *quicker* and more efficacious way by structuring the *work flow vs people* relationship in a logical fashion. I also suggested that stratified systems theory was mainly concerned with *space*—the spatial distance between organisational roles, particularly up and down the hierarchy.

This makes a kind of sense but you could as well put it the other way round. Work Structuring achieves its efficiencies by locating work groups at exactly the right distance from each other and by clarifying the location of the boundaries between them. To that extent, work structuring is as concerned with the spatial as the temporal. Similarly, the assessments of capability which flow from career path appreciations, and which get the spatial roles right, are based ultimately on Jacques' famous theory of the 'time-span of discretion'—a theory about the temporal implications of the decision-making involved in managerial work. The chief executive needs to be able to envision much longer time-frames than the front-line team leader. The CPA gets at that crucial capacity.

The fact is that time and space interact at every point. Any intervention in an organisation which fails to factor in both dimensions is likely to fail, because it will distort reality. Most BPR exercises fail in the end because their focus is too short-term—on *immediate* cost savings. Treating a complex system as if it were a bicycle disabled by a minor short-term mechanical problem is liable to damage the 'frog'—but the damage probably won't show for years. Or, the consultants sometimes 'fix' one part of the organisation, by 'downsizing' or even selling it, only to discover that there were subterranean connections with the rest of the organisation, a bit too deep for bright (but narrow) young consultants to discern. The result, once again, is a weakening of the big 'frog'. When the financial costs come home to roost, much time will have passed. By that time a new generation of optimistic youngsters may well be in charge, entirely without organisational memory. If they do not understand the meaning of the past for the present, they are doomed, as the saying goes, to repeat history. They will deal with 'new' financial difficulties as if they were novel, rather than the detritus left over from the innocence of their predecessors.

Experienced, high-capacity executives find it relatively easy to understand how the temporal and the spatial interact. Some major corporations, like Exxon, use Work Structuring on a more or less continuous basis—worldwide. Others, like ICI, use Career Path Appreciations worldwide. It is a virtuous circle. Corporations which grow their people organically and systematically, like a good farmer nurtures his crops, tend to end up with thoughtful, wise leaders at the top. They, in turn, buy in intelligent modes of intervention which are likely to sustain the natural cycles of renewal—in structures as well as people. It is a difficult matter to get the less canny leaders of less canny organisations actually to *understand* the preceding three paragraphs. It amounts to saying: *If you get good (i.e. smart and sane) people and you slot them into coherent structures and roles, things will go pretty well.* As the Americans say, it's not exactly rocket science.

HELPFUL HINT NO. 4: REFRAMING THE EXECUTIVE MIND

The Career Path Appreciation method flows from the theory of stratified system levels. Its useful output for the human resources director is an assessment of the current level of capability of the executive concerned and a prediction of the probable rate of ascent through the higher levels in years to come. I want to highlight now another method, called Executive Role Consultation, which is similar in some ways but has a different purpose. The purpose is to help the CEO to be actor and impresario at the same time—to manage with *passion* but to remain cool and clear as well. The combination of passion and detachment is the hallmark of the intelligent leader.

The Executive Role Consultation method is merely a formalisation of the natural process that takes place when one person (armed with a good system overview) helps another to 'reframe' his or her relationship with reality. Something of the kind goes on whenever anybody helps a friend, a colleague, a subordinate, a patient or a client to 'see' things differently. It is what 'natural leaders' do without knowing it. It is what Noel Waite does for people stuck in an unhappy or unproductive place, in order to help them to think their way out intelligently. Your best friend, after all, is someone who can be cruel to be kind, because he or she knows your habitual weaknesses. An important task for a role consultation is to *explain* the difference between:

- the *normative* or formal role (the job description, for example)
- the *experiential* role (what the executive *thinks* he or she is up to)
- the *phenomenal* role (how everybody else sees it)

These three roles are always different, sometimes grossly so. This is important and needs to be understood by the executive concerned.

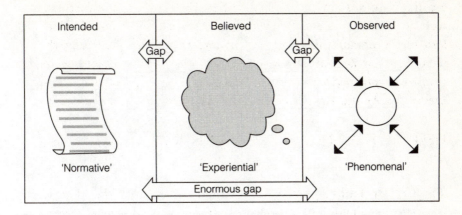

Figure 26   Three versions of an executive's role

> This sets out the logic for the Executive Role Consultation method.
> It is nearly always the case that the formal (or *normative*) role of an
> executive—the job description, for example—differs from his or her
> view of reality (the *experiential* role). This differential doesn't usually
> concern Anglo-Saxon executives—who tend to be keen on 'free-
> dom'—but it does worry German managers, who think that if the
> reality has drifted away from the intention it might be a good idea
> to update the job description. This makes sense. The extraordinary
> truth is that the *phenomenal* role (the activity pattern that everybody
> else observes) is nearly always wildly different from both the nor-
> mative and the experiential roles. If the executive concerned can get
> to understand the *meaning* of his or her *actual* activity pattern, then
> there is a good chance of exercising effective (because realistic)
> leadership. The so-called 'natural leaders' are always *naturally* real-
> istic—they don't delude themselves about the situation or about their
> own impact on the situation. This is fairly rare—which is why role
> consultation needs to exist.

A failure to understand this simply exports confusion into the system
because everybody else has to cope with three different versions of
the executive's 'role' (see Figure 26). An inexperienced or unsophis-
ticated personal assistant, for example, can confuse others by taking
the executive's formal role at face value. An adoring PA can infuriate
others by assuming that he or she is always right. The smart PA acts
as a kind of automatic transmission, meshing the external system to
the executive's peculiarities and fantasies.

When I conduct a role consultation, for example with a CEO, it
is generally described as 'mentoring'. I am not certain that that is

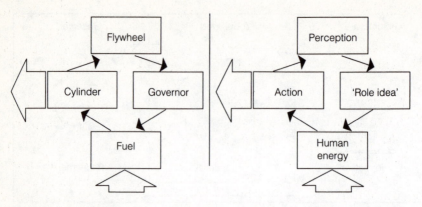

Figure 27 Executive role consultation: coping with change and initiating change

technically the correct term because the method is essentially *cognitive*. My client and I may have a stimulating time in the course of eight to ten meetings of up to three hours each—sometimes frustrating, sometimes hilarious—but the main focus is always on the executive's mindset: the way he or she 'constructs' the world. If a chief executive has a limited mental 'map' of the relevant territory— or a distorted one—then the entire organisation is certain to end up limited or distorted. *Nothing* is more important than the contents of the chief executive's head. An increasing number of chief (and other) executives are now calling on this sort of assistance. The previous generation of top managers might have seen the need for it as a weakness; the younger generation was brought up understanding much more about psychology, psychopathology, cybernetics and perception.

Figure 27 describes the process in cybernetic terms. I find that this form of explanation sometimes helps engineers to understand what a role consultation might be like, before the event. Otherwise, it sounds to them like therapy. The underlying theory is that the human mind runs on 'autopilot' most of the time. Just as an autonomic control system uses feedback loops to manage its task without constant supervision, so the executive's daily routine is generally programmed by surrounding routines and events. In the donkey-engine example on the left of the diagram, the source of energy enters the system as fuel. Combustion of the fuel drives the cylinder which, in turn, exports the 'work' or the added value. The flywheel senses the load, altering its aspect in line with demand on the system, and sends messages to the governor accordingly. If the message 'says', 'We're struggling here!', the governor is programmed to inject more fuel, thus maintaining the system in equilibrium. All control systems operate roughly like this—using *feedback* in order to adjust operations, within prespecified tolerances.

Using this metaphor, we can see that executive energy enters the system via the executive. 'High octane' executives simply bring in more physical energy. The 'work' of the executive is the actions taken, from which added value flows. The individual takes cognisance of the effects of the action taken, via normal perception (watching, evaluating, surmising)—this is the mental 'flywheel'. The really important element in the executive feedback loop is the *governor*—the preprogrammed set of assumptions which save the individual from laboriously delving into every detail. I call this the 'role-idea'—a completely individual assumption, belief, hunch, prejudice or 'map' about how the world is and what the impact of actions taken is. We can infer the existence of a role-idea from the way we behave but, other than that, we are mostly unaware of its existence.

The role-idea collects data from perception, according to habit. If it is inclined to collect only good news, it will collect only good news. The result will be complacency and increasing isolation. The role-idea also contains all the possible *excuses* for inaction or failure because it tells you what can't possibly be done. That news may relieve you of the responsibility for going outside your designated turf or for taking on a seriously frightening and risk-laden duty. If you enjoy certain kinds of work—hey presto!—the role-idea will record lots of need for that work to be done. If you dread certain work, the need for it may miss the role-idea completely.

All this is important for two main reasons:

- Chief executives are separated from reality by a raft of systems, routines and flunkeys. They infrequently meet the 'Imos' lower down the organisation who actually see at first hand the impact of top management decisions. They are forced to rely, therefore, on a working assumption about their own role in the system: where they might or should go to test reality; who they can trust inside and outside the organisation; what the Board wants; and so on.

287

- The role-idea actually *governs* behaviour. It is 'the governor'. The reason why people do what they do (even if it makes no sense at all to others) is that *it makes sense to them*—it is internally consistent with their mental map of the territory (which includes the individual himself or herself—in role).

If it is the case that behaviour is governed by the role-idea, then it follows that you cannot and will not alter behaviour unless you *get at* the role-idea, no matter how many management training courses you may attend. Altering *behaviour* in an intelligent direction is essentially the purpose of a role consultation. It will be clear that we are not talking about *formal* role, as specified in a job description. We are dealing with role in the theatrical sense as something that emerges from circumstances in a distinctive and individual way. If the surrounding system perceives you to be playing Iago, and deals with you accordingly, there is no point in your protesting that you are *really* Othello. Your real 'role' is determined by the perceptions of those surrounding you. This is why role consultation can be useful for leadership development; it helps the executive client to adopt a dynamic role that 'feels right' to all the followers.

Most of the important work in a role consultation takes place *between* the consultations, which are usually at two-week to four-week intervals. The first two or three consultations lay out the map of the territory, as it is constructed in the executive's head. That map represents a mixture of solid data and the 'spin' that the executive's mindset imparts to data. As the meetings progress, the consultant is formulating a series of hypotheses about what might be going on between the system and the client. All these hypotheses are testable. If you arrive at a hunch, you can always construct an experiment to test it. The testing is the job of the client executive in the spaces between meetings. In a recent consultation my client and I jointly devised a picture of the system which suggested that a much needed reform of work practices (long resisted by everybody and attempted unsuccessfully in the past) might be *easily* achieved in the present, unusual, circumstances of the system. Although it seemed to me that the supporting evidence for this was laid out in front of us (on a big piece of flip chart paper full of hieroglyphics, system models, hunches and other creative/artistic effusions), my client 'knew' that it was impossible.

Testing the hypothesis was easy. He walked into two key offices and *announced* the changes, the timetable for their completion, and the delegation of authority to carry them out. To his astonishment, it happened—the *system was ready!* At our next meeting, we went back to the hieroglyphics to revisit the *system* analysis. We satisfied ourselves that, while he had much reinforced his reputation for bold and incisive leadership, the truth was that it was *easy* to achieve because you could *see* the system was ready to tip in that direction. In a sense, I had been consulting directly to the *system* by way of the chief executive's perceptions. He learned two important lessons from this:

- at the basic level, he improved his 'map' of that particular territory at that time
- at the 'double-loop' level, he acknowledged that he had the mental *habit* of constructing particular *kinds* of unreliable maps, or fantasies

There is nothing like a good fantasy for distorting reality and turning followers off. He learned that it would be wise in the future to guard against the arousal of the same class of fantasy. In effect, what he had learned was that the 'role-idea' is mostly *unconscious*. It is there, inside our heads and shaping our actions. We *think* our actions are determined by 'reality' as we see it. The problem is that reality gets filtered through the role-idea and, sometimes, distorted. Role Consultation drags the role-idea, kicking and screaming, into consciousness.

No doubt I have failed to describe this process adequately. All of my past clients say that the experience is indescribable. However, when it works, it works spectacularly. To the outside world the outcome can look like a four to six month personality transformation from tentative and cautious technocrat to bold, confident and inspiring *leader*. The truth is that the executive client now simply has a better cognitive map—this effectively renders him or her more *intelligent*, thus creating the *impression* of bravery! If double-loop learning takes place, there should be no need to repeat the process. In fact, role consultation clients frequently return for a '10 000 kilometre service', as one put it, either to check that no cognitive bad habits have crept back or to seek assistance in unpacking a particularly messy situation.

In describing the role consultation process I have used the technical language of cognition, role and so on. The commonsense way of viewing this is in terms of *self-awareness*. Role consultation may simply be more helpful than instructing: *'Know thyself!'* Robert Keep (see earlier), was a *riveting* amateur actor because he really understood the *play*. All the characters in this book have a heroic quality for the same reason—self-awareness. Role consultation evidently improves awareness of self *and* system, in action, in the situation.

The new fashion for one-to-one mentoring, counselling and so on . . .

As faith in formal management education has dwindled, the use of one-to-one forms of executive support has grown, and continues to grow. The explanation for this is not difficult to determine.

1. At long last, it has dawned on corporate trainers and management developers that external management or business school programs are often wasteful, in the sense that their target is too broad for most of the students most of the time. Even the best external programs provide space for academics to tyrannise students, at great expense. This has been known for a long time but, lately, the money has got tighter.

2. More significantly, the 'downsized' organisation has created mana-gerial *vacuums*. A glance at Figure 22 above will show how the removal of a *necessary level* may lead to a dangerous loss of control. In the modern 'lean' organisation a lot of people are *under*managed. Their bosses are often away, usually on an aircraft, and they themselves have been promoted to a particular level of seniority, complexity and stress at a much younger age than would have been the case in years past. They have more subordinates to manage (because the spans of control have widened) and the subordinates themselves are younger and less experienced. Such a boss is going to want and need a helping hand—if not from another boss, then from a *mentor* or *coach*.

This is an interesting development. It is a necessary outcome of the super-lean organisation but it means that *loyalties* have been altered irrevocably. The social glue that held together organisations in the past had the parent-like relationship between boss and subordinate as a reinforcing structure which tied together all the peer groups. Now the trust that flows from personal understanding and continuity lies with an outsider—a professional mentor, coach or counsellor. Some organisations, recognising the limitations of the new managerial class, have opted for internal greybeards (sometimes recent retirees) to provide that social glue, in parallel with the managerial 'line'. It is difficult to make it work because even the detached greybeards tend to get drawn back into the organisational politics, particularly when they wish to promote the career cause of their protégés. Never forget that the lean organisation is usually a highly *political* organisation.

For these reasons, the one-to-one mentor/coach/counsellor is here to stay. The form varies. In California, as you might expect, much of the one-to-one work comes under the banner of 'creativity'. In the severely downsized organisation, the one-to-one supporter is often a 'stress counsellor' or, if not labelled as such, much the same thing. In the trendiest organisations, the executive mentor is modelled on the great sports coaches (like the golf guru David Leadbetter) and brandished about as a status symbol. My own approach to 'executive consultation' (see above) is essentially *cognitive* and attempts to enhance self-knowledge. It has much in common therefore with the sports coach model, because most sports success is 'in the mind'. Graham Alexander, one of the leaders in the field, proposes that: PERFORMANCE = POTENTIAL minus INTERFERENCE. I like that formulation. In the successful role consultation, the consultant and client jointly identify the sources of interference. Once identified, they can be managed or even eradicated.

What we have to face is that the emergence of all these one-to-one roles indicates the presence of an organisational vacuum created by weak leadership and dysfunctional structure. If the main 'demotivators' of managers in modern organisations (according to Institute of Management research) are *perceived incompetence of higher management* and *organisational politics,* then the calm, experienced, detached, sympathetic and frankly uncompromising mentor is bound to seem like an island of sanity in a sea of nonsense.

HELPFUL HINT NO. 5: THE ASSESSMENT/DEVELOPMENT CENTRE MODEL

I suggested above that the capacity for *judgement* is at the heart of our endeavours to fix problems and to plan for the future. Judgement is the key, whether you are engaged in assessment or in development of people. Why not combine assessment and development? If you put management trainees in classrooms and 'teach' them curricula, you run the obvious risk of turning off those who combine the spatial and interpersonal intelligences. As we have mooted, these may be the most capable people of all. If you select by psychometrics, you run the risk of excluding those with eccentric profiles. Again, if the examples in this book bear any weight, these may be the most valuable 'Imos'. We need a way, it seems, of putting people to *relevant* tests of their capability—and that means, if you accept the argument, tests of their capacity in *real time* to exercise judgement under conditions of uncertainty. 'Action Learning', the invention of Professor R. W. Revans, is the best known method of achieving this objective.

It was with these issues in mind that my colleagues and I in the IBM Corporation set about revamping our procedures for assessment, selection and promotion of all kinds of staff. This was in the United Kingdom company. The model we devised then has stood the test of time. It has been much copied, but *not copied enough* in my humble opinion. When we began this exercise, we had already inherited an 'assessment centre' model from our American parent. Like most American products, it was practical and sturdy, but without subtlety or style. It was, however, based on fairly exhaustive research into the observed traits of already successful IBM executives. The assessment centre design sought to replicate these success traits throughout the corporation. The difficulty with this is obvious—what you were good at formerly may not be what is required in a different future. This was at about the point in history when John Latham was beginning to expose the fixity of the IBM mindset.

In the United Kingdom company we had one or two advantages. One was that some of us had first-hand knowledge of the selection boards used by British organisations (including Unilever and the Civil Service), which were in direct line of descent from the original WOSBs (War Office Selection Boards) set up to identify *leadership capacity* in wartime. As a result of the WOSBs, the British Army had gone from almost invariably getting it wrong in officer selection to hardly ever making a mistake. The principal creator of the WOSBs was Wilfred Bion, who poured his insights about group dynamics and emotional leadership into the design. The American assessment centre movement grew from the same origins, but in different intellectual soil. 'Group dynamics' in the United States became an exploration of 'interpersonal authenticity' and power. The European descendant was mainly about the exercise of leadership judgement and *authority*.

IBM United Kingdom had another advantage—the presence of two Australian 'Imos', near enough culturally to the Brits to merge into the surroundings but different enough to *see* things in a tangential way, as from the proverbial 'helicopter'. I, of course, was one of them. The other was my then assistant, Julia Wansey. I wasn't all that clever in those days but I was smart enough to know how clever Wansey was. When she got a hunch, you gave her her head. Her great insight was that there was some kind of *pattern* to be found in the voluminous IBM records of all the selection and promotion exercises in the past. She also had the perseverance to plough through the archives, piecing together the pattern. No one had ever *bothered* before. The reader will see the parallel with Bob Clifford and Robert Keep, worrying away incessantly at a hunch. Her great discovery, amongst others, was that there were *two* branch sales managers in the system who had never, apparently, made a mistake in appointments and promotions.

Furthermore, they had not achieved this remarkable record by caution—these were the men who habitually pressed oddball sales-person candidates on to their colleagues with assurances that they would garner '300 per cent of quota', not just the target 100 per cent. Their advice was always taken because they were always right—they *knew* about these things. They were also very good at representing the IBM Corporation to the aspirants, so that the newcomers always understood what they were letting themselves in for, and settled in painlessly. These two branch managers were otherwise nondescript characters—competently carrying out an operational (but not strate-gic) job at Level III (see Figure 22). They were both somewhat older than the average branch manager and had been in the post for some years. They were *settled* and they clearly had a good contextual understanding of their branch's place in the wider scheme of things. This kind of stability probably wouldn't be allowed today.

Characteristically, I wasted a lot of time trying to find out *why* these two managers were thus gifted, and what it was they were doing right. *They* certainly didn't know how they did it, although they *did* know that they were much better than their colleagues in this respect. They were very grateful to us for making them famous for it. Julia Wansey was the one who instructed me to stop wasting time with research and to put the two of them to practical use. When we got our assessment/development program (called PDP—Personal Development Program) up and running, those two managers were routinely seeded into the six-person assessing group. We spread their insight around by a sort of osmosis. Over the years, they subtly acted upon the prejudices and confusions of their colleagues. The design that we came up with I now put forward as a simple and practical way of grappling with many of these important questions.

In designing an assessment centre model, we had to overcome certain characteristic weaknesses of the traditional approach:

- We were determined to overcome the 'cattle market' dynamic which arises when individual is pitted against individual in harsh competitive conditions. Some of the American assessment centres actually declare a 'winner' at the end of the week, which seemed to us counterproductive for eleven out of the twelve candidates. Acknowledging that there has to be a realistic competitive edge, we aimed to restore participants to a *colleague* relationship before the end of the program, because much of their everyday work demanded teamwork.

- However, we wanted each individual to have the benefit of *confidential* individual feedback on their performance during the week, parallel to the formal assessments.

- We were also determined that the group exercises, against which assessments are made, should be 'divergent' as well as 'convergent', in order to test ability to cope with ambiguity. Most of the American exercises we inherited were zero-sum games with more or less 'right' answers. Life is rarely like that. Our hunch was that IBM, as a world monopoly supplier of data processing hardware, had become much too convergent in its thinking. We had no business promoting more of the same.

- We also wanted everybody involved to use the opportunity to *learn* about the current situation of the overall system and to submit it to an exercise in collective 'systems thinking'.

- We deliberately set out to make the assessment process and criteria as transparent as possible. We saw this as part of the collective learning about 'how we do things around here' or, if you insist, the 'organisation culture'. After all, the main argument for assessment centres is that they make it possible to compare like with like in a fair and neutral setting. The unregarded 'Imo', tucked away in an obscure branch office, gets a chance.

The design that emerged spread over five days. The first three days were devoted to the assessments, some individual, most group-based, and all relatively open-ended. The Thursday was then given over to a combination of individual feedback and day-long group preparation for a 'management interaction' session on Friday morning. Friday contained the 'interaction' and the rest of the feedback. The first three days were for 'binary' competitiveness, but within suitably transparent 'ternary' game rules. The concluding two days were all 'ternary', concerning the system as a whole.

The two most distinctive features of this design were:

- The long and detailed process of system research preceding each program. The outcome of this work became the input to the group exercises. The participants worked on real, current problems rather than on warmed-up simulations of reality. The upside was the urgency and relevance of the work done, some of which had valuable outcomes in the real world. In effect, this was an Action Learning exercise. The obvious 'downside' was the enormous amount of prework required by management development staff to shape the materials for the exercises—though what else should management developers do? It was here that our analytic and design skills were stretched to the limit.

- The presence, throughout the Friday morning, of an open-ended group dynamics event involving the entire top management group of the relevant division of the company. This was modelled loosely on the Tavistock Institute 'Working Conference' design.

On each program, the participants were *presented* with their top management, to do with as they wished on the Friday morning. At the beginning, this was no less terrifying for the top management than for the participants. As the series rolled forward, both sides got the hang of it, building on the experience and reputations of previous groups. The participants could make presentations, ask questions, or do nothing if they chose. They could work collectively, or in sub-groups, or as individuals. They could create leadership and authority structures, or have a free-for-all. They could all try to speak, or they could delegate responsibility. The *content* of the event was up to them, at least until the top management team got going. All that was fixed was that they were collectively responsible for the management of the Friday morning event; the executive group, within reason, would do as it was told. We had turned the tables.

As noted, the preparation for the event took place on the Thursday. We left them to it but we offered them a consultancy service, on request. As they were confronting a pretty difficult management assignment, they usually availed themselves of that service. Although it wasn't part of the formal assessment, the real-time challenge of the looming top management interaction *really* sorted out sheep from goats. Those who rose to the intellectual challenge, whilst maintaining a good relationship with peers, were the natural leaders. Because, on the whole, we got the assessment exercises right (challenging, relevant, teamwork-based) the participants were just about ready to take on the Friday with a prospect of collective 'success'—a well-managed meeting which achieved the participants' stated objectives for it. Figure 28 shows the differential roles of participants and program staff.

This is a specific example of a particular program in a particular company, aimed at bringing together the twin aims of development and differentiation in a seamless whole. The details aren't important. Plainly, there are elements of Action Learning and action research, Schumacher's work restructuring, Tavistock group dynamics, Gardner's multiple intelligences and so on buried in this complex design. The principles and assumptions underpinning this initiative are still, in my opinion, interesting. Those principles have been applied repeatedly in my work over the years. One repeating theme is that it is always better to create a framework within which people can learn about their systems (by systems thinking) than to try to 'teach' them things, especially 'management techniques'. Whenever development is approached in this way, there is always a massive assessment outfall—you find out, quickly, who the natural 'Imos' are. They grasp the wider system properties quickly and then oscillate freely between the foreground and background. If all development were done this way, there wouldn't need to be any formal assessment

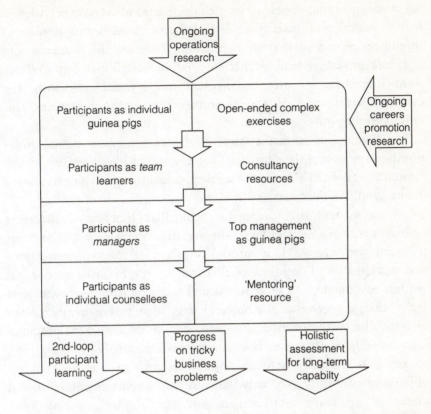

Figure 28 Assessment Centre model: respective roles of staff and participants

at all beyond the boss–subordinate process, with possibly a bit of 360 degree feedback thrown in.

HELPFUL HINT NO. 6: MENTORING THE SME CHIEF EXECUTIVE

All these helpful hints and ideas are aimed at bringing the advantages of natural development, as experienced by the 'natural leaders' in this book, to the large corporation. I direct the reader to Gifford Pinchot's 1985 bestseller, *Intrapreneuring,* and his 1993 book, *The End of Bureaucracy and the Rise of the Intelligent Organisation,* for further enlightenment on this subject. There is a groundswell of agreement that responsive organisations like Incat, Waite Consulting, Market Reality and Puddings On The Ritz show the way forward—as the big corporate behemoths shrink. It is a matter of importance, therefore, that new and developing SMEs (small to medium enterprises) should be kept in play so far as possible. They are the tender shoots of future growth. I believe that the Karpin Task Force has it about right here, by focusing mainly on one-to-one mentoring for owner/managers and on the creation of networks of mentors and entrepreneurs.

In 1992 I carried out a study of the entrepreneur–mentor relationship amongst SMEs for the Department of Employment in the United Kingdom. This piece of work parallels the observation (above) about people who always get it right.

It turned out that there was a smallish number of specialist consultants to SMEs who had a disproportionate impact on the firms involved with them. The multiplier effect of these interventions was remarkable. I studied one manufacturer of laboratory automation equipment whose business had been transformed by a fairly straightforward refocusing of objectives (involving all seventy employees) together with a statistically based quality improvement program. The owner/proprietor was basically an inventor, in partnership with an eminent surgeon. Between them they covered the technology/applications territory. Not only had this firm been transformed but a cluster of upstream supplier firms, in metal bashing, wiring loom supply, electronics and so on, had also been sharpened up by the impact of this work. In this case alone I calculated that an expense of £35 000, half of it public money, had resulted in *millions* of pounds worth of economic benefit to the local microeconomy.

In this case, as in many of the success story cases, the mentor was a *woman* of a certain age, consulting to a male owner about fifteen to twenty years her junior. This was a common pattern. Even more striking was the acknowledged success of this program in Scotland. I have remarked earlier how the Scots are superior to the English in most respects, and this should be factored into the equation. But the unusual feature here was that the government program was, by chance I think, administered by women in Scotland. The effect seems to have been that the *matching* of consultant/mentors to owner/managers was carried out with the same elan as displayed by the best society hostesses. Elsewhere, where the matchmaking was clumsier, the results were less impressive or, in quite a few cases, embarrassingly negative. In the course of the study my colleagues and I brought together a number of groups (six pairs at a time) of successful CEO/mentor pairs for two or three days in order to study the psychodynamics of the relationship at close hand. Not surprisingly, the psychometric patterns for CEOs and mentors were different (for readers familiar with the Myers-Briggs Type Inventory: CEO = STJ; Consultant = NFP). All the successful mentors were intuitively doing a form of 'role consultation' (see earlier)—helping the chief executives to view themselves from 'above'.

It seems to me that an outstanding woman *of a certain age* may well be better equipped to lean on a male owner/manager in an uncompromising ('tough but fair') way than another man is. For one thing, the female consultant usually seems to strike up a friendly relationship with *everybody* in the firm, cutting through any rigidities of hierarchy or turf wars. One female consultant had a confidential helpline established (via a letterbox in the entry vestibule) for all the predominantly female staff, without any sign of intrusion into the core CEO-mentoring role. People in the client firm say things like: '*She really cares!*'; '*She's one of the family!*'; *It's as if she's an employee!*'

It may not be fanciful to suggest that there is a family dynamic, or a potential one, in the small firm and that the absence of a strong female role model (or vice versa) is disturbing for the socio-technical system. In other words, in the SME, *leadership* has a special meaning, nearer to parenthood than to technocracy. If this all sounds mushy, it was this particular female mentor who virtually forced the CEO of the aforementioned firm to take the long overdue step of importing a hardedged chairman to the firm. The female mentor seems to embody the 'tough but fair' ternary model of leadership, in partnership with the boss.

Of course, the mentor need not be a woman. I simply pass on this intelligence for its possible relevance to the Australian case, where male owner/managers are also the norm.

On the basis of the above study, I would summarise the requirements for the SME consultant role as follows.

1. *Conceptual (systemic) thinking capability* The mentor/consultant must be *at least* the equal of the CEO in capacity level (using the Jaques stratified system scale). If the SME owner/manager is to manage strategic development effectively, he must be possessed of at least Level IV capability. If he is stuck at Level III, his consultant must

be at least Level IV in order to lead him into the strategic positioning arena. In that case, the consultant must be very sensitive, because the owner is somewhat exposed as his staff will certainly know, or sense, his limitations. The capability aspect, remember, has nothing to do with interpersonal skills or specialised knowledge; just the ability to exercise judgement and to process complexity.

2. *A bias to attachment*. The best of the SME consultants, in my experience, are people who positively dislike big companies, mostly as a result of spending too many years within them. Their enthusiasm for the SME sector is genuine and unfeigned. They are prepared to work very long hours for often inadequate reward, because of their close psychological *attachment* to the SME and its people. You could say that these consultants *need* the attachment. It is this factor, in my opinion, that leads to the admired and effective consultants always being described as having 'integrity'.

I hope the Karpin Task Force recommendations lead to good outcomes amongst Australian SMEs. Our evidence suggests that mentoring doesn't work when the capability/attachment equation is wrong, and when the mentor/CEO matching is insensitive. By the way, we proved to our own and our sponsors' satisfaction that the United Kingdom Government program to support SMEs financially via consultants was a great success. You needed only one in every ten projects to really take off to show a 'profit' on the scheme. Once we proved it, the government dropped it. I forget why, now; but I remember being unable to comprehend the muddled and illiterate justification for the decision. Nothing like that could happen in Australia!

HELPFUL HINT NO. 7: CREATIVE LEADERSHIP AND THEATRE

One of the persistent themes of this book has been the way in which certain kinds of creative people seem to be able to occupy two places at once. It may be the same capability that Howard Gardner describes as the 'intrapersonal intelligence' or capacity for self-awareness. All my heroes, varied as they are, are highly inventive but also highly expressive. This is not supposed to be the general case. Professor David McClelland once reviewed all the evidence he could muster about the psychological makeup of scientists—predominantly men, of course. He concluded that the key to scientists' personalities lies in the difficulty they experience in coping with aggression. Their work subjugates the external world to impersonal laws. This, he argued, is the symbolic expression of a destructiveness that might otherwise be vented on people.

McClelland noted that United States scientists tend to spring from strict if not Puritan backgrounds and try to avoid intimate physical contact with other people. It isn't that the scientist is anti-social but that he limits human contacts to a small number of a particular type which he feels able to deal with. When it comes to appreciation of the arts, apparently the 'typical' scientist prefers the impersonal representations of music and photography to the personal or allusive representations of painting and poetry. Of course, scientists are fascinated by the structure of the physical world. The more successful the scientist the more likely he is to work obsessively hard. There is an increasing number of successful female scientists, but they tend to be more like this type of male scientist than most women are.

I raise these questions in the context of the Federal Government's CRC (Cooperative Research Centre) program. At last count there were over sixty of these industry/research projects in existence, pulling in approximately $400 million per annum in funding from all sources, about a third of it from government. This strikes me as potentially of enormous value to Australia, *provided that* the scientists and the businesspeople and the potential users of outcomes can talk intelligently and intelligibly to each other. The Karpin inquiry, in my humble opinion, neglected the implications for business leadership of this important initiative. The people I have written about herein are exceptionally broad; they are all 'scientists' in the sense that they work systematically and rigorously with data of different kinds, but they can talk to anybody and make a fist of understanding anything. I wish their style could somehow infest the CRC program. It would not only be more effective, it would be more *fun*.

I have long been an admirer of the Swinburne University Innovation and Enterprise program in Melbourne. On one occasion that I presumed to 'teach' on that program there were, I think, three millionaires enrolled, mainly to discover what it was they were doing right. Now, in partnership with Ernst & Young, they have set up the

301

Centre for Innovation and Enterprise under the leadership of Professor Murray Gillin and Marcus Powe. I don't think there is much danger of their not having fun while they do good. The country needs more *connecting* of this sort to feed off the native inventiveness of Australians. The trick is to integrate the methodical with the expressive; not only are the people more rounded, but the work gets better—more subtle and complex.

I am currently engaged in a development program for very senior people with the objective of rounding out clever and dedicated people who have become too narrow. Our team contains a mix of management consultants and psychoanalysts and we think the key to our endeavours is the use of theatre. It is expressive, but it is disciplined. Our way of developing leadership is not to impose anything but to submit to what I call *God's typecasting*. If you want to carry weight as a leader, and impose your 'presence', you will never achieve it in a miscast part. If you find the right part that is true to your inner self, even if it is Iago or some other villain, then you have a good chance. The subjects who most need this treatment are the scientists by training. Perhaps the most exciting development at the time of writing is the new Centre for the Mind set up by (Prof.) Allan Snyder (see Chapter 13) in Canberra. This enterprise is designed to provide a home for the kinds of daring ideas which don't sit obviously or comfortably in any traditional disciplines. The Centre is pursuing the role of the unconscious in problem-solving and the role of emotion in discovery. In theatre the text is important, but it is in the creative rush of performance that the most important discoveries are made.

The key to this sort of *integration* really lies further upstream. If I were given dictatorial powers over Australia tomorrow, I would concentrate most of my effort and largesse on the *schools*. We have to get the young, *all of them*, in a fit state for Murray Gillin and Marcus Powe and, later on, for the CRC program, so as to put all that native wit on the road. I would put Allan Coman in charge of all education, because of the way his wonderful college pulled together all the disciplines of science with all the joy and expressiveness of the theatre. Short of socially engineering families (where most trouble starts), we have to rely on education and on its natural leaders to repair the damage in society.

Bibliography

Adair, John; *Great Leaders*, Talbot Adair Press, Guildford, 1989

Adorno, Theodore, et al; *The Authoritarian Personality*, Harper, New York, 1950

Ardrey, Robert; *The Social Contract*, Collins, London, 1970

Bateson, Gregory; 'Morale and National Character' in *Steps to an Ecology of Mind*, Paladin, London, 1978

—— *Mind and Nature: A Necessary Unity*, Dutton, New York, 1979

Bion, Wilfred; *Experiences in Groups*, Tavistock, London, 1961

Bronowski, Alison; *The Yellow Lady*, Oxford University Press Australia, Melbourne, 1992

Bronowski, Jacob; 'Knowledge: As Algorithm and as Metaphor', in *The Origins of Knowledge and Imagination*, Yale University Press, New Haven and London, 1978

Burns, James McGregor; *Leadership*, Harper & Row, New York, 1978

Carlsmith, Lyn; 'Effect of Early Father Absence on Scholastic Aptitude', in Hudson, Liam; *Human Beings: An Introduction to the Psychology of Human Experience*, Paladin, St Albans, 1978

Champy, James; *Reengineering Management*, Harper & Row, New York, 1995

Cleaver, Anthony; *Tomorrow's Company: The Role of Business in a Changing World*, Royal Society of Arts, London, 1995

Coopers & Lybrand; *The Middle Market Survey*, 1994

Cordiner King; *Taking Charge: Chief Executives Take Up the Reins*, Melbourne, 1996

Dixon, Norman F.; *On the Psychology of Military Incompetence*, Futura, London, 1979

Drucker, Peter; *The Practice of Management*, Pan Books, London, 1955

Emery, Fred and Trist, Eric; 'Socio-Technical Systems', in West, C. et al; *Management Sciences*, Pergamon, London, 1960

Fest, Joachim; *Hitler*, Pelican, London, 1977

Follett, Mary Parker; *Creative Experience*, Peter Smith, New York, 1951

—— *The New State: Group Organisation the Solution of Popular Government*, Longman, London, 1924

Frank, Robert; *The Winner-take-all Society*, The Free Press, New York, 1995

Fukuyama, Francis; *Trust: The Social Virtues and the Creation of Prosperity*, Hamish Hamilton, London, 1995

Gardner, Howard; *Frames of Mind, The Theory of Multiple Intelligences*, Basic Books, New York, 1993

—— *Leading Minds: An Anatomy of Leadership*, Harper Collins, London, 1996

—— *The Unschooled Mind*, Fontana, London, 1993

Garratt, Bob; *The Fish Rots from the Head*, Harper Collins, London, 1996

Ghoshal, Sumantra and Bartlett, Christopher; 'Rebuilding Behavioural Context—A Blueprint for Corporate Renewal', *Sloan Management Review*, vol 37, no 2, 1996

Goleman, Daniel; *Emotional Intelligence*, Bloomsbury, London, 1996

Golding, William; *Rites of Passage*, Faber & Faber, London, 1980

Graham, Pauline; *Mary Parker Follett: Prophet of Management*, Harvard Business School Press, 1994

Greer, Germaine; *Daddy, We Hardly Knew You*, Penguin, London, 1990

Hampden-Turner, Charles; *Corporate Culture*, Piatkus, London, 1994

Handy, Charles and Aitken, Robert; *Understanding Schools as Organisations*, Penguin, London, 1986

Harvey-Jones, John; *Getting It Together*, Heinemann, London, 1991

Hodgson, Godfrey; *In Our Time*, Macmillan, London, 1976

Hudson, Liam; *Human Beings: An Introduction to the Psychology of Human Experience*, Paladin, St Albans, 1978

Hughes, Robert; *The Culture of Complaint*, Warner Books, New York, 1994

Hutton, Will; *The State We're In*, Vintage, London, 1996

Industry Task Force on Leadership and Management Skills, *Enterprising Nation* (the Karpin Report), AGPS, Canberra, 1995

Janis, Irving; *Groupthink: Psychological Studies of Policy Discussions and Fiascos*, Houghton Mifflin, Boston, 1982

Jaques, Elliott; *Work, Creativity and Social Justice*, Heinemann, London, 1970

—— *Requisite Organisation*, Cason Hall, Arlington, 1989

—— *The Form of Time*, Heinemann, London, 1982

Kohlberg, Lawrence; 'The Child as a Moral Philosopher', *Psychology Today*, vol 2, 1968

Lifton, Robert J.; *The Nazi Doctors*, Macmillan, London, 1984

Mant, Alistair; *Leaders We Deserve*, Basil Blackwell, Oxford, 1985; Currency Productions, Melbourne, 1994

—— *The Dynamics of Management Education*, Gower, Aldershot, 1981

—— *The Rise and Fall of the British Manager*, Pan Macmillan, London, 1977

—— et al; *UK Management Consultants and the Small/Medium Firm*, HRD Partnership, HMSO, London, 1992

Mant, Catherine and Perner, Josef; 'The child's understanding of commitment', *Journal of Developmental Psychology*, vol 24, part 3, 1988

Marr, David; *Barwick*, Allen & Unwin, Sydney, 1980

McClelland, David; 'On the Psychodynamics of Creative Physical Scientists' in Hudson, Liam; *The Ecology of Human Intelligence*, Penguin, Harmondsworth, 1970

McGregor, Douglas; *The Human Side of Enterprise*, McGraw-Hill, New York 1960

McHugh, Siobhan; *The Snowy: The People Behind the Power*, Heinemann, Melbourne, 1989

Milgram, Stanley; 'Some Conditions of Obedience and Disobedience to Authority', *Human Relations*, vol 18, 1965

Mintzberg, Henry; *The Rise and Fall of Strategic Planning*, Prentice-Hall, New York, 1994

Mintzberg, Henry (with Quinn, James); *The Strategy Process*, Prentice-Hall, New York, 1996

Morris, Dick; *Behind the Oval Office*, Random House, New York, 1995

Mulgan, Geoff and Landry, Charles; *The Other Invisible Hand*, Demos, London, 1995

Mumford, Enid, *Systems Design; Ethical Tools for Ethical Change*, Macmillan, Basingstoke 1996

Nauright, John and Chandler, Timothy; *Making Men: Rugby and Masculine Identity*, Cass, London, 1996

Niall, Brenda; *Georgiana*, Melbourne University Press, Melbourne, 1994

Peters, Tom and Waterman, Robert; *In Search of Excellence*, Harper & Row, New York, 1982

Phillips, Angela; *The Trouble with Boys*, Pandora, London, 1993

Piaget, Jean; *The Moral Judgement of the Child*, Routledge & Kegan Paul, London, 1932

Pilger, John; *Heroes*, Jonathan Cape, London, 1986

Pinchot, Gifford; *Intrapreneuring*, Harper & Row, London, 1985

—— *The End of Bureaucracy and the Rise of the Intelligent Organisation*, Berrett & Kohler, New York, 1993

Porter, Michael E; *The Competitive Advantage of Nations*, Macmillan, London, 1990

Schumacher, E.F.; *Small is Beautiful*, Blond and Briggs, London, 1973

Schumpeter, Joseph; *Capitalism, Socialism and Democracy*, Allen & Unwin, London, 1976

Senge, Peter; *The Fifth Discipline*, Century Business, London, 1993

Sereny, Gitta; *Albert Speer: His Battle with Truth*, Picador, London, 1966

Sinclair, Amanda; *Trials at the Top*, The Australian Centre, University of Melbourne, 1994

Stamp, Gillian and Colin; 'Well Being at Work', *International Journal of Career Management*, vol 5, no. 3, 1993

Sulloway, Frank; *Born to Rebel*, Little Brown, London, 1996

Tiger, Lionel; *Men in Groups*, Random House, New York, 1969

Vickers, Geoffrey; *The Art of Judgement*, University Paperbacks, Methuen, 1968

Willis, Paul; *Learning to Labour*, Gower, London, 1980

Winterson, Jeanette; *Oranges Are Not the Only Fruit*, Vintage, London, 1991

Work Structuring Ltd. List of publications available from WSL, Church House, Church Lane, Godstone, Surrey RH9 8BW, UK or e-mail: admin@work-structuring.com

Wrangham, Richard and Peterson, Dale; *Demonic Males*, Houghton Mifflin, Boston, 1996

Index

307